A BODY of PRAISE

"'The body is his book' said the poet John Donne about human love, and in this excellent, nuanced, and well-timed study, David Taylor explains how the body is indeed the 'book' of our relationship with the love of God. The bodily dimensions of worship are explored with comprehensive empathy and scholarly depth. As we wrestle with the long-term impact of the pandemic on our worship practices, this work is an indispensable resource."

—**Rowan Williams**, former Archbishop of Canterbury

"The role of the human body in Christian worship has been neglected for too long but is now significantly enriched by Taylor's work. This book is wide in scope yet deep in wisdom. His writing displays a lifetime of scholarship and reflection, now brought together in mature form for the benefit of worshiping communities everywhere."

—**Constance M. Cherry**, Indiana Wesleyan University (emeritus); The Robert E. Webber Institute for Worship Studies

"Against our culture's increasingly transhumanist anthropology, Taylor reminds us that to be human means not merely to have a body but to *be* embodied. And at the heart of God's design for embodied persons made in his image is worship—worship that praises God, celebrates his good creation, and joyously engages every dimension of our corporeal and corporate existence."

—**Joel Scandrett**, Trinity School for Ministry

"Taylor has curated the story of the body throughout church history in a clear, concise, and compelling way. This book is for both lay leaders and the academic, with rigorous research that gives both a macro- and microperspective on what it means to live as bodies in a world aching for the redemption of all things. The collective minds and hearts of Christians need this book as we learn and relearn what the body has known all along."

—**Lore Ferguson Wilbert**, author of *A Curious Faith* and *Handle with Care*

"Taylor's thoughtful and highly readable work shows that, whether it's 'free church' or 'liturgical,' holistic worship must engage the whole body in all its senses. He makes his case by drawing from a wide range of studies: from Scripture and Christian tradition to the arts and sciences. This book should effectively put to rest the notion that online worship can be an adequate substitute."

—**Simon Chan**, former lecturer, Trinity Theological College, Singapore; editor of *Asia Journal of Theology*

"The topics of this book are close to my heart and close to the needs of the church today. Taylor knows that good theology and good practice form a whole, and he lays that out in ways that will bless us body and soul. This book will be useful across a wide variety of worshiping traditions."

—**Beth Felker Jones**, Northern Seminary

"This well-written, vivid study on the role of our bodies in corporate worship is timely and helpful in the wake of our recovery from the COVID-19 pandemic. Taylor correlates the theological and pastoral wisdom of the church with the findings and insights of the arts and sciences to show how the triune God interacts with his people bodily in worship and engages them spiritually with their physical senses of sight, smell, sound, taste, and touch."

—**John W. Kleinig**, Australian Lutheran College (emeritus); author of *Wonderfully Made: A Protestant Theology of the Body*

"As striking as Ezekiel's vision of enfleshing bones, Taylor knits together the motivating force of grief in a world reluctantly awakened to our common fragility. Involved in the human-God story through the provocation of perplexing questions, we are encouraged to trust and begin to live into the gifted smallness of our bodies as we reflect the glory of the divine image. Through overcoming the wounds we pile on others and ourselves by a host of misconceptions, this book, at once exhortation and evidence, invites us into newness and renewal. No longer dry, we rise."

—**Cecilia González-Andrieu**, Loyola Marymount University; author of *Bridge to Wonder: Art as a Gospel of Beauty*

A BODY of PRAISE

UNDERSTANDING THE ROLE OF OUR PHYSICAL BODIES IN WORSHIP

W. DAVID O. TAYLOR

Baker Academic

a division of Baker Publishing Group
Grand Rapids, Michigan

© 2023 by W. David O. Taylor

Published by Baker Academic
a division of Baker Publishing Group
Grand Rapids, Michigan
www.bakeracademic.com

All rights reserved. No part of this publication may be reproduced, stored in a retrieval system, or transmitted in any form or by any means—for example, electronic, photocopy, recording—without the prior written permission of the publisher. The only exception is brief quotations in printed reviews.

Library of Congress Cataloging-in-Publication Data
Names: Taylor, W. David O., 1972– author.
Title: A body of praise : understanding the role of our physical bodies in worship / W. David O. Taylor.
Description: Grand Rapids, Michigan : Baker Academic, a division of Baker Publishing Group, 2023. | Includes bibliographical references and index.
Identifiers: LCCN 2022030399 | ISBN 9781540963093 (paperback) | ISBN 9781540966483 (casebound) | ISBN 9781493440177 (ebook) | ISBN 9781493440184 (pdf)
Subjects: LCSH: Worship. | Public worship. | Human body—Religious aspects—Christianity.
Classification: LCC BV15 .T39 2023 | DDC 264—dc23/eng/20220801
LC record available at https://lccn.loc.gov/2022030399

Unless otherwise indicated, Scripture quotations are from the New Revised Standard Version of the Bible, copyright © 1989 National Council of the Churches of Christ in the United States of America. Used by permission. All rights reserved.

Scripture quotations labeled CEB are from the Common English Bible. © Copyright 2011 by the Common English Bible. All rights reserved. Used by permission.

Scripture quotations labeled ESV are from The Holy Bible, English Standard Version® (ESV®), copyright © 2001 by Crossway, a publishing ministry of Good News Publishers. Used by permission. All rights reserved. ESV Text Edition: 2016

Scripture quotations labeled The Message are taken from THE MESSAGE, copyright © 1993, 2002, 2018 by Eugene H. Peterson. Used by permission of NavPress. All rights reserved. Represented by Tyndale House Publishers, Inc.

Scripture quotations labeled NLT are taken from the Holy Bible, New Living Translation, copyright © 1996, 2004, 2015 by Tyndale House Foundation. Used by permission of Tyndale House Publishers, Inc., Carol Stream, Illinois 60188. All rights reserved.

Scripture quotations labeled Phillips are from The New Testament in Modern English by J. B. Phillips copyright © 1960, 1972 J. B. Phillips. Administered by The Archbishops' Council of the Church of England. Used by permission.

Baker Publishing Group publications use paper produced from sustainable forestry practices and post-consumer waste whenever possible.

23 24 25 26 27 28 29   7 6 5 4 3 2 1

To dancers:
who teach us how to be a body

Contents

Acknowledgments xi

1. **The Glory of the Body** 1
   An Introduction to the Body in Worship

2. **The Map of the Body** 15
   Mapping Out the Landscape of the Body in Worship

3. **The Story of the Body** 29
   Historical Perspectives on the Body in Worship

4. **The Benediction of the Body** 43
   Biblical Perspectives on the Body in Worship (Part 1)

5. **The Future of the Body** 55
   Biblical Perspectives on the Body in Worship (Part 2)

6. **The True Image of the Body** 67
   Theological Perspectives on the Body in Worship

7. **The Nature of the Body** 81
   Scientific Perspectives on the Body in Worship

8. **The Art of the Body** 95
   Artistic Perspectives on the Body in Worship

9. **The Way of the Body** 109
   Ethical Perspectives on the Body in Worship

10. **The Discipline of the Body**   125
    The Prescriptive Body in Worship
11. **The Freedom of the Body**   139
    The Spontaneous Body in Worship
12. **The End of the Body**   153
    A Conclusion to the Body in Worship

Notes   165

Scripture Index   201

Subject Index   205

Acknowledgments

This book has been twenty-five years in the making and goes back to a ThM thesis that I wrote in the late 1990s for New Testament scholar Rikk E. Watts at Regent College, which explored the significance of Jesus's healing miracles for our physical bodies. It is Rikk whom I wish to thank first for nurturing my interest in biblical scholarship and in the theological meaning of our bodies. This thesis served as the beginning of my interest in human bodies. I am also grateful to Jeremy Begbie for introducing me to Karl Barth and Colin Gunton and, through them, to a theology of creation that fosters a robust vision for all things physical: our bodies, the spaces we inhabit, works of art, and care of the environment.

Special thanks are also owed to Celeste Snowber, who kindly told me in 1999 that I was not too old to learn how to dance. I am grateful to Kathy Dunn Hamrick, who in the spring of 2001 led a ten-week class in modern dance in Austin, Texas, wherein I learned how to dance, even though I felt too old and too tall to do it right. A heartfelt thanks to Ceci Proeger, Annette Christopher, and Shari Brown during the early years of my time as a pastor at Hope Chapel in Austin, for being such good sports to create modern dance pieces not only for our gathered worship but also for my sermons.

I am particularly grateful to the churches that have shaped me over the years:

- To Centro Biblico El Camino in Guatemala City, for showing me what unadulterated joy looks like within the praises of a congregation

- To First Assembly of God in Russellville, Arkansas, and to Thomas Hale in particular, for teaching me what no one had ever taught me, namely, that my hands had something good to do in worship, which only hands could and should do
- To Hope Chapel in Austin, Texas, and to Jack and Debbie Dorman specifically, for creating such a gentle space in worship in which a kid who grew up in a dispensationalist world could give himself without fear to God in full-bodied worship
- I am likewise grateful to the team at Hope Chapel that helped create the monthly Compline services, which included incense and silence, choral music and visual art, beauty and contemplative prayer
- To the Vineyard Church in Evanston, Illinois, for showing me that it is possible to be leisurely with God in praise
- To Saint Matthew's Episcopal Church in Austin, for introducing me to the "beauty of holiness"
- To Saint Martin's Lutheran Church in Würzburg, Germany, for showing me that it is possible to be fully charismatic and fully liturgical at the same time
- To Holy Trinity in Vancouver, British Columbia, for teaching me that something deeply good can happen in the liturgy, even if only seven people show up
- To All Saints Church in Durham, North Carolina, for blessing my calling to the priesthood
- To Redeemer Presbyterian in Houston, Texas, for showing me the rich points of connection between liturgy and the Reformed tradition
- To Church of the Cross in Austin, for beautifully modeling a commitment to Scripture, sacrament, and the Spirit

Thanks also to the keen-eyed comments of Tamara Murphy, Jeanmarie Tade, Blake Alan Mathews, Travis Hines, Terri Fisher, Lore Ferguson Wilbert, Victoria Emily Jones, Brian Moss, Matthew Aughtry, Krista Vossler, Bill and Yvonne Taylor, Kimberly Deckel, Sarah Smith, Peter Coelho, and Anna Russell Thornton. A sincere thanks to Viktor Toth as well for his excellent and generous-spirited work on the indexes for this book.

To the marvelous team at Baker Academic: to Bob Hosack for your persistent support of my work, reaching back to the summer of 2000;

to Paula Gibson for your extraordinary generosity of spirit; and to Julie Zahm for your incisive edits that made the book better than I could have imagined on my own.

To Blythe and Sebastian for yet again bearing with a physically and mentally absentee father in the final weeks of writing.

To Phaedra for being my ideal reader and my faithful companion.

1

The Glory of the Body

An Introduction to the Body in Worship

By our faithful, bodily participation in congregational worship, we receive God's incarnate Son and all the blessings of his incarnation.

—John Kleinig, Wonderfully Made

We are writing to you about something which has always existed yet which we ourselves actually saw and heard: something which we had an opportunity to observe closely and even to hold in our hands, and yet, as we know now, was something of the very Word of life himself!

—1 John 1:1 (Phillips)

A Disembodied Funeral

My aunt Grace, my father's only sister, died on April 30, 2020, at the age of eighty-one. She passed in the hospice-care home where she had spent the final six years of her struggle against Alzheimer's disease. Because her death had occurred during the period of social isolation that COVID-19 required of us in the United States, no in-person funeral would take place. My aunt, in fact, had wanted no flowers or fuss. She had desired no worship service to commemorate her passing. She had wanted only to be left alone.

But for us as her family, locked down in our homes across the city of Austin, Texas, hundreds of miles away from Decatur, Georgia, we had not wanted to be left alone in our grief. We had wanted something—*anything*—to process the awful fact of a death in our family. But that was not to be. My aunt got her wishes. No liturgy would bear witness to the sound of voices singing their lament. There would be no hugs to absorb the sorrow, no hands to hold our grief, no casket to touch. No earth would be felt in the hand or dropped into the grave, carved out of the Georgia red clay, where we might have heard the words from the Book of Common Prayer:

> We are mortal, formed of the earth, and unto earth shall we return. For so thou didst ordain when thou createdst me, saying, "Dust thou art, and unto dust shalt thou return."[1]

If it is true that touch has a memory, as the poet John Keats once observed, what will our family be unable to remember about my aunt's life, or our own, on account of this missing liturgical rite? What emptiness will always haunt our memory of her? What wound will never be healed? What, in the end, will we lose because no corporate body bore witness to death's sting in the corporeal form of Grace Taylor Ihrig and to Christ's defeat of that painful sting in a liturgy for the burial of the dead?

Our experience, of course, was far from unusual. The coronavirus pandemic that brought the world to a sudden halt in the spring of 2020, demanding that people shelter in place, involved a massive rupture of common life. Among other things, it profoundly affected the embodied liturgy of the church. We exchanged no friendly handshakes on entering a physical space of worship. We received no heartfelt hugs in the passing of the peace. We neither sat, nor stood, nor knelt in one another's company. We heard no raucous praise erupting out of the mouths of parishioners standing near at hand. And we went for months without tasting the eucharistic bread or savoring the contents of Christ's cup.

While church leaders are to be commended for going to great lengths to learn new forms of technology in order to provide meaningful opportunities for corporate worship, the experience of exclusively digitally mediated worship could not satisfy the God-given need for embodied communal worship. The Body was atomized, its corporeal fellowship was fragmented,

An Introduction to the Body in Worship

and the effects of this rupture are still, today, being calculated by scientists and psychologists. What happened to us was not simply something unfortunate; it was something, in fact, that profoundly affected our ability to be truly and wholly human.

In his study of the effects of trauma on the body, *The Body Keeps the Score: Brain, Mind, and Body in the Healing of Trauma*, Dutch psychiatrist Bessel van der Kolk argues that if meaningful physical contact, the need for which is hardwired into our biology, is absent for long periods in our lives, our humanity suffers.[2] On this point, a 2015 study conducted at Brigham Young University showed how chronic social isolation increased the risk of mortality by almost 30 percent; it was akin, the authors noted, to smoking fifteen cigarettes a day.[3] Scientists from across a variety of disciplines have shown how prolonged physical isolation leads to accelerated cognitive decline, poor cardiovascular function, and impaired immunity at every stage of life.[4] Psychologists have coined a term to describe the experience of deficient physical contact: "touch deficiency syndrome."[5] If left untreated, it leads to a shriveling up of life.

A Disembodied Worship?

A curious result of the COVID-19 lockdown, I found, was the opportunity it afforded us to experiment with what I might call "soul only" worship. Such worship, underwritten by a theology that regards the soul as metaphysically superior to the body, prioritizes the interior and invisible activities of the heart and mind, where the "real" action of worship is believed to occur. Radio stations broadcast preachers' words directly to our minds. Computer laptops delivered the music straight to our hearts. Sounds and images traveled through our televisions straight to our souls. And our bodies, resting passively at home, served as mere receptacles of spiritual data. On the thinking of "soul only" worship, we could, in principle, thrive without the need to gather in our bodies in a common physical space in order to worship God together.

But that is not how God has designed us as human beings or how the Spirit has wired us to be Christ's Body. Nor, for that matter, did many of us experience this socially isolated period as life-giving; we experienced it as life-shrinking in manifold ways. Over against "soul only" worship, I argue here that our bodily participation in worship is essential not just to faithful worship but also to a fullness and richness of corporate life. God, I contend, has created us to worship with our whole bodily selves: hands and feet, eyes and ears, nose and mouth, along with every cell and sense in our physical bodies. All of it gets caught up in the worship of the triune God. And while care-filled attention must always be given to the specific needs of those who are sick, homebound, elderly, or experience physical limitations, the fact remains that God has created us to flourish in the experience of gathering liturgically in our good bodies alongside the bodies of others as Christ's own Body.

The Glory of the Body at Worship

This book, then, is about the unique glory of the physical body in corporate worship. In it I engage two lines of argument. First, I argue against the idea that our bodies are merely neutral spectators or a problem to be escaped at worship; there is, in fact, *nothing* neutral whatsoever about the bodies that we bring to worship. We bring bodies that fear failure, rejection, or being out of control. We bring bodies that are burdened by sickness and self-hatred. We bring disfigured and dispirited bodies. We bring bodies that have been scarred *by* touch and bodies that have been starved *of* touch. And on account of the insidious effects of sin, we bring broken ways of relating to our own bodies and to the bodies of others who gather with us in a common space of worship.

> **The question before the church today is not whether our liturgical prayer will be embodied but how.**
> —John Baldovin, "An Embodied Eucharistic Prayer"

Against a widespread presumption that our bodies are neutral or passive agents in corporate worship, I argue that they, in fact, have something *to do*, which only they can and must do by God's design.[6] In worship we *sense* and are *resensitized* to the grace of God. In worship we get a *feel* for the story of God through our *hearing* of the word of God. We *see* the cross and *behold* love divine, all loves excelling. We *taste* the Lord's Supper and *see* thereby that the Lord is good (Ps. 34:8). And we get in *touch* with the work of the Spirit through the ministries of healing prayer and reconciliation, among other ways. The body in this way "is liturgy's native language," as Nathan Mitchell observes, and—existing in a mutually responsive relationship to the heart, mind, and will—it actively participates in the transformative work of God within the context of worship.[7]

This conviction is grounded, among other reasons, in God's good purposes for our bodies at worship. The body that we bring to corporate worship is not a problem to be solved, requiring the powers of the soul to put it in its place. Neither is the body's purpose to get out of the way so that the heart and mind can get on with the job of properly praising God. The purpose of the body is to offer to God what only it can offer—what *must* be offered to God. The body on this thinking offers itself as an agent of good in the formation of Christlikeness in worship. It does so not by its own power alone but by the power of the Spirit who enables our bodies to become tabernacles for God's palpable presence. It does so by participating in the incarnate life of our risen Lord, through whom we become flesh of his flesh (see Gen. 2:23). And it does so because it pleases the Father to make our bodies sacramental sites for holiness so that we might become wholly ourselves and a blessing to our neighbor.

What, then, is the body's glory in the context of worship? To borrow the language of Irenaeus, it is a body that is fully alive in the Spirit-ed company of other bodies who have gathered to worship God as Christ's own body.[8]

The above argument represents the first part of my thesis. The second part, hewing more closely to a pattern of thought in Holy Scripture, argues this line of thought: (1) that we *must* worship God with our bodies, (2) that we *need to* worship God with our bodies, and (3) that we *get to* worship God with our bodies.

First, then, we are commanded to worship God in our bodies. The Psalter, the church's determinative worship book, is full of such language. Psalm 33:8 says, "Let all the inhabitants of the world stand in awe of him." Psalm 47:1 adds, "Clap your hands, all you peoples." And in Psalm 95:6 the faithful are enjoined to "kneel before the Lord, our maker!" None of this is suggestive language; it is normative language, and it points to a nonnegotiable requirement for human beings. Eugene Peterson brings this point to light in his translation of 1 Corinthians 6:20: "The physical part of you is not some piece of property belonging to the spiritual part of you. God owns the whole works. So let people see God in and through your body" (The Message). Putting the point more generally, my body is not my property. It is neither my possession nor a thing that I own. It does not exist at the behest of my mind or under the hegemonic rule of my personality type. It is the Lord's, and it is his to command. And in gratitude I willingly glorify God with my body.

But the matter of our bodies in worship is not simply a matter of imperatives. It is also a matter of necessity. God has designed our bodies to flourish under specific conditions. They are not designed to be muted or to be muzzled in worship; our bodies are designed instead to be yielded fully to God in worship. Our bodies are like sunflowers made to turn their faces to the sun. If they refuse to do so, they deny their very nature and eventually wilt. John Calvin remarks how the little birds "sing of God; the beasts clamor for him; the elements dread him, the mountains echo him, and the grass and flowers laugh before him."[9] This is what they do by nature; it is what they *need* to do to fulfill their blessed creaturely purposes. So too our hands are made to rise in a response of love, our knees to kneel in humility, and our feet to dance and to parade and to process. Our bodies are made to love God in *bodily* ways. This is their created purpose. This is what they must do—for life's sake.

Beyond these fundamental reasons to worship God in our bodies, there is also a *get to* quality to our embodied liturgy. In 2 Samuel 6, David dances as the ark of the covenant is carried into Jerusalem. The text says twice that he dances before the Lord "with great abandon." In witnessing it, his wife Michal upbraids him for such "vulgar" behavior. In response, David says, "In GOD's presence I'll dance all I want!" (v. 21 The Message). This phrasing captures the "excessive" character of life in God's world. In God's world there is always more than enough. There is a glut of color, a profligacy of sound, and a surfeit of things to taste. There is an excess of bread and a surplus of wine. The point is this: we raise our hands to God because such a sign of honor is his due. But we also *get to* raise our hands in a spontaneous expression of affection for God. We choose to kneel because it befits a posture of humility before our Maker. But we also *get to* kneel because love yields itself gladly to such a gracious God. We get to do all such things with our bodies in worship because this is their true end.

The Problem of the Body

The problem is that Christians have not always rightly understood the purposes of the body in worship. In manifold ways and at different times,

Christians have feared the body, distrusted it, or despised it. They have suppressed or indulged the body. They have sought to transcend their own bodies, and they have objectified the bodies of others. They have engaged in superstitious or flippant uses of the body in worship. They have deemed their own culture's approach to the body at prayer and praise as superior to other cultural practices of the body. They have believed that bodies exist solely "to transport our heads from place to place . . . otherwise we would have no need for them," as a character in a Jules Feiffer cartoon once joked.[10] And in plenty of instances, Christians have simply muddled their way through, never really understanding why they do what they do with their bodies in worship.[11]

This cocktail of deficient, defective, and demonic approaches to the body has marked the church's worship from its earliest days. Part of this broken legacy is owed to Gnostic ideas about the body that dominated during the early centuries of the church; part of it to ruinous notions that reigned during the medieval era; part of it to the mixed messages that Christians received about the body during the Reformation period; part of it to Descartes's metaphysics that stressed the categorical superiority of reason over physicality; part of it to a perverse hierarchical arrangement of colored bodies that marks modern Western history, with White bodies at the top and non-White bodies at the bottom; and part of it to the utterly confused view of the body that marks our contemporary era. This last distortion is true both in the secular setting, with its simultaneous absolute gratification and absolute hatred of the body, and in Christian circles, where the body is burdened by bad exegesis, faulty theology, and a defective spirituality.[12]

The Task Ahead

To what end, then, did God give us this composite of cells, tissues, and organs, all of it composed of decayable matter? Why not make human beings like angels—creatures needing no genes, glands, or genitals? And what lessons might we take from church history about the manifold uses of our physical bodies in worship? What does the Bible tell us about these fleshy bodies of ours? How might Christ's body determine the true meaning of all human bodies? How might the science of smell enable us to acquire the intoxicating scent of God in worship? What might dancers teach us about the faithful use of our bodies in worship? How might both prescriptive and spontaneous uses of our body in worship positively contribute to our discipleship before God? And to what end do we offer our bodies to God before a watching world?

The task of this book is to make good sense of these questions, and others like them, in order to persuade readers that our physical bodies play a far more decisive role in the context of corporate worship than they may have previously imagined. Throughout the book, I use the language of *corporate worship* to mean the same thing as *liturgy*, assuming that all churches work with an order of worship that remains, for them, definitive and ritualized from week to week. I remain focused on this particular context of *corporate* worship, eschewing any treatment of worship that might occur at a retreat or conference or small group, and I aim to help not just so-called liturgical churches but all manner of congregations—Presbyterian, Baptist, charismatic, and the rest. And in a very practical sense, I wish to bring to readers' attention relevant resources on the body in worship that offer invaluable insights on what could and should be done with our bodies.

The outline of the book is as follows. In chapter 2, I map out what I am calling the landscape of the body at worship. In chapters 3 through 6, I investigate the substantially determinative insights of church history, the Bible, and theology. In chapters 7 and 8, I show how the sciences and the arts offer invaluable insights on our topic. In chapter 9, I raise a number of ethical concerns surrounding the nature of our bodies, along with the potential misuses and abuses of our bodies in worship. In chapters 10 and 11, I explain how both prescriptive and spontaneous uses of the body offer good news to both sides of the aisle: to the "liturgical" folk and the "free church" folk alike. Finally, in chapter 12, I contend that our postures, gestures, and movements in worship become a way to train us in Christlikeness, to bear witness to God's good purposes for our bodies to a watching world, and to participate in the glorious, Spirit-ed ends of our bodies.

Mayra Rivera, in her book *Poetics of the Flesh*, writes that "words about bodies create social relations."[13] This deceptively simple observation about body talk best represents my goal for this book. My hope is not simply to persuade readers to think differently about the uses of our bodies in worship; my hope is to write in such a way that our bodily worship might change the way that we worship together for the better.[14] I should also say that my interest does not simply lie in the nuts and bolts of bodily worship—what we do or do not do with our bodies in worship on any given Sunday (or Saturday or otherwise).[15] My interest instead is to offer a constructive and a practical vision for the body at worship that serves to inspire a more meaningful engagement of our physical bodies in a corporate worship context. My hope is that Christians will actively look for ways to expand their repertoire of embodied worship in such a way that it more deeply forms them in the triune life.

What This Book Does Not Attempt to Do

It is virtually impossible to write a treatment of the body in worship without frustrating readers from any number of liturgical traditions. Readers may find their own tradition represented only minimally or not at all. Certain topics will be set aside, such as fasting and sexuality, or receive no chapter of their own, such as the topic of worship and culture. This, of course, is the nature of a situated and perspectival treatment of the topic. Only so much can be said, and what is said will be necessarily socially located.[16] This is not to excuse any deficiencies that a reader may find in this book; it is simply to state the obvious about a subject that remains frequently disputed across Christian denominations. Where some readers may regret that I did not address a particular topic, my hope is that the resources in the endnotes will offer an opportunity to pursue the matter further.

I should also say that I write this book as both an ordained pastor and an academic theologian. The audience that I presume for this book is accordingly both ecclesial and academic. I bring to this task, as such, a vested interest in the real-life outcomes of this project, not just for classroom settings but also for congregational ones. While as a scholar I take seriously the need to analyze texts from a variety of disciplines in critical, careful, and charitable fashion, I also take seriously my vocation as a priest, which involves a primary responsibility to the people of God, gathered and scattered across a range of liturgical contexts. It is for this reason that I write not so much to prescribe a single way to worship in our bodies but to cast a vision for what *might be* within any given church context. Finally, although scholarly readers may wish that I had provided more about certain matters and lay readers may wish that I had provided less, my hope is that both will discover enough here to whet their appetite to read further.

The Body as the "Second Book" of God

One last thing deserves mention in this introduction. I would like to offer an explanation for why I appeal to the arts and sciences for guidance on the role of our bodies in worship. Why not simply stick to the usual suspects of Bible, history, and theology? I do so on the conviction that the Holy Trinity has revealed the divine purposes for our bodies not only through the determinative sources of special revelation as well as by way of direct responses to that revelation (what we might call tradition and doctrine) but also through what has often been nicknamed God's "Second Book"—that is, the physical creation and what humans have been charged to make of it through the distinctive activities of "culture making." This is a concept that goes back to Augustine and, before him, to the writings of the psalmists and of the apostle Paul.

Psalm 19:1–2 says, for example, "The heavens are telling the glory of God; and the firmament proclaims his handiwork. Day to day pours forth speech, and night to night declares knowledge." A similar idea is articulated throughout the collection of so-called creation psalms (Pss. 8, 104, 148, etc.). Eugene Peterson renders memorably the idea of creation as a "book of nature" in his translation of Psalm 111:2–3: "GOD's works are so great, worth a lifetime of study—endless enjoyment! Splendor and beauty mark his craft" (The Message). Paul assumes this feature of God's creation in the opening section of his argument in his letter to the believers at Rome (Rom. 1:19–20), and Augustine (354–430) picks up on this biblical motif in a sermon preached toward the end of his life: "Some people read books in order to find God. Yet there is a great book, the very appearance of created things. Look above you; look below you! Note it; read it! God, whom you wish to find, never wrote that book with ink. Instead, He set before your eyes the things that He had made. Can you ask for a louder voice than that? Why, heaven and earth cry out to you: 'God made me!'"[17]

The idea that creation, along with its many wonders, deserves a "lifetime of study" is teased out in one of John Chrysostom's (347–407) letters, where he describes nature as a "volume" that all may look to in order to receive "a sufficient lesson" about God's works.[18] Genevan Reformer John Calvin (1509–1564) articulates something similar in his *Institutes of the Christian Religion* eleven centuries later: "The contemplation of heaven and earth is the very school of God's children."[19] Under the "tuition" of creation, he adds, all people can learn about the things of God and the things that God has made.[20] Franciscan theologian Bonaventure (1217–1274) describes the human creature specifically as "a book with writing front and back."[21] But it is the Spanish theologian Raymond of Sabunde (c. 1385–1436) who more fully develops the idea in his fifteenth-century book *Theologia Naturalis*:

> Hence there are two books given to us by God, the one being the book of the whole collection of creatures or the book of nature, and the other being the book of sacred scripture. The first book was given to human beings in the beginning, when the universe of creatures was created, since no creature exists that is not a certain letter, written by the finger of God, and from many creatures as from many letters is composed one book, which is called the book of the creatures. Within this book is included humanity itself, and human beings are the first letters of this book. But the second book, Scripture, was given to human beings secondarily to correct the deficiencies of the first book, which humanity could not read because it is blind. The first book is common to everyone, but the second book is not common to all.[22]

What each of these statements points to is a conviction that the revelation of God is both consistent and coherent. God has not revealed something in the book of Scripture that fundamentally contradicts what the Creator has revealed in the book of creation. According to Deborah Haarsma: "Since God reveals himself in both nature and Scripture, these cannot be in conflict; both must speak truly of God and his creation."[23] Because God has created a world that bears witness to him, then, and because he has called and capacitated human beings to delight, to discover, and to discern the meaning of creation, we can be confident that the results of our investigations from the sciences and the arts, humbly undertaken, will lead to wisdom in the way that we worship corporately as well as to wonder in the beauty and variety of all God's sensory works in our liturgical settings.

In concrete terms, there is a logic and an integrity to these bodies of ours, which the disciplines of neuroscience, genetics, and psychology—along with the visual, kinetic, and musical arts, to name a few—may bring to light in a way that remains consonant with the theological truth about our bodies in the Bible. What ideally should result from such explorations? Chiefly, it should evoke in us a profound sense of delight that we are indeed fearfully and wonderfully made as human beings. Such an exploration should also show us more clearly the broken condition of our fallen bodies. It should, that is, poignantly and painfully bring to light the ways in which we wound and are wounded by others in our bodies. And it should help us to perceive ways that God's purposes for creation and the new creation intermingle in both surprising and salutary ways.[24]

The Destiny of the Body

In an essay on the relationship between creation and eschatology, Daniel Hardy writes that the intention of worship ought to be "a direct anticipation of the fullness of the *eschaton*, often through the enactment of present participation in the heavenly banquet."[25] As it relates to the purposes of this book, I very much hope for something similar. I hope that all our bodily activities of worship might to be done under the light of the end of worship, namely, the fulsome praise of the entire cosmos and our wholly uninhibited bodily worship. As the book of Psalms expresses it, such worship does not involve a partial gift of praise; it involves *everything* that has breath praising the Lord (see, e.g., Pss. 145–50). It is a body of praise in a maximal register.

And as the book of Revelation, the Bible's other "book of worship," envisions it, the goal of such worship is not how we might offer the *least* of ourselves to God. For it is not simply "four living creatures" or only the voice of "myriads of myriads" of angels that sing "with full voice" in the company of heaven (Rev. 4:6; 5:11, 12). It is "every creature in heaven and on earth and under the earth" (Rev. 5:13) that sings before the Lamb of God in worship. The language here cannot get any more comprehensive than this. The goal of all true worship, then, ought to be the offering of our *whole* bodily self in self-surrendered worship of God. No part of our physical self is left on the cutting-room floor of our prayer and praises. It is every jot and tittle of our bodies praising their Maker in their own way:

sight and sound, touch and taste, scent and sense, gesture and posture, hands and feet, and the rest. It is in this way, I suggest, that our bodies fulfill their creaturely and liturgical purposes. And it is with this end in mind that we embark on our study of the body in the corporate worship of the church.

2

The Map of the Body

Mapping Out the Landscape of the Body in Worship

The human body . . . is intrinsically polyphonic; it speaks several languages simultaneously, just as liturgy and ritual do.

—Nathan Mitchell, Meeting Mystery

And so, dear brothers and sisters, I plead with you to give your bodies to God because of all he has done for you. Let them be a living and holy sacrifice—the kind he will find acceptable. This is truly the way to worship him.

—Romans 12:1 (NLT)

A Map of the Body

I am conscious of the fact that this may feel like one of those chapters that could be skimmed through in order to get to the more "exciting" material of the book. It is, granted, a chapter that deals with the definition of terms, that outlines a variety of functions for the body, that ventures a summary of the peculiar powers of the body, and that then seemingly detours into an investigation of the bodily basis of human meaning. But as tempting as it may feel to skip ahead, I would ask the reader to stay with me as there has been a great deal of confusion around the role of the physical body in worship due to a lack of clarity around very basic things.

Is the "body" the good part of us and the "flesh" the bad part of us? Or are they both bad and good under the right circumstances? What do "personal space" and "crying like a girl" have to do with our bodies in worship? What does it mean to "know something in your bones" when you pray for one another? And in what sense does "being in touch" with God depend on our ability to receive touch from others in positive, meaningful ways in our liturgical gatherings? These are the questions that this chapter aims to answer as a way to achieve a measure of clarity around the complex topic of this book. They are, lamentably, questions that rarely get asked in books of this sort, chiefly because authors frequently assume that readers will agree to the terms of discussion that seem most obvious to them but are anything *but* obvious. If the history of the body at worship teaches us anything, however, it is that we should not assume such things.

The purpose of this chapter, then, is to draw up a map of the body at worship so that readers will understand clearly what I mean throughout the book. This is another way of saying that writing about the body at worship always requires careful qualification, because a body is never *merely* a body. A body is always a body bound up in a tangle of contested meanings and in a maelstrom of forces, and these influences exercise a power over us that often remains invisible to us, frequently to our detriment and to the detriment of others. Our bodies are always "talking," and it is important to understand what they are saying so that we can make sure that our bodies are saying the things that remain commensurate with our calling to faithfully be the Body of the risen Lord in our postures and processions, our gestures and movements, and in every sense that we bring to corporate worship.

The Terms of the Body

A first thing to say here is that there is no such thing as a neutral, universally agreed on idea of what a "body" is. Swedish theologian Ola Sigurdson helpfully describes our experience of the physical body as "a matter of entering into a multilayered labyrinth of meanings, contradictions, and half-sensed connections."[1] In other words, the body has many histories and many senses that we do well to discern and to define as carefully as possible, lest we talk past or needlessly clash with one another.

A first sense of the term "body" is the body that biologists study: the *biological body*. This is a body, significantly, that is subject to external forces such as gravity and weather as well as to internal forces such as genetic codes and chemical imbalances. What is of interest to this book is the way in which our biological bodies are vulnerable rather than invincible. If to be embodied is to be embedded, not least within one's physical environment, how have our practices of worship ignored or resisted God's good purposes for our vulnerable bodies, leading us to believe that we are the indominable masters of our bodies and physically invulnerable to powers above, below, and beyond us—such as circadian rhythms, barometric pressure, gut microbiota, electromagnetic radiation, noise pollution, and the rest?

> *We are in touch with our world at a visceral level, and it is the quality of our "being in touch" that importantly defines what our world is like and who we are.*
> —Mark Johnson, The Meaning of the Body

As a case in point, when electricity was introduced to corporate worship around the turn of the twentieth century, it allowed Christians to obviate the rhythms of creation and to triumph over the limitations of nature. In practice, it meant that Christians could worship night and day with the help of electric lights, and worship leaders could make their voices sound clearly across a distance by way of a microphone. Our calling to make culture no doubt underwrites such inventions, and others like them, and certainly much good has come to the church's worship because of them. But in what way have such technologies, shored up by often unquestioned ideas about the good life, undermined God's gift of vulnerability to our bodily lives, the grace of physical limitations, and our ability to be attentive to the God-given wisdom of our bodies?[2]

Another sense of the body is the *cultural body*. This term describes how a specific culture shapes one's idea of the physical body. This sense of the body is captured in phrases such as "Boys don't cry" and "Act like a lady." It is experienced in practices of social etiquette (such as good manners) and of personal space (what is considered "too near" or "too far"). And it manifests itself in frequently contested dress codes ("formal" vs. "informal"), codes of conduct for men and women (weeping publicly vs. privately), and in hotly charged ideas around "proper" body image.[3]

Closely related is the idea of the *social body*, which draws our attention specifically to the powerful ways that the experience of our own bodies is shaped by our social interactions with others, whether that involves our families of origin, our present friendships and professional circles, or our interactions with society at large.[4]

With respect to the church's worship, these two senses of the body have informed where men and women might sit in the sanctuary (whether separate or together), what forms of touch are appropriate between people (often maximal for Latin American cultures and minimal for Asian cultures), how children may be excluded from the "serious business" of worship, when a display of emotion is perceived as welcomed or indecorous, why the inclusion of a Black Jesus in the iconography of a worship space may be experienced as countercultural or contextually necessary, and other similar sociocultural matters.

With respect to more specifically biblical language about the body, the language of *the body of Christ*, small *b*, usually indicates the physical body of Jesus, while capital *B*, *the Body of Christ*, points to the corporate form of the church.[5] There is also the often-confusing language of *flesh* (Greek: *sarx*) in the New Testament that, while frequently overlapping with the language of ***body*** (Greek: *sōma*), is its own unique thing in Paul's Letters. Both can be good or bad, depending on the circumstances. Beyond these Bible-specific terms, the language of ***ritual body*** and ***mystical body*** often shows up in discussions around the body in worship—the former referring to what Christians do from beginning to end of corporate worship and the latter describing how God is sacramentally present and available to Christians by grace.

This leads us to the complicated territory of *sign*, *symbol*, and *sacrament*. While I cannot fully address the rich complexity that these three terms demand, for the purposes of this book I wish to clarify a few things here. First, the word ***sign*** means one thing in the Texas Department of Transportation and a very different thing in the Gospel of John. In the TxDOT, a highway sign serves one purpose only: to tell us what city lies ahead and how many miles we must travel to get there. The sign, in this way, *points away from itself* and holds only the power of information: El Paso, 851 miles ahead. In the Gospel of John, by contrast, a sign (Greek: *sēmeia*), like the water that Jesus changes into wine at Cana in John 2, *retains in itself the power which it symbolizes*. These signs disclose Jesus's unique identity in, and not despite, the material thing itself. Sign (water-to-wine) and the thing signified (revelation of Christ's glory) are inextricably linked. God's glory is thus revealed through rather than beyond the physical.

It is in this sense that signs in John are more like a *symbol* in our common understanding of the term. Unlike a road sign, a national flag has the power of symbol behind it. It does not simply indicate a thing (a history, a people, a value); it also participates in the reality to which it points. It is for this reason that burning a national flag causes such strong emotion, even violence, as this may be perceived as a threat to a country's identity, while the burning of a road sign may only result in an inconvenience to the people who are required to replace it. It is in this sense that there is no such thing as a "mere symbol" in the Bible. There are only symbols—visible, visceral, tangible symbols—through which we experience the true knowledge of God.

As it relates to corporate worship, contested symbols may include people who appear in sacred paintings (like biblical figures of questionable moral character), the presence or absence of Jesus's body on a cross that hangs in a sanctuary, the official clothes that pastors wear, or the specific placement of a baptismal font in the church. The language of *sacrament*, finally, includes the sense of a symbol, but with the added idea that it emphasizes the sensory experience of God's grace—of tasting, touching, seeing, hearing, and smelling such a grace.[6] In Augustinian terms, a sacrament is a visible sign of an invisible grace, and it not only discloses to us the true knowledge of God but also communicates the grace of God *through* physical things.[7]

In the usual discussions of sacraments, this involves baptism and Communion, among other things. In a broader sense, the term "sacramental" describes the way in which all material things are suffused with divine grace.[8] With respect to the purposes of this book, a sacramental vision for the body at worship brings to light the unified work of the Trinity.[9] The Father delights to work through all aspects of our physical humanity in order to redeem and to sanctify us. In the Son we witness how this is so, where not only hearts and minds are changed but also bodies. And it is the Spirit who makes it possible for us to actually experience God's grace through physical things, bringing about our restoration not just through preaching and praying and such, but also through the God-given insights of such fields as psychology and physiotherapy, neuroscience and art therapy.[10] It is not one or the other; it is both-and.[11]

The Functions of the Body

With these definitions in mind, what are the different functions of the body at worship? What, that is, are the sorts of things that a body might do in a liturgical context? In general terms, I suggest that the body can do two basic things. First, it can assume an active role through postures (such as standing and kneeling), gestures (such as bowing and the sign of the cross), and movement (such as clapping, jumping, processing, and choreographed dance). Second, it can shape our experience of worship through our five senses. What forms our sense of God is not simply how we move or position our bodies in worship but also what our bodies see (or never see), what they hear (or hear only rarely), and what they smell, taste, and touch (as the case may be).[12]

As it relates to specific functions that a physical body might perform in corporate worship, there are five that we might highlight here. One function of the body is *aesthetic*. A Messianic Jewish circle dance, for example, may be done for the sake of delight, while a hip-hop performance might be done for the pleasure that a congregation experiences in response to the miraculous rescue of God.[13] The same may be true in the experience of an exquisite postlude that features the music of Mozart, a joyful eruption of applause following the baptism of a member of the community, or the inclusion of purely decorative elements such as embellished colonnades or stained glass in the architecture of a building. Aesthetic delight is one of God's gifts to our bodies.

A second function of the body in worship is *didactic*. Sandra Organ-Solis, a former ballerina for the Houston Ballet, has created a choreographed version of the Nicene Creed that she often performs for congregations during worship. The piece involves her speaking a phrase from the Creed and accompanying that phrase with interpretive movement. This serves, for her, not as a substitute for the verbal confession of the Creed but as a way to perceive the kinetic contours of faith. Celeste Schroeder reinforces this view, noting that faith "does not go in a straight line but turns, falls, sinks, pulls, pushes, releases, clings, pauses, leaps, and dances."[14] The gestures that a pastor uses in a celebration of the Lord's Supper are another didactic function of the body.

A third function is ***devotional***. Walking a labyrinth, for instance, is a way for the body to move in prayer, as many Christians have experienced firsthand.[15] As the body moves through the spiral of lines, the heart contemplates the things of God. Walking in and around a contoured path, the body offers a space for the heart to be kindled with affection for God. The posture of stillness may be another way for the body to serve the purposes of devotion. Stillness can be a way for the Christian to know certain things about God that cannot be known in any other way apart from a quieting of the body that, in turn, opens a space for the mind to attend to God (Ps. 46:10).

The body may also serve a specific ***activity*** of the liturgy. At Church of the Servant in Grand Rapids, Michigan, for example, liturgical dancers carry the elements of the Lord's Supper from the back of the sanctuary to the front. This is done to symbolize the movement of bread and wine as a gift *from* God *to* the people of God—as well as *from* the raw materials of the earth and the human hands that make something of the earth *to* the table of God, where Christ offers himself as bread for the life of the world and the Spirit remakes us so that we might become the hands and feet of Christ to the hungry and thirsty of our world.

The body may be enlisted, lastly, for ***missional*** purposes. In fourth-century Jerusalem, a procession of Christians moved through the city streets during major holy days, testifying thereby of the expansive scope of God's reign on earth.[16] As their physical bodies moved from place to place, they symbolically reenacted the pilgrimage of Christians on earth and their calling to bear the image of God in every time and place. A similar thing occurred with the "March for Jesus" movement that started in the late twentieth century, which included processions of Christians around the world singing and praying, carrying banners, and lifting joyful shouts into the air as they marched through the streets and demonstrated the *public* aspect of distinctly Christian worship.

The Powers of the Body

In order to appreciate the specific ways that our bodies form us in worship, we need to also have a clear sense of the unique powers that they possess. These include, among other things, body knowledge, muscle memory, nonverbal communication, the enculturated nature of our bodies, and embodied presence. These powers show up in common figures of speech, such as "I know it in my bones," or "It's like riding a bicycle," or "Her face says it all." All such figures of speech describe the ways we figure out the world through our bodies and through the powers that they possess to form us, for better and for worse.

What the Body Knows

A first power of the body is **body knowledge**. This is a kind of knowledge that athletes and farmers know a great deal about. An athlete acquires a form of kinetic intelligence after a lifetime of repetitive physical exercises. A farmer obtains a sense for the weather after a lifetime of seeing the sky and smelling the air. With both, the body acquires a feel for a way of being in the world through direct and recurring sensory experience. In other cases, the body may acquire negative knowledge through addictive behaviors, chronic stressors, and traumatic experiences, the latter of which leave a person feeling powerless and profoundly debilitated, as with those who suffer from PTSD (post-traumatic stress disorder).[17]

When Christians repeatedly open their hands to receive the pastor's benediction, it is a way for them to get a *handle* on a life that remains always open to God's blessing. Or when members of a multiethnic congregation exchange hugs and kisses at the passing of the peace Sunday after Sunday, they acquire a sense of God's reconciling work that ought to characterize their whole bodily selves. Or the freshly baked bread that I take in my hands, then bless, break, and offer to the congregation, serves to form in me a feel for a eucharistically shaped life. In doing all such things over time, we gain a *body knowledge* of our identity as the true Body of Christ.

What the Body Remembers

A second power of the body is **muscle memory**. A pianist's fingers, for example, acquire memory of a piece of music through careful repetition, in such a way that the piece can eventually be played without deliberate thought. Musicians might say things like "my hands have a mind of their own" to express this experience. The same is true of typing on a keyboard. Eventually each finger knows exactly where to go without needing to consult the brain each time a key is pressed. What the body remembers applies to things like tying one's shoes, knitting scarves, or braiding hair. After repeated, conscious, and intelligent practice, such things can be performed automatically.[18]

One also hopes that such things will result in our bodily actions at worship. When members of a multigenerational congregation, for example, lay hands on one another during the prayer ministry that follows a sermon, the hope is that this repeated action—as a tactile sign of the re-membering work of the Spirit—might generate holy muscle memory in moments when these same members might be tempted to judge and to find one another wanting in some fashion beyond the context of corporate worship. The prayer is that such members will not have to think twice about the sacrificial love that ought to mark each generation of Christ's Body.

What the Body Says on Its Own

Not only does the body remember things but it also says things of its own accord, in the form of ***nonverbal communication*** that may or may not match what we have communicated with words. We may say one thing with our mouth, for instance, such as "I trust you," but a contrary thing with our eyes, "I don't trust you," and the latter will often be believed as the more reliable indicator of the person's intent. Crossed arms may communicate a closed-off disposition, a knowing glance is usually understood between friends, and very different messages are given by a weak handshake, a warm bear hug, a patronizing pat on the head, or a controlling grip on the arm. Our bodies are always talking, whether we realize it or not, and they may be saying things that support or contradict our acts of verbal communication.

Within a context of corporate worship, nonverbal communication plays an outsized role. For example, a typically American Christian may interpret the actions of a typically Japanese Christian during the passing of the peace as a sign of disinterest because a large personal space was maintained in the exchange. Or a highly variable volume of voice and the use of nonverbal noises (such as grunting or sighing) may communicate sincerity in a sermon in one context but may provoke negative feelings in another context because such speech is perceived as "melodramatic" or "sensationalist."[19] And, as was common in 2021, when many congregations gathered in person but chose to remain masked, pastors preached to people whose faces remained inscrutable. All the usual nonverbal cues that a mouth might make stayed hidden, and a vital sense of connection was lost.

What the Body Says in Context

A fourth power of the body is its capacity to communicate meaning in *culturally contextual* ways. At a general level, this will include ideas about "who my people are" by virtue of what is done with the body and "who is with me in this moment" because of how the bodies of the many are coordinated in action.[20] It includes ideas about what it means to be a "strong man" or a "submissive woman." It includes things such as eye contact (usually perceived in the West as a sign of confidence but in Middle Eastern cultures as rude or challenging), kisses between and across genders (more common in Latin American and European cultures), and the volume of one's voice in conversation (often louder in Arab cultures and softer in Southeast Asian ones).

Within a liturgical context, it includes ideas around what counts as appropriate church attire. In some contexts, for example, casual clothing will be regarded as proper dress for one who has entered the "domestic" house of God, marked by the authentic gathering of family members who congregate in communion with Christ the Host. In other contexts, more formal clothing will be viewed as suitable for a visit to the "majestic" house of God, where royalty determines one's attire in the presence of Christ the King.[21] Or with many African churches, it is in dance "that the African can best be himself."[22] To be an African Christian is to be a Christian who moves freely in worship. This stands in sharp contrast to what the German Joseph Cardinal Ratzinger (formerly Pope Benedict XVI) argues—namely, that dancing cannot be regarded as an appropriate form of expression for *any* Christian at worship.[23]

What the Body Senses Near at Hand

A final power of the body is the power of *embodied presence*. This is the body that is immediately and physically present to the body of another. Politicians, for instance, know that there is no substitute for the tireless travel that takes them on the campaign trail from town to town—shaking hands, sharing meals, and listening to people's stories—rather than only communicating to them by way of print, television, or internet. Similarly, while a pastor may call a sick parishioner over the phone in order to pray for her, a unique power is experienced when the pastor visits and prays with her in person—holding her hand, looking her in the eye, remaining near at hand. This also holds true for practices of communal song, the administration of the Lord's Supper, and healing prayer where face-to-face exchanges and the possibility of physical touch are perceived as essential.

In the end, all the singular powers of the body add up to the experience of a bodily inertia. This describes a certain way of being in the world in our physical bodies that we take for granted and do not readily or consciously question unless our bodily inertia itself is questioned and reordered by an encounter with a new idea or way of being in our bodies.[24]

The Meanings of the Body

The way in which our bodies make our experience of worship intelligible and meaningful is another aspect of the body that requires a bit of clarity. A common assumption among Christians in the West is that what *really* matters in worship is what we think and what we say. Words and ideas are everything. What we do with our bodies, so the thinking goes, is, at best, a bonus aspect of worship or, at worst, a negligible and inhibiting thing to true worship. But as philosopher Mark Johnson argues in his book *The Meaning of the Body*, what we experience as meaningful in the world "reaches deep down into our corporeal encounter with our environment."[25] In other words, we are not disembodied minds or talking machines; we are holistic creatures whose corporeal experiences of the world determine how we think about reality itself and live meaningfully in it.[26]

For example, the idea of "up" as "happy" does not come from nowhere; it comes instead from our experience of the world, where physically erect postures typically match to a positive emotional state.[27] Conversely, when we let gravity have its way with us, it usually results in the experience of being pulled down, and it is for this reason that we correlate sadness with feeling "down," because of how "low" we may feel. Or the statement "I have grasped a concept" makes sense only because we have first grasped a physical thing in our hands: held it, touched it, felt its weight and texture, assessed it, and so on.[28] If I "grasp an idea," this means that I have understood it; if I "lose my grip" on reality, then I am somehow failing to understand a thing.[29] Human language is rooted in physical realities.

Our bodily experiences of the world also generate metaphorical fodder for how we think about what is "normal" or "good."[30] In the context of the Bible, for example, we find such metaphors as "the body is a temple" (1 Cor. 6:19) and "the eye is the lamp of the body" (Matt. 6:22). The physical body is not, of course, literally a stone structure, and it is physiologically impossible for the eye to light something up. But nor are we to think that these are "mere" metaphors.[31] Meaning is discovered *through* the metaphor, not despite it. It is also true that these metaphors are meaningful only because we have had experiences of actual physical buildings and lamps. Such bodily rooted metaphors disclose things about our new identity as Christ's Body that we could not know in any other way. And like the rest of the features of our embodied life that we have explored in this chapter, they amount to a form of "intelligence in the flesh," without which we cannot live a full or meaningful life as human beings.[32]

The Gift of the Body

The whole point here is that our physical bodies powerfully shape our experience of the world around us. Our bodies are not a bonus, and they are never neutral. They are a gift. They may not, of course, feel like a gift at times, but, like all the gifts of God's creation, our bodies represent tangible evidence of the grace of God, evidenced supremely in the flesh of Jesus. Because they are a gift, our bodies are to be stewarded rather than to be "possessed"; cherished as a microcosm of God's glory, not manipulated like disposable "things"; and embraced as wounded but beloved sites for the Spirit's work of healing, not shunned or shamed. And when we offer our bodies wholly to God in worship, it is a way for us to begin to discover what bodies are *for*—what they *can* and *must* do in order to fulfill their unique creaturely purposes.

To worship well with our bodies, in the end, requires understanding our bodies rightly. And though much more could have been said on the matter, my hope is that readers will feel inspired to discover in the chapters that follow all the good work that the Trinity has entrusted to our bodies in the corporate worship of the church. I also hope that those who feel alienated from their bodies might discover themselves becoming more at home with their God-given bodies and with the bodies of other members of Christ's Body, as they gather together liturgically.[33] Finally, my hope is that readers will not feel their "too, too solid flesh," as Shakespeare's Hamlet calls it, as onerous but rather as a blessed locus for communion with God in the praises and prayers of the people of God.

3

The Story of the Body

Historical Perspectives on the Body in Worship

For as the body is clad in the cloth, and the flesh in the skin, and the bones in the flesh, and the heart in the whole, so are we, soul and body, clad in the Goodness of God, and enclosed.

—Julian of Norwich

So then, brothers and sisters, stand firm and hold fast to the traditions that you were taught by us, either by word of mouth or by our letter.

—2 Thessalonians 2:15

The Wisdom of History

What wisdom might church history offer to us on the role of the body in worship? Allow me first to summarize some of this wisdom before I address a number of key issues at greater length, in order that we might make the most of the wisdom that church history offers to us in our own liturgical times and places.

First, history is neither the holy grail of ready-to-wear absolute truth about the body in worship nor a complete wasteland of hodge-podge data about the body's role in worship—nor is it a waste of our time, as some in free church traditions may suppose. The study of church history can serve to illumine how Christians in different times and places have appropriated the data of Scripture to worship God in bodily faithful fashion; it can serve as an occasion for the recovery of practices of the body that may have been lost or neglected, as Anglo-Catholics during the Gothic Revival of the nineteenth century concluded; and it can serve to inspire and instruct as well as to reorder and reimagine our own uses of the body in corporate worship, as Pentecostals have experienced firsthand.

Second, however the body was used in worship in the early centuries of the church, the body mattered.[1] Over against Gnostic assertions to the contrary, the body mattered to early Christianity because it was seen to occupy a sacramental space in which the goodness of the physical world had received God's definitive benediction and through which the grace of God was palpably experienced. In opposition to body-denying claims of the time, Christians believed that the body mattered because Jesus Christ had taken on human flesh and *retained* that flesh in his resurrected humanity, albeit in a Spirit-refashioned form. And counter to all metaphysical dualist beliefs of that period, Christians believed that the Spirit remained steadfastly committed to the renewal of the whole of material existence. This is important for contemporary Christians to remember because the temptation to regard the body in Gnostic fashion is one that every generation of Christians must learn to actively resist.

Third, the body will always find itself in a complicated relationship with worship and culture. The early third-century *Epistle to Diognetus* describes the Christians of that day in a way that illumines this complicated relationship: "They are at home in their own countries, but as sojourners. They participate in all things as citizens and they endure all things as foreigners. Every country is their homeland and every homeland is a foreign country."[2] While God has made our bodies to be "at home" and to "make sense" within a particular time and place, our bodies by virtue of belonging to Christ will also find themselves at odds with our own home cultures—broken as they are.[3] Always we must seek to discern how the body in worship might remain contextually rooted, cross-culturally and transculturally meaningful, and serve as a countercultural force in Jesus's name.

With these summary thoughts in mind, it is important to state that the purpose of this chapter is not to be exhaustive but rather to offer an abridged and perspectival trip through church history that might inspire in us a more richly full engagement of our bodies in corporate worship.⁴ It should also be said that while the study of church history is fundamentally important to a faithful liturgical use of the body, serving both to ground and to orient our own embodied practices today, such a study is marked by murky passages that resist easy interpretation and data that is shrouded in the mists of time and that is often polemically charged.⁵ On this point, liturgical scholar Paul Bradshaw urges readers to be alert to any "unconscious projections back into ancient times of later practices."⁶ If there is anything that we can assert with complete confidence, then, it is that the data of history is far more complex than is often assumed.⁷

> **Let no one tell you that this body of ours is a stranger to God.**
> —Cyril of Jerusalem, **Catechetical Homilies**

Context Is Everything

The first thing that must be said, at the risk of stating the obvious, is that context is everything. Perhaps less obvious is that there are very different ways in which context illumines the history of the body in worship. The meaning of terms to describe the bodily activities of worship, for instance, may change with the times and require that we attend carefully to meaning in linguistic context. The distinctive contexts in which kinetic activities are exercised—whether in formal corporate worship or in familial and communal activities of worship—also come into play. And it is crucial that we not misinterpret the relative absence of certain embodied practices of worship during the pre-Constantinian era, when Christians would have been denied opportunities for a fulsome public worship on account of political, social, or economic hardship.⁸

In his book *Liturgical Dance*, J. G. Davies offers two examples of terms with meanings that have changed over time: *praesul* and *chorus*. The first term, *praesul*, in its original pre-Christian Greek context described the practice of a priest of the god Mars, who performed a war dance in honor of the god; however, in the early medieval era it denoted a person of eminence or authority, such as a judge or a bishop. "As far as the word 'chorus' is concerned," Davies writes, "it is simply not true that wherever it appears in the writings of either the Greek or Latin Fathers dancing is always denoted. There is no denying the fact that in its beginnings, over five hundred years before Christ, the Greek chorus danced—so Plato: 'the chorus is made up of two parts, dance and song.'"[9] But by the time of the patristic era, the term nearly exclusively pointed to the practice of singing, not dancing.

These two points suggest a need for restraint in our deployment of "dance" quotes from the patristic era. Whereas many English translations of Clement of Alexandria (150–215), for example, have the church father saying that Christians raise "a sober choral dance," Davies insists that a more accurate translation of the Greek is, "stirring up a solemn choral chant."[10] And although Gregory of Nazianzus readily calls the citizens of heaven a people who "dance an eternal dance," there is no indication that he recommended the practice of dance in the liturgical worship of his day. In fact, the language of dance often appears as shorthand for a variety of *non-dancing* activities: as a roundabout way of talking about good works (Augustine), as a euphemism for the joyful soul (Ambrose), and as a figurative way of talking about the holy life (Gregory of Nazianzus).

To believe that the patristic era enthusiastically welcomed dance into the church's worship, as casual readers of history might do, is to misunderstand how language worked during this time period and to misappropriate a statement for purposes that remain foreign to its authors.[11]

It is likewise important that we not assume a single context for embodied practices of worship. What may flourish in paraliturgical contexts, such as at a wedding service, may not equally flourish in official liturgical contexts. Martin Luther (1483–1546), for instance, made allowance for dance at weddings in Protestant Germany, so long as young people engaged in it in modest ways. In a sermon from John 2:1–11, which he preached in 1525, he writes: "Whether the Jews had dances I do not know; but since it is the custom of the country, like inviting guests, decorating, eating and drinking and being merry, I see no reason to condemn it, save its excess when it goes beyond decency and moderation."[12]

John Chrysostom, by contrast, had no tolerance for dance at weddings under any circumstances. In a comment on Isaac's marriage with Rebecca, he writes, "Consider here how there was no satanical pomp, no cymbals, and piping, and dancing, no satanical feasting, no scurrilous buffoonery of filthy discourse, but all was gravity, wisdom and modesty."[13] He says much the same with respect to Jacob and Leah's wedding. For both Luther and Chrysostom, the culture of their time played a determinative role.

A final area that requires careful contextual thinking is around practices that would have occurred pre- and post-Constantine. In a pre-Constantinian era, prior to AD 313, only certain things will have easily flourished under conditions of duress and in the face of Greco-Roman cultural pressures. Other things, such as works of church architecture on a grand scale, could not be built under such circumstances. Church leaders of the time also would have worried about syncretistic entanglements with pagan worship practices, such as religious dances, which would have included drunken revelry as well as the veneration of Greek and Roman gods.[14] Ecclesiastical leaders would have feared that embracing dance in Christian worship would have been tantamount to idolatry, and an absolute prohibition was believed to be the only pastorally prudent thing to do.[15]

What changed in the post-Constantinian era? Plenty. What was once done behind closed doors for fear of persecution now goes public. "In a monopoly position," writes Davies, "the church could now afford to be generous towards pagan practices; its identity could not be blurred because it had no rivals."[16] The use of incense, for example, is now reconceived under the light of Christ's coming and finds easier entrance into the church's public worship. Susan Harvey, who chronicles the explosion of material artifacts during the post-Constantinian era in her book *Scenting Salvation*, summarizes things this way: "At every turn, Christianity encouraged and engaged a tangible, palpable piety physically experienced and expressed."[17]

It is important, however, when reading this account in church history that we not hastily adopt a narrative of decline or of unqualified glory. The transition from a condition of persecution, marked by a minority position in society, to a condition of privilege, marked by a majority position, must not necessarily be seen as a hopeless corruption of the faith or as the unequivocal "Triumph of the Church," underwritten in full by divine providence. Both may be true, but not without serious qualification. It should also be stated that what occurs in the fourth century is not unusual to church history. Christians of every era adapt and adopt the practices of a local culture, freighted with meaning that may remain strange or sympathetic to faithful corporate worship.

Adaptions and Adoptions

Two ways in which a local culture informs the embodied practices of corporate worship include the notion of *stately conduct* in Greco-Roman society and the ideas of feudal *honor* in the medieval era. With respect to the first, historians generally agree that for early Christianity there was a greater dependence on the "high culture" of upper-class Romans than on the somatically expansive worship of Judaism.[18] Joseph Cardinal Ratzinger explains how kneeling, for instance, was viewed as "unworthy of a free man, unsuitable for the culture of Greece."[19] It was considered barbaric and superstitious, unbecoming of a noble human being, with the practice of expressive dancing being even more so.

In contrast to an embodied Jewish worship rooted in a creation spirituality and typified in the demonstrative actions of Miriam and David, in the Greco-Roman world of Galen and Marcus Aurelius a true Greek scholar remained sober-minded and physically restrained. "Gradually," explains African theologian Elochukwu Uzukwu, "from antiquity down to the Middle Ages, the ideal of godlike immobility was preferred by the elite to body movement."[20] More passionate, spontaneous bodily activities might be rejected as "undignified" or "indecorous."[21] Subtlety of gesture, precision of posture, and moderation of movement represented the ideal philosopher in the culture of Greco-Roman antiquity, and this, in time, would also become regarded as "the genius" of the Roman rite in the West, with its emphasis on a "sober" and "solemn" liturgy.[22]

Another posture of worship that owes a good deal to its immediate culture is the posture of praying while kneeling, with hands folded.[23] Although the act of praying standing had served as the dominant posture for prayer for the first thousand years of the Western church, kneeling in the liturgy had replaced it as the ideal posture by the time of the medieval era. Ratzinger writes how this posture derives from the world of feudalism, wherein the "recipient of a feudal estate, on taking tenure, placed his joined hands in those of his lord."[24] Although the act of kneeling at Sunday worship was met with great resistance in some places, not least because the fourth-century Council of Nicaea had explicitly prohibited it, it eventually won the day as the preferred posture for liturgical worship.[25]

The Confusions of Culture

What is the point here? The point is not that culture is a problem. Culture is simply the creaturely form in which the worship of God takes concrete shape.[26] Nor is the point that worship should not find a home in the heart language of a particular culture.[27] There is, in fact, no culture-less form of worship in which the words, actions, and forms of worship do not become meaningful to a particular people—neither in Abraham's time nor in Paul's nor in our own. The point is that the culture of a time and place makes certain bodily activities of worship more *plausible* and *desirable* to a particular group of people, rather than preposterous and unimaginable.

It is equally important to point out that Christians of every time and place will both *borrow* and *reject* local customs for use in worship, which, when introduced into Christian worship, may also take on a "life of their own."[28] For example, the *orans*, or standing posture for prayer, while inherited from Greco-Roman culture, would now be reinterpreted in light of the cross.[29] A similar thing occurs with the exchange of a kiss in worship: while once shared only among members of the same social class, it would now function as a decisive sign of the peace that Christ had brought and with it a breaking down of walls of separation between members of society.[30]

If there is a problem to be reckoned with, it is the way in which the culture of a particular time or place presumes that its worship is culture-less and therefore universally binding for all people in a way that undermines the telos of the church (see Rev. 21:24–26).[31] Uzukwu rightly argues, for instance, how the physically "unaffected" comportment of priests in the Roman Catholic liturgy, rooted as it is in a specifically European history that valorizes an economy of movement, bears no resemblance to the quintessential African experience, wherein dynamic rhythms, expressive gestures, and spontaneous movements are regarded as integral to the public worship of the church.[32]

In a war against superstition, paganism, and idolatry that took place during the colonial period in the West, the unique spirit of African worship was rejected wholesale. And although Vatican II officially stated that in matters related to the liturgy, the Catholic Church does "respect and foster the genius and talents of the various races and peoples,"[33] the reality is that at the time of the writing of Uzukwu's book in 1997, "the score sheet on inculturation or the localization of the Church in Africa remains unimpressive."[34] This is a story that can be retold in any number of denominational contexts, from Baptist to Presbyterian to Lutheran, and with respect to plenty of cultural contexts globally.

It is one thing, of course, to fully indwell one's own culture; this is good and right. It is another thing to assume a hegemonic attitude with respect to one's own amalgam of worship and culture. To argue, as some in the Protestant and Catholic West have done, that a restraint in gestures is merely a way to remain faithful to how the church has "always" worshiped is to underestimate one's own culture's capacity for self-deception and to misjudge a culture's fundamental need to be ever-reformed by the Holy Spirit. This issue, in turn, raises the question of what I am calling the double-edged sword of originalism.

The Double-Edged Sword of Originalism

An "originalist" reading of worship in church history, as I define it here, has two sides to it. On one side is the idea that if we can find a practice of worship in the early centuries of the church, then it must remain normative for the church's worship today. On the other side is the conviction that if we cannot find an expression of worship in the early centuries of the church, then it does not belong in our worship today. An example of the former is fully naked baptism in third-century North Africa and citywide processions in fourth-century Jerusalem, while an example of the latter would be the inclusion of organs and pews, which became central to the church's public worship in the West only in the tenth and thirteenth centuries, respectively.[35] And if an originalist argument were applied to all postures, gestures, and movements of corporate worship, none of us might be kneeling at any point in the celebration of the Lord's Supper or standing during the Lenten season.[36]

The same set of arguments can be made with respect to the place of dance in corporate worship. Whereas the patristic era eschewed liturgical dance altogether, in the medieval era a proliferation of dance occurred in the form of choral dances, labyrinthine dances, ring dances, and, most famously, the Dance of Death and the Feast of Fools.[37] The evidence for dance is so extensive, Davies writes, "that it would be tedious for the reader to be faced with detailed descriptions."[38] In the periods that followed, dance waxed and waned in public worship, while the modern era sees a near-complete absence of it within the main bodies of Catholic and Protestant churches.[39]

With the advent of the twentieth century, dance slowly made its way back into corporate worship, culminating in an explosion of choreographic and scholarly work in the 1970s and '80s. Whether it is the Dance of the Cross in the Ethiopian Church, the liturgical dance ministry of the Abyssinian Baptist Church, or the hip-hop dance ministry of Hillsong Church, a wide variety of contemporary churches are making a place for dance in corporate worship by appealing to its oldest origins: the Old Testament.

While one side of the church, then, may argue that the absence of dance in the early centuries of the church in both the East and the West legitimizes its present exclusion from corporate worship, the other side may argue that its presence in Israel's worship demonstrates its most ancient, God-ordained origin and thus its continuing liturgical benefit today.[40] My point here is not to make a case for or against dance—or any other particular bodily activity of worship. My point is simply to invite the reader to a more chastened understanding regarding the origins of any specific embodied practices of worship. Both slavish repetition and impulsive rejection ought to be avoided. In its stead we ought to read church history judiciously and to discern the mind of God as revealed in Holy Scripture in conversation with the wise saints of eras past—which is to say, with church tradition—so that our embodied worship might remain faithful to God and coherent to a particular people in a particular time.

Holy Scripture and Tradition

This raises the rather complicated issue of the relationship between the Bible and tradition as they relate to the body in worship. In many ways the Bible is the Rorschach test of church history: one often sees what one is *predisposed* to see on account of one's social location. For instance, even though the New Testament includes no explicit practice or prescription for the use of musical instruments in corporate worship, plenty of churches have justified their inclusion for reasons that remain exegetically foreign to the Gospels and Epistles themselves. Yet other bodily activities of worship, such as dancing or the use of incense, both of which are commended in the Old Testament, are often excluded for reasons that remain directly tied to cultural predilections and theological prejudices of one sort or another. Likewise, one is hard-pressed to find a liturgical tradition that has attempted to implement every single instance of bodily worship in the Bible—full prostration *and* speaking in tongues *and* wearing head-coverings *and* shouting to God in praise *and* exchanging a physical kiss, and so on.

Although there is no way to adequately address the complex relationship between Bible and tradition in this chapter, perhaps St. Basil's (330–379) reflection on embodied worship might offer us a word of wisdom.[41] In his treatise on the Holy Spirit, Basil anticipates a question that his imagined interlocutor asks of him: On what basis do we use our bodies in the liturgy when Scripture makes no mention of actions, such as the sign of the cross, or turning eastward for prayer, or immersing people three times in the baptismal waters? In answer to this question, Basil writes that certain things are stated plainly for all to see in the Bible but that other things have been "received in mystery as the teachings of the traditions of the apostles." Such teachings, he argues, represent "the very vital parts of the Gospel"—that is, the good purposes of God for the church.[42]

Basil likewise notes how these embodied activities are subject to multiple meanings, and that such meanings remain integral to the warp and woof of the Bible itself. Why, for instance, do Christians say their prayers standing on the first day of the week? Basil answers, "By standing for prayer we remind ourselves of the grace given to us on the day of the resurrection, as if we are rising to stand with Christ and being bound to seek what is above." We stand both to cultivate hope during this earthly pilgrimage and to turn the mind to future things in the "age to come." We pray standing, finally, "so that we would not neglect the provisions for our journey to everlasting life by a constant reminder of it."[43] For all such reasons, the Christian stands on Sunday because it remains commensurate with the mind of Scripture and befits the posture of sanctified humanity before God.

In the end, Basil does not limit himself to explicit prescriptive or proscriptive statements about bodily worship in Scripture; he also commends principles and practices that can be inferred from Scripture. In the same way that we rightly confess our faith in the Trinity as true to the nature of God, even though that term is not found in Scripture, Basil argues that bodily practices that come to us without an explicit scriptural warrant but are commended to us by the apostles and fathers should rightly be embraced because they remain faithful to the God of Scripture. Basil in this way seeks to remain faithful to the mind of the church, which is to say to a Spirit-authorized, Spirit-authenticated tradition. In this too he seeks to remain faithful to the Bible itself, for example, to passages such as 2 Thessalonians 2:15: "So then, brothers and sisters, stand firm and hold fast to the traditions that you were taught by us, either by word of mouth or by our letter" (cf. 1 Cor. 11:1–2; 2 Thess. 3:6).

The lesson for us is this: if a bodily practice of worship, which has been handed down "by word of mouth," increases God's glory, then it has fulfilled God's written word. If it increases Christlikeness in us, then it has realized the good purposes of the Word made flesh. And where it may in some fashion fail to increase such Christlikeness, then we welcome the Spirit of God, in conversation with Christ's global Body, to interrogate and to interrupt our traditions in order to draw us back to the heart of Scripture, which is also the heart of the triune God.

Abusus Non Tollit Usum

What happens, however, when an embodied practice of worship, regardless of its direct ties to Scripture or tradition, is misused or abused and leads not to Christlikeness but to the harm of our humanity and the rupture of Christ's Body? This tragically occurs all too often throughout church history. Precision of posture becomes pompous performance. Sensory-rich movement becomes spectacle. Expressive gesturing turns self-indulgent, while ecstatic dancing becomes sensationalistic. Physical self-discipline devolves to hatred of the body. Corporate movement grows manipulative and coercive. And the body's ability to lead us astray is seen to hold a greater power than the Spirit's power to transform our bodies, so it is sidelined and suppressed.

The possibility for mistreatment of the body in worship remains a constant danger for churches in every tradition and context. The human tendency to abuse material aids to worship is "a contagion disease of sorts," as Calvin once described it.[44] This includes, most fundamentally, any instance of idolatrous, hypocritical, and superstitious uses of the body that involve attempts to manipulate God or that result in mindless or heartless worship. It includes the unnecessary engorgement of bodily activities as well as the impoverishment of bodily activities. And it includes the possibility of racist, ableist, and sexist cultures and behaviors, which deny the full humanity of people's particular bodies.

Eastern Orthodox bishop Kallistos Ware is especially frank, for example, about the complicated legacy of women's bodies in Orthodox worship.[45] While the fundamental goodness of the body is always upheld in Greek Christianity, Ware acknowledges that a recurrent feature of monasticism from the fourth century onward is a "suspicion of the body, and more especially of women's bodies."[46] More broadly, the historian Caroline Walker Bynum shows how in both the patristic and medieval eras women were more closely associated with the alleged evils of the body, "which needed to be punished or expiated."[47] Men tended to be linked to soul, mind, and the "orderly" intellect, while women were usually tied to the "inferior" faculties of body, heart, and the "disorderly" passions.[48] Great harm has resulted from such false dualisms and faulty anthropologies, for which church leaders should readily repent.

Humility will always be needed to guide our employment of the physical body in worship in light of these harms and dangers. Wise leadership, pastoral care, constant education, growth in virtue—these too are essential. This is a work that is best accomplished when we welcome other members of Christ's Body to examine our own practices in order to show us where we may have confused gospel and culture, or failed to inhabit the fullness of the gospel, or undermined the beauty of the gospel in other members of Christ's global Body. It should also be said, however, that the possibility of misuse of our bodies in worship does not necessarily require the elimination of that use (in the Latin: *abusus non tollit usum*), even if for a season Christians may find its exclusion from corporate worship pastorally, theologically, or psychologically necessary.

In all these things wisdom is paramount.

A Body of Grace

Church history offers to us all one final lesson: grace must have the last word in all things that we do with our bodies in worship. In his treatise on prayer, *De Oratione*, Origen makes a forceful case for standing as the proper posture for Sunday worship, but he also reckons with circumstances, such as sickness, where praying sitting or lying down may be good and right. Such is the way of grace. The North African theologian

Tertullian (c. 155–220) likewise commends grace in his homily on prayer, in which he offers insight into the bodily postures that were common to his day and to the disagreements that Christians apparently held around these matters: "As regards kneeling, prayer finds a variety of practice in the action of a certain very few who refrain from kneeling on the Saturday. At the very moment when this difference of opinion is pleading its cause in the churches, the Lord will give His grace that they may either yield or, without proving a stumbling-block to others, follow their own opinion."[49] Augustine writes in a similar spirit, "We are made aware by a number of examples that there is no objection to how the body is positioned for prayer, as long as the mind is present to God and fixes its attention [upon God]."[50] Whatever the circumstances may be, grace must show us the way forward. And while some may see no benefit to the study of history around our uses of the body of worship, and while others may believe that the matter has been settled by ecumenical councils or the decrees of confessions, we do well to embrace the charity that 1 Peter 4:8 commends to us and that church history, at its best, exemplifies, trusting that if the love of Christ be our guide, all will be well.

4

The Benediction of the Body

Biblical Perspectives on the Body in Worship (Part 1)

Human flesh is, then, brought into being and maintained as flesh by touch from other flesh.

—Paul Griffiths, Christian Flesh

"Truly I tell you, whoever does not receive the kingdom of God as a little child will never enter it." And he took them up in his arms, laid his hands on them, and blessed them.

—Mark 10:15–16

A Body of Two Tales

One of the more persistent ways that Christians have read the biblical account of the physical body is as a narrative of decline. The tale goes something like this. At one time in the primordial past, in a pristine time that only two human beings were given to enjoy, the body was good. It was good for tasting delectable foods; it was good for tilling the garden; it was good for becoming "one flesh." But then sin entered the world and ruined everything. Most especially, it ruined the body. The body became the root of every bad thing that happened to humans: disordered relations, disordered work, disordered love of creaturely things, disordered imaginations, and, of course, disordered worship. And because of its unruly powers, the body would now need to be tamed, tortured, or transcended, as the circumstances demanded.

In the specific case of Israel's experience, this particular tale sees their physical aids to worship as a divine concession to their "weak" need for such things: things to look at, such as the tabernacle's tapestries; things to make sound with, like trumpets and timpani; things to do with their bodies, like skip, jump, and dance. All such aids, though necessary under the conditions of the old covenant, invariably caused them to cling to earthly things and to believe that God was automatically pleased by their material offerings of worship. But a time would come, this tale tells, when the people of God would mature and no longer need such "lesser" physical things to worship God faithfully.[1] They would need only their hearts and minds, invisible and interior things both, in order to enter into communion with the immaterial essence of God—spirit to Spirit, as it were.

On this telling of the body's tale, the good bodies of Genesis 1 become the unfortunate bodies of Romans 7. The blessed flesh of humans in Genesis 2 turns into the dangerous flesh of the saints in Romans 8. The kinetic bodies of Miriam and David turn into the reserved bodies of the Christians at Corinth. The maximalist bodies of the Psalter are exchanged for the modest bodies of 1 Timothy. And the sensuous bodies of Israel's worship are swapped for the sober bodies of the early church's worship, while the activities of our current "body of humiliation" in the liturgy of the church are seen to have nothing whatsoever to do with our future body in the glorious liturgy of heaven.

The tale that I wish to tell in this chapter and the next, however, is a very different tale of the body in the Bible. It is the tale of a body that, while disfigured by sin, does not lose its image-bearing glory. It is the tale of a body that is defined by the body of Jesus and that is determined by the economy of the Spirit. It is the tale of a body that gives and receives the healing touch of God. It is the tale of a body whose fundamental problem is not its fleshiness but rather its captivity to the forces of sin and death. It is the tale of a body that experiences now a Spirit-ed foretaste of our new creation bodies, prefigured in the glorified flesh of Christ. And it is the tale of a good body that remains central to the re-creative purposes of the Trinity, here and now, in the worship of the church.

Inasmuch as the Bible has played an integral role in how Christians across theological and liturgical lines have thought about the body, it is important that we revisit key biblical texts in order to challenge poor understandings of the physical body and to propose alternative interpretations that result not just in a positive estimation of the body in worship but also in a more biblically sound one. One chapter, however, can hardly do justice to this important task, which is why I have split the biblical investigation of our topic into two chapters. And while the Bible does not afford us an exhaustive blueprint for the right use of the body in a liturgical context, it does afford us a coherent and compelling picture of what the body is *for* in the church's worship.

> *It is not that incarnation is a means to divine ends but rather that incarnation is God's way of loving material creation and at the same time God's way of loving us.*
> —*Marilyn McCord Adams,*
> *"For Better for Worse Solidarity"*

What I am after here, then, is a judicious reading of broad patterns and unifying threads in Scripture in order to discern a proper role for the physical body in the church's worship.² To argue that patterns play a determinative role in our conception of the liturgical body is to argue that, while both prescriptive and proscriptive statements about the body matter, along with any number of key principles, they should be interpreted in relation to the relevant patterns that run throughout the Bible and in a way that remains coherent to a trinitarian conception of the body. It is also to argue that these patterns will suggest inertias and trajectories for right understandings and wise uses of the body in worship, rather than self-evident plans or compulsory formulae.

I begin my study at the beginning, then, where all bad ideas get their start: in Genesis.

Good Bodies

The first argument I wish to make here is that our physical bodies are not separate or secondary to the divine image that we bear as human beings. They are fundamental to the *imago Dei*. It is for this reason that we ought to give greater weight to what we do with our bodies in worship, because it is in and through our bodies, not despite or beyond them, that we make manifest God's glory. My argument here owes a specific debt to the work of biblical scholars of the past century who have persuasively shown how the corporeal dimension of the divine image is far more central to our humanity than had been thought possible or desirable by previous generations of theologians. They arrived at this conclusion by reading the biblical text in context rather than by superimposing on the text philosophical assumptions that were, and remain still, alien to the biblical world.

Starting with the publication of Herman Gunkel's critical work on Genesis in 1901, a great majority of biblical scholars have moved away from what is often called a "substantialist" reading of the image of God and more toward a "royalist" reading of it. A substantialist view goes something like this. If humans are created in the image of God, then whatever it is that God and humans share in common, that is what comprises the image. And since God has no physical body, then only the nonphysical parts of our humanity—such as rationality, freedom, morality, volition, etc., in short, the "higher" faculties of the soul—truly represent the divine image. Augustine gives representative voice to this view: "For not in the body but in the mind was man made in the image of God."[3]

Against this view, many biblical scholars have argued that a more accurate understanding of divine image language is to be sought in the text itself and in conversation with comparable cosmological documents of the time, in a way that makes good sense of the image language in Genesis and of the way that Genesis also subverts such language. In brief, the language of "image" and "likeness" that recurred in ancient Near Eastern literature of the time tended to view the king as the exclusive embodiment of the divinity. Wherever the king was, there also was the god. And as the image of that god (think here Nebuchadnezzar in Daniel 3), the king's person functioned as a "royal" representative of the god. Divine image language, in this particular context, described the whole person rather than only a part of the person.

One of the remarkable things about the Genesis story of creation, however, is the way in which the divine image is radically democratized. It is now *all* human beings, not just the king, who truly image God. But what the biblical account holds in common with similar accounts of the time is the idea that the whole person, not just specific faculties of the person, represented the divine one.[4] This too is a view that the rest of the Old Testament assumes. Claus Westermann summarizes the point this way:

"Gen 1:26f is concerned neither with the corporeal nor with the spiritual qualities of people; it is concerned only with the person as a whole."[5]

On this understanding of the *imago Dei*, then, human beings do not *have* the image of God inside them; instead, they *are* God's image, from head to toe and inside out.[6] The function of the *imago*, moreover, is not to depict something in God but rather to express the character of God in and through our whole humanity. Our vocation accordingly is to represent the life of God in our own native sphere: the physical creation. Wherever we find ourselves, in public or private, with others or in solitude, we bear the image of God.[7] John Kleinig comments, "The body of each person was made for theophany, for God's human manifestation on earth, the visible disclosure of his glory in human terms. That is what human bodies were designed to do and what they have failed to do ever since the rebellion of our primordial parents (Rom. 3:23). And that is what Jesus regained for all humanity to compensate for that failure (John 1:14, 16–18)."[8]

Another point of relevance for our study here is the way in which the author of Genesis brings into intimate relationship creation and worship. In a biblical perspective, there is no sharp divide between the two.[9] The linguistic parallels between Genesis and Israel's worship help us to see the interplay between the physical creation and the liturgical practices of the tabernacle. God's command to Adam "to till and keep" the garden (Gen. 2:15), for example, is the same language used in Exodus 3:12 and Numbers 28:2 to describe sacrificial offerings. Eden functions like a sanctuary, with Adam and Eve serving as archetypal Levites.[10] The Hebrew verb *hithallek* (to walk to and fro) in Genesis 3:8, additionally, is the same term used to describe the divine presence in the later tent sanctuaries of Leviticus 26:12, Deuteronomy 23:15, and 2 Samuel 7:6–7.

Other parallels include the cherubim that guard the east entrance to the garden and which would bring to mind for the original reader the cherubim of Solomon's temple that guard the entrance to the inner sanctuary (1 Kings 6:23–28).[11] The tree of life adumbrates the menorah candelabrum, while God clothes Adam and Eve in a manner similar to the way that Moses clothes the priests (Exod. 28:41; 29:8; 40:14; Lev. 8:13).[12] And the seventh day of rest, in an ancient Near Eastern context, symbolized the day when the gods, by entering the temple place, took control of the cosmos.[13] The garden, as a microcosm of the heavens and the earth, represents in this way the house of God, a place of ordered flourishing under the personal rule of Yahweh.[14]

What the Bible commends to us, then, is a holistic vision of creation and worship. There is no metaphysical bifurcation here. There is no creation "over here" and worship "over there." There is no *body* doing one thing and *soul* doing another separate thing. There is only our whole humanity created and called to worship God with all our heart, mind, and strength in our own unique creaturely ways. Worship occurs in and through creation because it is God's continual pleasure to call forth praise in "the very beautiful fabric of the world," as John Calvin once put it.[15] This, I suggest, is the consistent testimony in Scripture, not just in the Pentateuch but also in the Psalms, the prophetic visions of Isaiah and Jeremiah, and the New Testament.

What, then, do we make of the vocabulary of "soul," "heart," "spirit," and the rest in the Bible? Does it not suggest that certain parts of our humanity are more important than others? Not at all. When Scripture speaks of one dimension of human life, it does so usually to emphasize not a part but the whole *from a certain point of view*. While *psychē* (soul), for instance, may refer to the whole person in terms of its inner life, *sōma* (body) is a way of understanding our humanity from a physical perspective.[16] Though the physical body does not play the same role in the redemptive work of God as either the soul, spirit, or heart, it nonetheless plays its own crucial role.[17] N. T. Wright offers this helpful insight into Paul's anthropology: "When Paul thinks of human beings, he sees every angle of vision as contributing to the whole, and the whole from every angle of vision. All lead to the one, the one is seen in the all. And, most importantly, each and every aspect of the human being is addressed by God, is claimed by God, is loved by God, and can respond to God."[18]

The basic point is this. A right understanding of the image of God in the Bible involves an affirmation of our whole humanity.[19] To be truly human on this reading is not to have a body that exists in a metaphysically lesser role to that of the soul; it is to be a some*body* through whom the image of God is made present to others. My body is not like a pair of sunglasses that I put on and off at will. My body instead is what makes me uniquely *me*. To affirm this is to affirm that the divine image is communicated through our bodily actions, not just our so-called soulish activities. It is to affirm, finally, that our bodies are the place where others get to see what God is like. It is in this sense that we both *reflect* and *represent* God through our bodies. Our good bodies on this understanding have good work to do.

Kinetic Bodies

Part of that good bodily work takes place in corporate worship. This is something we witness repeatedly throughout the book of Psalms. Against the assumption that the kind of kinetic extravagance that we find in the Psalter represents a lesser or excessive form of embodied worship, I argue here that it represents an integral vision for faithful worship, wherein our physical bodies participate fully in the movement of heart and mind, along with the movement of heaven and earth, in the fulsome worship of God. I suggest also that the authors of Scripture are no less attuned than subsequent generations of Christians to the dangers of embodied worship. The concern, it must be stressed, lies always with the renewal of worship, not with the abrogation or diminishment of bodily acts of worship.

What sort of bodily worship do the psalmists describe and commend to us? Among other things, the faithful bow down (Ps. 5:7; 45:11), they stand (Ps. 33:8), and they kneel (Ps. 95:6). They raise their hands (Ps. 88:9) and they clap their hands (Ps. 47:1). They rise (Ps. 119:62) and they fall before the Lord (Ps. 72:11). Miriam dances (Exod. 15:20). Jephthah's daughter dances (Judg. 11:34). So does David (2 Sam. 6:5) and the Shulammite woman (Song 6:13). The psalmists throughout enjoin us to dance (Pss. 30:11; 149:3; 150:4), while the teacher of Ecclesiastes suggests that there is always an appropriate time to dance, just as there is always an appropriate time to mourn (Eccles. 3:4; cf. Jer. 31:4, 13; Lam. 5:15).

Holy Scripture is replete with such movement language. In the original Hebrew, such language captures a rich variety of movement that our English translations may obscure. There is, for instance, *hagag*, "to dance in circles" (Ps. 42:5); *sabab*, "to encircle, turn about" (Jer. 31:22); *raqad*, "to skip" (Ps. 29:6); *qippus*, "to jump" (Song 2:8); *kirker*, "to whirl, pirouette" (2 Sam. 6:14); *pizzez*, "to skip" (2 Sam. 6:16); *pasah*, "to limp dance" (1 Kings 18:26); and *siheq*, "to dance, play" (2 Sam. 6:14).[20] All throughout we find the language of shouting, bursting, reveling, resounding, clapping, thundering, crying, exulting, and dancing to describe the activities of worship. These are not internal and invisible activities; these are decidedly embodied and expressive activities.

Although this rich vocabulary in the Psalter does not by itself prescribe an absolute way that the church ought to worship God on any given Sunday, it does suggest a pattern of embodied worship that the Bible assumes throughout (see Eph. 3:14; 1 Tim. 2:8; 2 Tim. 1:6; 1 Pet. 5:14; Rev. 7:9–10).[21] It also represents perhaps a model for the kind of worship that Christians may wish to enact in their own liturgical contexts, inasmuch as it models for us a kinetically purposeful worship. Breath and mouth, hands and feet, body and soul: all of these have something *to do* in the personal and communal praises of God's people, and in their laments, thanksgivings, and confessions as well. At the very least, the Psalter offers us an invitation to consider what the body *might be* in worship, both now and in the age to come. It does so on account of a God who wills to make and to remake our physical bodies not only through the gestures, postures, and movements of our physical bodies, but also through care-filled touch.

Touchy-Feely Bodies

The care of God that we discover in the haptic (from the Greek *haptikos*, "to touch") ministry of Jesus, I argue, does not represent a concession to a "weak" need for physical touch, nor does it represent a rare practice in the redemptive and reconciling work of Jesus. It represents instead a consistent and definitive means by which Jesus communicates felt love in order to deepen our experience of felt communion with God, both in our common life and in our liturgical life. This habit of God's goes back to the beginning.

In the beginning, God touches dirt (*adamah*) in order to make the human creature (the *Adam*). From this earth, God makes earthen vessels, capable of bearing the divine image, and he makes us trustees of this treasure, to borrow Paul's language in 2 Corinthians 4:7. When God breathes his breath into this flesh, it becomes living flesh, *nephesh hayah*. The early church father Tertullian imagined this episode in Genesis 2 as if God were a kind of ceramicist. Humanity could not come alive, Tertullian argued, by mere oxygen. Something far more potent would be needed. He described God's breath as a fiery breath, "competent as it were to bake clay into a different quality, into flesh as though into earthenware."[22]

From this man's flesh (*Ish*), moreover, God takes a rib, and then sews up the gash in the man's wounded side. With the rib, God now makes a different kind of creature—a woman creature (*Ishah*). Holding this human-dirt in hand, so to speak, God possesses the human creature wholly, echoing in this way the language of Psalm 139:13, where God is said to knit the psalmist in his mother's womb. It is the picture of God as weaver, making human beings out of a plait of bone, sinew, and vein (cf. Ps. 119:73; Job 10:11).[23]

While this represents a miraculous aspect of each human birth, what is even more astonishing—a mystery, in fact—is that the Second Person of the Trinity experiences a comprehensive touch of his own body in the womb of his mother, Mary. In this place of "the depths" (Ps. 139:15), Jesus is utterly embraced at every point of his flesh. An amniotic sac protects his developing body and regulates his temperature; Mary's placenta supplies oxygen and nutrients by way of his umbilical cord; and day by day he is woven into shape. It is a place of complete somatic care. And it is in his ministry that we witness Jesus offering to others what he himself has received: a comprehensive care-filled touch.

By habit, Jesus chooses to touch people to heal their sicknesses, to deliver them from demonic forces, and to communicate God's generous love to the least, the last, and the lost.[24] He does so because it remains integral to the character of God to communicate love through the immediate means of physical contact. The hands of Jesus, then, are the means by which human beings experience God's proximate solicitude. They are also the means by which we experience God's vulnerability.[25] In choosing to touch "unclean" bodies, such as the bodies of the diseased, the dead, and the undesirable, Jesus makes himself vulnerable to becoming unclean himself. He risks being rejected, misunderstood, or taken for granted, as we see, for example, in the story of the healing of the lepers in Luke 17:11–19.

This is a risk he accepts, for such is the nature of God. He touches those with skin diseases (Matt. 8:3; Luke 5:13). He touches Peter's mother-in-law (Matt. 8:15). He touches the severed ear of the high priest's slave (Luke 22:50–51). He touches the eyes of the blind (Matt. 9:29; 20:34) and the tongue and ears of the mute (Mark 7:33). He touches the bodies of the dead (Matt. 9:25; Luke 7:14) and the demon-oppressed (Mark 9:27). He permits a woman with an "issue of blood" to touch him (Luke 8:43–48), and he lets the sick masses touch the fringe of his cloak so that they might be healed (Matt. 14:35–36). He also rebukes his disciples for preventing the little children from receiving a blessing in the form of an affectionate touch (Mark 10:13–15).

One of the most memorable moments of physical contact occurs in Luke 7, where Jesus allows himself to be touched in a profoundly sensual manner. A nameless woman, whom the reader meets as "sinner" (likely a prostitute), approaches Jesus at the house of a Pharisee named Simon. Biblical scholars explain that by entering his home, the woman will likely have introduced a contagion in the form of ritual impurity. This does not stop her from approaching Jesus, nor does it provoke any concern on the part of the narrator. Standing behind Jesus, silent, weeping, she begins to bathe his feet with her tears. This task completed, she dries his feet with her hair and commences to kiss them.

She concludes her act of devotion by anointing his feet with an expensive ointment. Hands, hair, and lips have all been pressed in service of Christ's body. The touch is intimate as well as vulnerable, but it is not manipulative. It is sensual but by no means sexual, the prejudices of the observers notwithstanding.[26] Possessing no source of water other than her tears, no towel, nor any of the customary olive oil, and by kissing not his cheek or hand but his feet, this woman fulfills the law of hospitality and functions for the reader as a sign of true devotion. Aspects of this episode will play itself out again in John 13, but in that case Jesus will be the one who touches the disciples' feet, washing and drying them with his own hands.

Our Lord wills to be touched, and he leaves us an example that we should follow. In doing so, he shows us the way of loving, restorative touch that ought to characterize the life of the church at worship. German poet Rainer Maria Rilke expresses memorably the essence of such touch: "Have you noticed how scorned, lowly things revive when they come into the willing gentle hands of someone solitary? They are like small birds to which the warmth returns; they stir, waken, and a heart begins to beat in them, rising and falling in those hearkening hands like the utmost wave of a mighty ocean."[27]

In Luke 24:39–40 the resurrected Christ invites his frightened disciples to touch him: "Look at my hands and my feet; see that it is I myself. Touch me and see; for a ghost does not have flesh and bones as you see that I have." Over and again the flesh of Jesus touches other human bodies and is touched by other human bodies. Paul Griffiths writes,

> Between birth and death the Gospels mention Jesus being touched by and touching the flesh of others at least twenty times. He is circumcised,

baptized, hugged by Simeon, has his feet anointed by Mary of Bethany and wiped with her hair, is bound and whipped and crucified, is kissed, washes the feet of others, caresses children, and heals the flesh of others by touching it. The Gospels don't provide a full account of Jesus's fleshly exchanges, but what they do give us shows almost no embarrassment about these fleshly exchanges.[28]

In the Lord's Supper, the faithful experience a similarly intimate encounter with Christ's body. His body and blood are exchanged between members of Christ's own Body. They are beheld in love and commended to us as a sign of our spiritual health. If the bread is freshly made and the wine newly poured, it is smelled in the nose and relished in the mouth, and then it is tasted on the tongue and consumed wholly in oneself. Martin Luther expresses the matter beautifully in a sermon on the Gospel of John:

> God has given us Baptism, the Sacrament of the Altar, and absolution to bring Christ very close to us, so that we can have Him not only in our heart but also on our tongue, so that we can feel Him, grasp Him, and touch Him. . . . For He wants to come to you, plant Himself before your very eyes, press Himself into your hands, and say: "Just listen to Me and take hold of Me, give Me eye and ear; there you have Baptism and the Sacrament of the Altar. Open your mouth, let Me place My hand on your head. I give you this water which I sprinkle over your head."[29]

At the end of all things, in John of Patmos's account of the last things, we read of a God who touches the faces of the saints in order to wipe every tear from their eyes (Rev. 21:3–4).[30] Its figurative sense notwithstanding, this is further evidence of the intimate physical care of our Creator.

What does all of this have to do with our bodies in worship? I maintain here that the deepest desire of human beings, among other things, is to be known and to be loved through positive, care-filled touch: by family and friends, by neighbors and strangers, and ultimately by our bodily resurrected Lord.[31] In Jesus, we witness a God who is no stranger to physical touch. We encounter a God who is neither afraid of touch nor embarrassed by touch.[32] We meet a God who chooses to communicate love in "touchy-feely" ways and in so doing enables us to get a feel for the love of God through our Spirit-mediated experiences of touch—the touch of healing hands, the touch of compassionate service, the touch of a warm greeting, the touch of blessing. We experience a God who enables our embodied worship to become resensitized to the triune life.

We are wrong, then, to reject the physical ways of our Lord, and we do well to make space in our corporate worship for the kind of physical touch that bears witness to the tactile care of Jesus. Hands held together during the recitation of the Lord's Prayer, hands that rest on the bodies of the sick and dying, hands that receive in gratitude the gift of bread and wine, hands that reach out in a gesture of reconciliation with an estranged brother or sister: these are good things. We do well also to remain alert to all forms of abusive and insensitive touch.[33] Such forms of touch violate the law of love and result in experiences of violence against the body. We do well to protect the innocent and to defend the injured who have been traumatized in such ways. We do well, finally, to guard the sacred nature of vulnerability that is involved in the exchange of physical touch between people.

In doing all such things, I suggest that we witness the work of the Spirit in our communal worship, enabling us to become at home in our own skin, however broken or disappointing it may feel to us, and to be fully present to others in their own skin, in the face of all the forces that threaten such vulnerable living. This, too, is what bodies are for.

5

The Future of the Body

Biblical Perspectives on the Body in Worship (Part 2)

What Christians presently do with their bodies matters, matters eschatologically.
—N. T. Wright, The Resurrection of the Son of God

For no one ever hates his own body [sarx], but he nourishes and tenderly cares for it, just as Christ does for the church, because we are members of his body [sōma].
—Ephesians 5:29–30

Trinitarian Bodies

There is probably no biblical text that has exercised such an outsized influence on how Christians think about the physical character of worship in particular as John 4:23–24. In this passage, which occurs immediately following Jesus's encounter with Nicodemus and the richly trinitarian language that concludes the third chapter of John, Jesus engages a Samaritan woman in a high-level discussion of the past, present, and future of worship. To her comment that mountains are everything in the history of Samaritan and Jewish worship, Jesus declares in 4:22–24:

> Woman, believe me, the hour is coming when you will worship the Father neither on this mountain nor in Jerusalem. You worship what you do not

know; we worship what we know, for salvation is from the Jews. But the hour is coming, and is now here, when the true worshipers will worship the Father in spirit and truth, for the Father seeks such as these to worship him. God is spirit, and those who worship him must worship in spirit and truth.

Two basic traditions of interpretation have characterized the church's reading of this text. In one tradition, the words of Jesus are seen to point to the essential nature of God as well as to the interior condition of the human worshiper.[1] On this reading, physical and material things are regarded, at best, as negligible and irrelevant, and, at worst, as problematic and hostile to true worship. Reformed Baptist pastor John Piper's conclusion is typical of this particular tradition: "What we find in the New Testament, perhaps to our amazement, is an utterly stunning degree of indifference to worship as an outward ritual, and an utterly radical intensification of worship as an inward experience of the heart."[2]

> Love must have a body. Joy, peace, patience, kindness, goodness, faithfulness, gentleness, and self-control all must have a body. Without the body, such fruits are not only empty concepts; they are not available to the other members of the body of Christ.
> —Beth Felker Jones, Marks of His Wounds

A second tradition of interpretation comes to a decidedly different conclusion. Here the language of John's Gospel is understood to point to the activities of the triune God.[3] The matter of the physical condition of worship is seen, at the very least, to be irrelevant to the point that Jesus seems to be making and, at the very most, caught up in a larger argument of John's Gospel that invests material things with a sacramental and theological value that exceeds what we, as readers, may have imagined possible. New Testament scholar Marianne Meye Thompson offers this representative comment: "That Jesus speaks of an alternative worship does not demonstrate that Christian worship of God renders irrelevant protected sacred space and holy places; precisely the opposite."[4]

While I am sympathetic to this second tradition of interpretation, I wish to suggest in this chapter that a more positive assessment of the physical aspect of worship and thus also of our physical bodies might emerge out of our reading of John 4.[5] I argue here that Jesus's words to the woman at the well open for us a trinitarian vision for our bodies in the liturgy of the church. I follow this lengthy exposition of John 4:23–24 with a brief treatment of "flesh" and "body" language in Paul's Letters, and I end our biblical tour of the body by showing how our future bodies ought to inform what we do with our present bodily engagement of worship. While the previous chapter looked at the role that our good bodies play in the kinetic and haptic dimensions of corporate worship, this chapter aims to show how our bodies are ultimately caught up in the movement of the triune God and thereby enabled to fulfill their true end.

We begin with the enigmatic words of Jesus in John 4:24: "God is Spirit."

"God Is Spirit"

Like the passage as a whole, the phrase "God is Spirit," which I have purposefully chosen to capitalize in this discussion even though it is lowercase in many translations, has also been understood along two interpretive veins. One vein of interpretation has seen in Jesus's statement an assertion about the essential nature of God.[6] Leon Morris, on this view, suggests that the Samaritan woman's attempt to steer the conversation in a new direction "serves to open up the way for Jesus to speak of the essential nature of God and of the worship that should be offered him."[7]

A very different vein of interpretation argues that 4:24 presents the reader with a picture of God's triune activity. What we observe here, as also elsewhere in the Johannine narrative, is a picture of God's work in creation, not of God in himself. Lesslie Newbigin remarks: "This action of the Father [to seek true worshipers] is the Father himself in action, for God is Spirit, and Spirit is action—the mighty action which is 'from above' and which, like the wind, is invisible and yet unmistakable in its presence and its powerful effects. God is not essence but action. His being is action, and the action is the seeking of true worshippers out of Jewry and out of Samaria and out of every nation."[8]

Similar to such phrases as "God is light" and "God is love," then, the phrase "God is Spirit" can be seen here to describe an activity of God.[9] These are things God *does*, and in so doing we witness who God *is*. Four points can be adduced on behalf of such a reading of "God is Spirit" (*pneuma ho theos*).

First, it is unlikely that God's nonmaterial nature would have been in serious doubt for faithful Samaritans or Jews.[10] Did this woman *really* need reminding that God has no physical body, that "God is invisible and unknowable," or that "the mystery of divine invisibility" was key?[11] Arguments such as these fail to persuade in light of the historical context for John 4, especially if we are right in assuming a Jewish background rather than an exclusively Greek background for John's Gospel.[12]

Second, an essentialist reading is unwarranted from the narrative itself. The woman does not need a rebuke of anthropomorphic projections of God; what she needs is living water (John 4:7–15; cf. Isa. 55:1; Rev. 22:17). What she gets is a revelation of the Messiah (4:25–30). Jesus's answer to her question, then, remains consistent with his answer to Nicodemus (3:1–21): the work of the Spirit, whom Jesus equates with "living water" in 7:37–39, is required in order to enter into God's kingdom.

Third, it is a strange hermeneutical move to assert that the nonmaterial nature of God (God *as* spirit) establishes the basis for right-hearted worship (by way of the human *spirit*).[13] In what way exactly does God's immaterial essence necessarily *generate* heartfelt worship? It is a confusion of apples and oranges, as it were, believing that spiritual—or "sincere"—worship will result from an affirmation of God as a nonmaterial being.

Fourth, the primary sense of "spirit" in John does not stand in opposition to matter.[14] Nor is such language intended to describe the immanent activities of God, whereby the divine Spirit communicates directly with the human spirit.[15] Instead, the Johannine language of *pneuma* consistently describes the sovereign activities of God over against a dark and broken world.[16] For John, participation in life "from above" is possible only by the Spirit (20:31),[17] and it is God's Spirit who calls forth true worship.[18] Dale Bruner puts the point this way: "Worship is only secondarily and reflexively humans seeking *God*; it is, first of all and creatively, the divine Father, through Jesus the Truth, by the Fountain Spirit—the one God seeking humans and moving them upward to him."[19]

A similar idea is at work, I believe, in the phrase " in Spirit and Truth."

"In Spirit and Truth"

As with "God is Spirit" in John 4:24, the phrase "in Spirit and Truth" (*en pneumati kai alētheia*) in verse 23 involves two divergent lines of thought in church history. One view is that this phrase describes a facet of human beings.[20] It points, more precisely, to an internal and invisible condition of the rightly oriented worshiper. C. H. Dodd writes, for example, that "*alētheia* has in the Fourth Gospel in general its Hellenistic sense of reality, reality as apprehended, or knowledge of reality. Thus *pneuma* has some very close relation to reality, unseen and eternal."[21] George Johnston similarly states that "the outlook and mentality of John strongly indicate that we are to interpret 'worship in spirit' as inward worship, the offering of the heart, done out of love and not within a legal system like that of the Synagogue."[22] The concern of this view, in sum, is for a sincere heart and a right-thinking mind.[23]

Against this reading, I contend that the phrase describes not something that the worshiper *does*, but rather something that happens *to* the worshiper.[24] Raymond Brown rightly argues that the phrase has little to do with the inner recesses of the worshiper precisely because "the Spirit is the Spirit of God, not the spirit of man."[25] Central for John is not the heart of the worshiper but the work of Christ and the Spirit, who together enable a person to enter the kingdom of God.[26] It is the Spirit, Jesus tells the woman, who makes worship possible in "the hour [that] is coming, and now is."[27] The Spirit who descends and remains upon Jesus is the same Spirit who accomplishes the will of the Father in the ones who believe in the Son.[28] Thompson argues this case from the logic of the narrative:

> Both [the narrative of Nicodemus and of the woman] point the reader away from the human being as self-sufficient actor to the human being as recipient of the activity and Spirit of God. It would then seem odd if in conversation with the Samaritan woman Jesus were to urge her to "look within," as it were, for the strength and capacity to offer true worship. Quite the contrary, one is brought into the eschatological hour by God's caring activity in Jesus and by the divinely sent Spirit of God.[29]

How, then, should the phrase be understood? I suggest that we should see it as a word image that depicts the integral work of Jesus and the Spirit in the worship that the Father now seeks.[30] In John's narrative, Jesus is presented as the fullness of truth (1:14), the revelation of the truth of God (5:25–33; 8:45–46; 17:17; 18:37), the *Truth* himself (8:32; 14:6), and the one who bestows the Spirit of truth upon his disciples (15:26; 16:13). In

John it is *both* "the truth shall make you free" (8:32) *and* "if the Son makes you free, you will be free indeed" (8:36). The Spirit, in turn, is the one who bears witness to the Truth and who makes the presence of Jesus real to his disciples. The Spirit is the "other" helper—helping by advocating, comforting, revealing, uniting, and so on—inasmuch as Jesus is regarded in John as the "first" helper (14:16–18).[31]

The kind of worship the Father seeks, therefore, has a clear Christocentric and pneumatic shape. It is *in* the Truth, not merely *of* the truth, and it is by *the* Spirit, not by *any* spirit. Worship in this new hour arises out of a right orientation to the person of Jesus rather than to "the way things really are,"[32] and it requires the work of the Spirit, rather than the sincerity of the human heart—as important as that may be—to orient the worshiper to the Father.[33] Over against *truth*, in John, moreover, stands not untruth but "un-Jesus," and the opposite of *spirit* is not hypocrisy but false spirits (cf. 1 John 4). The "hour," then, that Jesus discloses to his disciples invites an intimate relationship with God *as* Father, through Jesus himself *as* Truth, and by the Spirit *as* Paraclete.

Here we begin to discern the trinitarian shape of Jesus's exchange with the Samaritan woman.[34] Worship "in this new time" occurs in the Spirit, who bears witness to Jesus, the perfect Son of the Father, while the Son is the one who both mediates worship to the Father and is himself a proper object of worship.[35] *Truth* and *Spirit* are not, I argue, two poles around which the church's worship orbits: a human "head" pole and a human "heart" pole. The church's worship orbits instead around the unified work of Son and Spirit, who together enable the faithful to offer acceptable worship to the Father.

If this trinitarian reading of John 4:23–24 is largely correct, what exactly does worship in the sphere of the Spirit and the Truth imply for our physical bodies in worship?[36]

The first thing that we can say here is that John 4:23–24 remains silent on the question of physicality per se. The physical aspects of worship obtain neither a negative nor a positive judgment in Jesus's statement. An antiphysical polemic, in fact, can only be inferred from the text, which is what usually happens with preachers and theologians. All that the text declares explicitly is that the exclusive geographical places that Gerizim and Jerusalem occupied in Samaritan and Jewish worship will no longer serve the purposes of the Father in this eschatological hour.[37] Something different will be needed in light of the advent of Christ and the gift of the Holy Spirit.[38]

A second thing that can be said is that worship in a Johannine perspective is never an immediate encounter with the essence of God—between nonmaterial human spirit and nonmaterial divine spirit. It is always a materially and symbolically mediated thing. The call to obedience, for example, is incarnated in the practice of foot-washing.[39] The gift of the Spirit in the form of "living waters" is experienced in sensory fashion in the practice of baptism. And God's abundant life is given expression both in the physical body of Christ, poured out for the life of the world, and in the eucharistic body that, "like a rich and inexhaustible fountain," pours into us the very life of God.[40]

Over against the common perception of John as otherworldly and ethereal, I contend, with Richard Hays, that "this gospel's aesthetic vision is deeply grounded in the *particular*, the *palpable*, and the *embodied*."[41] The old physical ways of worshiping God are not replaced by the allegedly superior nonmaterial activities of the soul; instead, new practices, new symbols, and new embodiments of a distinctly trinitarian faith will be required to give expression to worship in this "new hour."[42] Put otherwise, our physical bodies still have important work to do, but this work will now take place in the name of the triune God and by participating in the triune life.

This leads us to a third point. Whatever role our bodies play in worship in Johannine perspective, it will not be a role that they play on their own. It will be a role that they play by being taken up into the dynamic life of the "Two Hands" of God, as Irenaeus called Christ and the Spirit. Our physical bodies are caught up in the physical body of Jesus, to which the Spirit makes us partakers through a power that we do not possess on our own.

In the definitive flesh of Christ, which appears "full of grace and truth" (John 1:14), God's glory is supremely witnessed, and it is through this flesh, tabernacling briefly among us (John 2:21), that the purpose of all flesh is apprehended: communion with God (John 17:21). In Christ's body we also discover the One who empathizes with our own frail and bewildered bodies (John 19:28–30, 34; 20:27) as well as the possibility of an infusion of divine life, insofar as we partake of his flesh and blood (John 6:51–58).[43] This is a Spirit-ual work, the Gospel of John tells us repeatedly.

The Spirit rests upon the body of Jesus and so also upon our own bodies at baptism (John 1:32–33; 3:5). In John 6:63 we witness how the Spirit animates lifeless flesh, and in John 20:22 Jesus breathes the Spirit on the disciples in a way that recalls hereby the language of Genesis 2:7, where God breathes humanity into being. As scholars point out, what John intends to evoke in the mind of the reader is new creation imagery.[44] What was once promised in Ezekiel 37 is now being fulfilled in John 20. Jesus breathes upon the disciples the breath of life so that sinew, flesh, bone, and skin (see Ezek. 37:7–10) might become bodies that are hypercharged with the life of the eschatological Spirit.

In John's Gospel, in sum, there is never *mere* materiality; there is always materiality caught up in the life of Jesus and the Spirit. There is never only an invisible and interior expression of belief; there is always and everywhere a visceral and visible exercise of faith. And there is never any sign of a disparagement of physical bodies; there is only an affirmation of physical bodies and the possibility of bodies that have been imbued with the life of Christ and the Spirit. In this sense we can say here, too, that for John our bodies are always *for* something: they are for Christ's work of showing us the true image of bodily life, and they are for the Spirit's work of resensitizing us to the life of God.

Fleshy Bodies

Part of the reason why Christians have balked at a full embrace of the physical aspects of worship is due to a misunderstanding of Paul's language about flesh and body.[45] As often as not, Christians assume that *flesh* is simply a synonym for *body* and that the former is wholly flawed and the primary cause of our human misery. Plenty of Christians likewise assume that *soul* stands exclusively on the good side of our recovery of a life that is pleasing to God. To assume such things is not only to tell a defective tale about the body in Paul's writings, it also leads to an inability to imagine a positive place for the physical body in worship. The body will be seen either as a fundamental hindrance to faithful worship or as a negligible help to such worship. But such assumptions run directly counter to the careful manner in which the New Testament speaks about flesh and body and the positive role that they play in our liturgical discipleship as Christians.[46]

With respect to the vocabulary of "flesh" (*sarx*), it is important to point out that the term signifies two basic realities in the New Testament. It can describe our humanity in its creaturely status (Rom. 4:1; 1 Cor. 9:11; Gal. 4:23, 29), and it can describe our humanity in its sinful condition (Rom. 7:14; 8:5, 9–11; 2 Cor. 10:2–3).[47] Depending on the textual circumstances, flesh can describe what we have in common with animals, birds, and fish, or it can serve as a technical term to describe what we suffer as human beings on account of sin.[48] When these two senses are not clearly distinguished, it becomes all too easy to assume that flesh as flesh is our primary problem. And when our flesh is perceived chiefly as a prison to our souls, as Christians have done throughout the centuries, then bodies will at worst be rejected and at best be regarded with a suspicion within the context of corporate worship.[49]

With respect to the language of body (*sōma*) in the New Testament, it too is employed in complex ways. In some cases it is used to describe the conditions of our sin-warped bodies, such as a "body of sin" (Rom. 6:6) or a "body of death" (Rom. 7:24). In other cases, it points to the unique active agency that they possess to form Christlikeness in us. In this latter sense, our bodies represent the concrete place for life in Christ to be worked out—quite literally.[50] For it is in and through our God-given bodies that worship and mission, work and play, relationship and service are fully realized. And it is for this reason that Paul enjoins us to honor God with our bodies, in every time and place, for this is how Christ himself is made seen and known and eminently desirable.[51] For writers such as Paul, this is the normative way to enact human life before God.[52]

The problem of the human body, then, is not materiality. Its problem, as with the mind and heart, is its enslavement to sin. Left to their own broken devices, our minds become a factory of idols, as John Calvin once described it.[53] Our hearts, when likewise left to their own broken devices, become deceiving and self-deceiving, causing us to become strangers to ourselves and stunting our ability to love God and neighbor both. The same lot befalls our souls and spirits and wills. The body's fundamental need is accordingly transformation rather than rejection or suppression.[54] As it relates to worship, Christians ought not to overestimate the warping powers of sinful flesh—nor ought they to underestimate the Holy Spirit's power to rightly order our bodily passions. Christians should let their bodies do what they have been created to do: worship God fully and freely.

It is under this light that Christians should seek to live well "in the flesh" but not "according to the flesh" (2 Cor. 10:2–3 ESV) and in this way imitate Jesus who tabernacled in the world as "flesh" but not "according to the flesh" (John 1:14; 8:15 ESV). We offer our bodies freely and fully to God in worship, therefore, because our confidence rests in the Spirit's power to guide and to govern our physical bodies—even as that same divine power binds together Christ's diverse Body in ways that seem miraculous but that are standard procedure for life in the family of God at worship. The regrettable fact is that too many Christians ascribe to the human body a subordinate role in corporate worship for fear that it will inevitably lead us into dangerous and destructive territory. This stands in contrast to the picture that the New Testament envisions for us and for our future bodies.[55]

Future Bodies

"What Christians presently do with their bodies matters, matters eschatologically," writes N. T. Wright in *The Resurrection of the Son of God*.[56] It matters precisely because our bodies have been caught up in the resurrected body of Christ, through which the purpose of all flesh has been apprehended and whose true end is glimpsed, even if only through a glass darkly, as a body fashioned by the Spirit for life in the new creation (1 Cor. 15:44).[57] How precisely do we partake of Christ's resurrected body here and now? And how do we participate in the embodied aspects of worship in such a way that we experience together a foretaste of our new creation bodies? In short: by the Spirit. In 1 Corinthians 6:19, Paul writes, "Do you not know that your body is a temple of the Holy Spirit?" Paul uses this same temple language to describe the Spirit-shaped Body of Christ.

What does this mean practically for the body at worship? First, it means that our physical body, as a temple of the Spirit, experiences now the power of the age to come. The vitality of Christ's own imperishable, immortal, resurrected body does not remain a future-only reality; it becomes accessible to us *here and now* by the same Spirit who raised Jesus from the dead (Rom. 8:11; 1 Cor. 15:42–49). Second, inasmuch as the Spirit infuses our bodies with a taste of the age to come, we are to live in our bodies *now* in light of God's good future for our bodies.[58] It is for this reason that the New Testament urges believers to "present" their members to righteousness (Rom. 6:13), to "offer" their bodies as living sacrifices

(Rom. 12:1 NIV), and to "glorify" God with their bodies (1 Cor. 6:20). A new metaphysics, as it were, requires a new ethics, a new liturgics, and a new physics.

Although our physical bodies suffer the entropic forces of life in a sinful world, they also experience the categorically greater benefit of the Spirit's revivifying power. And though it may seem that we are only wasting away in these sad, broken-down bodies of ours, waiting for that far-flung day when all shall be made new, the New Testament reminds us that our resurrected life does not remain inaccessible to us today. By God's Spirit it remains miraculously and mysteriously near at hand: in the body and blood of Jesus, in tangible acts of reconciling love, in gestures of peace, in postures of humility, in movements of gracious care, and in works of liturgical art that offer us a glimpse and foretaste of the new creation.[59] In the end, we practice resurrection today in our corporate worship, not tomorrow or some far-distant day, because the Spirit has breathed into our mortal bodies the death-defying life of God and energized our bodies with Christ's own resurrection life.[60]

Gifted Bodies

If our physical bodies are viewed as the joint work of Christ and the Spirit, as I have argued in this chapter, then the church at worship is looking not to escape the physical condition of our lives but rather at the preservation, healing, and liberation of all things physical, so that our own physical bodies can become what the Father has eternally purposed for them. Rather than being seen as accommodations to human weakness, our bodies ought to be seen as God-given instruments that fittingly serve the church's worship in light of the resurrection. And instead of being regarded as hopelessly warped, "fleshy" things this side of the eschaton, our bodies can be regarded as God-given gifts that remain commensurate with our God-given creaturely condition, through which we experience a foretaste of the age to come.

Our physical bodies, in short, do not diminish corporate worship, nor do they endanger "acceptable" worship of God. Instead, they ably serve the good purposes of God in the public praise of God, as a portrait of God's glory in and through our physical lives. Our bodies serve as normative—rather than incidental—aids to the church's work of prayer and praise, singing and supplication, confession of sin and confession of faith. They complement and enhance—rather than merely illustrate—the mental, emotional, verbal, and volitional activities of worship. And they enable us to bring our whole humanity in an enactment of faithful worship before the triune God, for the sake of the whole world. What is the appropriate response to such a divine gift? It is gratitude in the form of stewarding our bodies well and offering them back to God in love.

6

The True Image of the Body

Theological Perspectives on the Body in Worship

I believe that God has made me and all creatures; that He has given me my body and soul, eyes, ears, and all my members, my reason and all my senses, and still takes care of them.

—Martin Luther, Luther's Small Catechism

For in him dwells all the fullness of the Godhead in bodily form.
—Colossians 2:9

I wish to make a bold and perhaps counterintuitive, but far from original, claim at the start of this chapter. In order to know what human bodies are for, we should not go back to the beginning—that is, to the first chapter of Genesis—as invaluable as that task may be. Nor should we go to the end, to the book of Revelation, where we get a glimpse of our glorified bodies. We should go instead to the middle, to the very center of things: to the paradigmatic body of Jesus. For it is this body that tells us the true meaning and true nature of all human bodies.[1] Like all aspects of our human life, not just our bodily life, we cannot know our truest purposes on our own. No amount of empirical research or earnest self-examination will disclose to us why and what we really are. It must be revealed to us.

Put otherwise, it is not just the Maker of heaven and earth who must be known by faith, as the Nicene Creed reminds us in its opening lines.

It is also our own human selves that can only be known by faith, and it is Jesus who discloses this true knowledge of our selves. By faith we perceive the true nature of Jesus Christ; by faith we perceive the true nature of his human body; and by faith we perceive the true nature of our own human bodies in light of his own body. Whatever doubts we may hold about the data of Genesis or the cryptic language of Revelation to tell us the meaning of our physical bodies, those doubts are categorically dispelled by the One who became flesh of our flesh and bone of our bone and thus made crystal clear the good purposes of our own flesh and bone.

> **I do not worship matter; I worship the Creator of matter who became matter for my sake, who willed to take his abode in matter; who worked out my salvation through matter. Never will I cease honoring the matter which wrought my salvation!**
> —John of Damascus,
> On the Divine Images

One of the crucial insights that Christ's body makes clear to us is that true bodily life is neither self-generated nor free to do as it pleases. It is instead a body that the Father pleases to give him, born also of the Virgin Mary, and it is a body that the Spirit enlivens so that it might accomplish the good, pleasing, and perfect will of the Trinity. What follows, then, for our embodied worship from the fact that the Father pronounces a categorical blessing upon our bodies in the beginning? What significance does the resurrected and ascended but still scarred body of Jesus hold for what we do with our bodies in prayer and praise? And in what way does the Spirit's work of making and remaking our bodies inform how we *sense* our way through worship in gestures, postures, and movements?

The task of this chapter is to answer these questions in such a way that we rightly perceive the trinitarian shape and significance of our bodies in corporate worship.

The Good Body

The first thing that we discover in a trinitarian theology of the body is that it is an expression of the pleasure of God the Father. Swiss theologian Karl Barth once remarked that it is the Christian's duty "to love and praise the created order, because, as is made manifest in Jesus Christ, it is so mysteriously well-pleasing to God."[2] To take pleasure in our physical bodies, then, is to take pleasure in *God's* own pleasure in our bodies, a marvelously created thing he made and on which he pronounces a definitive benediction: not just somewhat good, or conditionally good, but *very good*. Robert Farrar Capon, in *The Romance of the Word*, imaginatively captures the delightful and delight-inducing work of God in the original act of creation. It is worth quoting at length here:

> Let me tell you why God made the world. One afternoon, before anything was made, God the Father, God the Son, and God the Holy Spirit sat around in the unity of their Godhead discussing one of the Father's fixations. From all eternity, it seems, he had had this thing about being. He would keep thinking up all kinds of unnecessary things—new ways of being and new kinds of beings to be.
>
> And as they talked, God the Son suddenly said, "Really, this is absolutely great stuff. Why don't I go out and mix up a batch?" And God the Holy Spirit said, "Terrific! I'll help you." So they all pitched in, and after supper that night, the Son and the Holy Spirit put on this tremendous show of being for the Father. It was full of water and light and frogs; pine cones kept dropping all over the place and crazy fish swam around in the wineglasses. There were mushrooms and mastodons, grapes and geese, tornadoes and tigers—and men and women everywhere to taste them, to juggle them, to join them and to love them.
>
> And God the Father looked at the whole wild party and said, "Wonderful! Just what I had in mind! *Tov! Tov! Tov!*" And all God the Son and God the Holy Spirit could think of to say was the same thing, "*Tov! Tov! Tov!*" So they shouted together "*Tov meod!*" and they laughed for ages and ages, saying things like how great it was for beings to be and how clever of the Father to think of the idea, and how kind of the Son to go to all that trouble putting it together, and how considerate of the Spirit to spend so much time directing and choreographing.
>
> And for ever and ever they told old jokes, and the Father and the Son drank their wine *in unitate Spiritus Sancti*, and they all threw ripe olives and pickled mushrooms at each other *per omnia saecula saeculorum. Amen.*[3]

Capon readily admits that this is a crass analogy and that no one should *ever* believe that God is three old men throwing olives at one another. But not everyone, he argues, "is equally clear that God is not a cosmic force or principle of being," which is to say, that God is not a distant and dispassionate Maker or that God makes a world because that's simply the business of divine beings.[4] God instead is an exuberant Maker who delights in what he has made. Capon's crass analogy serves one purpose only, and that is to draw our attention to something we rarely, if ever, think: that the whole of creation is the result of a trinitarian bash.

Because our pleasure in our bodies is grounded in God's own pleasure in our bodies, then, the use of our bodies within the context of corporate worship is first and foremost an occasion for delight, not just a dutiful requirement. It is an invitation to wonder-filled adoration rather than only a solemn obligation to fulfill before a divine Ruler; it is a way to get in on the exceeding joy that God derives in making things *be*, rather than not be. We delight in all the powers and possibilities of the body in worship, in other words, because we believe that the physical body most fundamentally belongs, for love's sake, to God's economy of grace.[5]

A Graced Body

This is another way of saying that God was not compelled to make our bodies. Our bodies do not *need* to exist in order for God to feel fulfilled. They are from first to last *sheer gift*.[6] As such, they represent a means to experience God's grace firsthand: to taste and to touch it, to see and to hear it (cf. Ps. 34:8). On account of this, the church at worship gets to revel in the bounty of our bodily life before God. The church gets to raise a hallelujah with joyful noises and sonorous choirs; it gets to adorn the cross with sweet-smelling flowers at Easter; it gets to impress our foreheads with ashes as a sign of our mortality; it gets to revel on "God's Great Dance Floor"[7] and to lie prostrate in reverent silence before the Holy One who sits enthroned above the cherubim.

In other words, we *get to* make something of our bodies in worship; we do not only *have to*.[8] We have to make clothes for protection against the elements, but we get to make cassocks and bonnets and paisley ties that are "pleasing to the eye" (Gen. 2:9). We have to build shelters, but we get to build chapels and cathedrals in order to situate our corporeal life before God in symbolically meaningful spaces of worship. We have to give glory to God—because our lives depend on it—but we get to do so with a wealth of physical goods: pipe organs and syncopated jazz, holy water and anointing oil, Palm Sunday processions and Praise Marches. The Body of Christ gets to participate in a fullness of bodily worship, in short, because it participates in a sacramental universe that is marked throughout by the gratuity of God's creative work and saturated with the excessive grace of God.

A Culture-Making Body

Yet whatever it is that we believe that our physical bodies ought to be doing in corporate worship, they must be grounded in the good purposes of God for human work. Made in the image of a Creator who makes both gardens and cities, both clothes and civilizations, we likewise make things *in* the world in order to make something *of* the world.[9] In specifically trinitarian terms, the Father invites us to discover, to attend, to name, to cultivate, and to care for things in creation. In Christ we discover how to do this manifold work well, and in the Spirit we are empowered to make culture for the sake of the world that God so loves. Among other things, this calling involves giving loving attention to the logic of our bodies, to the powers of our bodies, to the possibilities of our bodies, and to the beauty of our bodies in a liturgical context.[10]

With the help of tools and machines that we have imagined, designed, and created ourselves, we make well-crafted chairs and pews for the comfort of our bodies. With an eye for light and line, we make illuminated Bibles in order to inspire our vision of God, and we make digital projections to facilitate our view of sayable and singable words. With an ear for dialogue, we make mystery plays, and with a feel for plot, we tell our own stories of hardship and healing so that our ears might hear afresh the good stories of God. With our feet, we make processional rituals in order for the elements of bread and wine to be carried *from* the people *to* the table of the Lord. With our mouths, we make songs of both praise and lament. And with our noses, we get a whiff of the presence of God in the use of incense and flowers.

All such things and more represent the blessed work that we have been called to do by a God who both commands us to till the ground (Gen. 2:15) and graces us to fulfill that sacred vocation (Eph. 2:10).

A Marred Body

As we are reminded in Genesis, however, this work is marred by toil and sweat on account of the distorting effects of sin (3:17–19). Little evidence is needed of this fact in our daily lives. We glimpse at every turn the tragic effects of sin on our bodies and on the bodies of others. Yet it is only in Christ that we see how terribly broken our bodies are, for they are caught up not simply in the forces of entropy but more critically in the forces of sin.[11] Sin insidiously disfigures our bodily life as well as our bodily relations. Sin causes us to become alienated from God in our bodies, to become strangers to our own bodies, to become at odds with the bodies of others, and to be perpetually at war with the physical world around us.

As it relates to the role of our bodies in corporate worship, the effects of sin involve a constant risk of idolatry. This might manifest itself in the inordinate love of physical things over against divine things. Or it might involve hypocrisy where we engage the body without heart and mind, or superstition where we invest the body with a power that is not its own to possess, or an engorgement or an impoverishment of our bodily worship that results in an indulgence of both gluttonous and miserly habits, or of the near-infinite possibility for misuse of our bodies in worship that causes us to do harm to our own bodies and to the bodies of others in Christ's own Body.

What is required to heal our bodies is the initiative of God. In Christ's own initiative, then, to become "flesh from our flesh," we discover not only the extent of our body's brokenness but also its true belovedness. In Christ we discern not only the comprehensive corruption that our bodies suffer but also their destiny to be hale and holy, able now to become vehicles of Spirit-enabled healing. The point that must be stressed here is that, as corrosive and dangerous as sin may be, it does not have the last word on our bodies at worship. The grace of God does.

And while the tragedies and traumas that our bodies suffer must be taken seriously and may require years of patient and persevering therapeutic care, those wounds do not have the final say on our bodies. The grace of God does. The goodness of Christ does. The power of the Spirit does. It is in Christ's body that we discover our body's original tragedy, yes, but it is also in Christ's own physical body that we discover our eschatological destiny, where we are capable yet again of intimate fellowship with the Father through the Spirit.

The Flesh of God

What else does Christ's body tell us about all human bodies? It tells us what it means to be a *fleshy, particular* body, marked by the glorious scars of his own *wounded* body.

A Fleshy Body

First, Christ's body is flesh, or *sarx*. Such a body recalls the flesh that Adam beholds in his counterpart, Eve, flesh of my flesh (Gen. 2:23). Made from the *adamah*, this body is subject to the rhythms of creation: of waking and sleeping, of working and resting, of hungering and thirsting, of feeling and wanting, of growing and decaying.[12] In the definitive flesh of Christ, which appears "full of grace and truth" (John 1:14), God's glory is supremely witnessed.[13] Paul puts it this way in Colossians 2:9: "In [Christ] all the fullness of Deity dwells in bodily form [*sōmatikōs*]" (NIV). It is positively a *fleshy* flesh: "It is I myself. Touch me and see; for a ghost does not have flesh and bones as you see that I have" (Luke 24:39).[14] This flesh is seen and touched (1 John 1:1), and by its touch, it heals other bodies (Luke 13:13).[15]

What is the significance of this point for our embodied worship? Against every Gnostic presumption to the contrary, God gladly assumes human flesh in order to redeem all flesh, and it is through this flesh that the definitive purpose of all flesh is apprehended: intimate communion with God, whom we know now "in part" but whom we shall one day behold "face to face" (1 Cor. 13:12; cf. Gen. 32:30; Num. 12:8; Deut. 34:10). All of what we do with our bodies in worship now is grounded in the grace of God and in the grace that we witness in the incarnation of God. "Nothing compels God to take flesh," writes Ian McFarland in *The Word Made Flesh*.[16] It is *from* grace and *for* grace that God becomes enfleshed. John Kleinig summarizes the point this way:

> [Christ's body is] the place where God shows his glory to all people, in order to give them access to his grace. Through his human body Jesus shares his own divine life with us; through his human face, as in a mirror, he shows us the face of God the Father; through his human mouth and limbs he speaks the Father's words to us, both by what he says and by what he does. With his human hands he delivers the Father's gifts to us. He resides with us bodily so that we can receive God's grace and truth. He is the bodily theophany of the Father (Heb. 1:3); by seeing him, we see the Father (John 14:9).[17]

A Particular Body

Second, Christ's body is very much a particular body, not a generic body. By this I mean that Christ's body belongs to a particular mother, a particular family history, a particular people, a particular culture, and a particular tradition, among other things.[18] This is both the scandal and the glory of his body. His is a Jewish body, "born of a woman, born under the law" (Gal. 4:4). His is a body that is "born into the world in a flood of blood and water and mucus and agony, as all babies are,"[19] and in this way his body comes to us as a vulnerable body: vulnerable to all the vicissitudes of infancy, vulnerable to the injury of his friends and to the insults of strangers, vulnerable to the powers of Rome and to death on a cross.[20] The point to be stressed here is that, as with Christ's earthly body, vulnerability remains a central feature of our bodies, rather than a regrettable one that we ought to resist or to escape at all costs in our communal worship.

To say that Jesus possesses a particular body also involves an acknowledgment of the limitations of his body. During his earthly sojourn, Jesus goes to this town but not that town, he heals this person but not that one, he embraces some but not all.[21] He requires rest and sleep. He needs food and drink. He comes to Israel for the sake of the nations, yet he restricts his ministry to an astonishingly small geographic space. He does not accomplish all that ever could be done in a body (we have no record, for instance, of him playing sports or farming the land) but only that which accomplishes the will of the Father, which is his will also. And, in his ascension, Christ's body remains a particular body, seated at the right hand of the Father—not as a specter but as a body that occupies a delimited place in God's world.

Over against the aspirations of transhumanism, with its project to free the mind entirely from the "imprisoning" limitations of the body (as depicted, e.g., in the movie *Transcendence*), and in contrast to assertions around the body's absolute plasticity, subject finally to human desire to make of the body whatever it wills (as with, for instance, the illusory promise of the virtual reality "OASIS" in Ernest Cline's novel *Ready Player One*), I argue here that the limitations of our own particular bodies are a good thing and that we ought to work with, rather than against, such limitations.[22] In specifically theological terms, limits are always *for* something, rather than a *lack* of something, and they serve always as a context for God's grace to be felt in the real circumstances of our lives, instead of something that we should seek to escape for the sake of a life that we might imagine for ourselves *beyond* the particularity of our own physical bodies.[23]

A Wounded Body

Third, Christ's body is marked by both continuity and discontinuity. One point of continuity between Christ's crucified body and his resurrected body is his wounds. In John's Gospel, Jesus takes the initiative to exhibit his wounds, "his hands and his side" (John 20:20), which is an action that comes in response not to doubt but rather to a word of "peace" (John 20:19). It is a positive commendation of his body, not a concession to weak faith.[24] For it is this wounded body that constitutes the identity of the Second Person of the Trinity in perpetuity. Yet in view of the fact that Jesus receives the gift of a "Spirit-ual body," a *sōma pneumatikon*, to use the language of Paul in 1 Corinthians 15:44, this new body exists in sharp discontinuity with the body that bore the "likeness of sinful flesh" (Rom. 8:3). The Spirit fashions for Christ an incorruptible body, "a body for the realm of the Spirit,"[25] which is not simply alive but "hyperalive, excessively alive."[26]

Of significance for corporate worship is the way in which the wounds of our risen Lord serve to remind us of something essential about our own wounded bodies (cf. Gen. 32:24–32). In assuming a body "in the likeness of sinful flesh" (Rom. 8:3), Christ becomes intimately familiar with our infirmities, in order that he might remain a sympathetic priest upon the "throne of grace" (Heb. 4:16). In Christ, we encounter the One who in his own wounded body empathizes with weak and bewildered bodies, which groan for their full redemption (Rom. 8:23). Instead of ignoring our wounded bodies, then, we ought to make ample space in our practices of worship to come as we are—broken but confident that we approach a God who retains the "dear tokens of his passion" and who draws our gaze to his "glorious scars."[27] In doing so we make space for the restorative work of the Spirit of God within the Body of Christ.

The Spirit-ed Body

The double entendre expressed in the phrase "the body of Christ" points significantly to the somatic and ecclesial nature of the redemptive work that the Spirit of Christ accomplishes in us. In Pauline terms, as Udo Schnelle observes, "there is no crucified One (Rom. 7:4) or exalted One (Phil. 3:21) without his body, just as conversely participation in the body of Christ is not imaginable without the glorification of God in the body of the believer."[28] How specifically does the Holy Spirit enable human bodies to become partakers of Christ's body and thereby achieve their God-given end in worship?

An Incorporated Body

First, the Scriptures make clear that to be "in Christ" is to be "with Christ," which in turn is to be integrated to the Body of Christ in both senses.[29] To be in Christ means nothing less and nothing more than that we are in Christ's Body. This, Paul tells us repeatedly, is the Spirit-ual work of God. John Calvin helpfully observes: "Though every one of us is said to be the temple of God and is so described, yet all must be united together in one, and joined together by mutual love, so that one temple may be made of us all. Since it is true that each one is a temple in which God dwells by His Spirit, so all ought to be so fitted together, that they may form the structure of one universal temple."[30]

The point here is that the relationship between our bodies and Christ's Body is far more intimate than many of us have allowed. This intimate relationship is vividly witnessed in our participation in Christ's own body and blood. Christians throughout history have used a variety of phrases to describe this relationship, calling it a "wonderful exchange" (Calvin),[31] a "happy exchange," and a "beautiful exchange" (Maximus the Confessor).[32] Irenaeus believed that Jesus's blood directly strengthens our blood, just as his body strengthens our bodies.[33] Far from despising these creaturely bodies of ours, then, Christ makes himself accessible to us through blessedly earthy things, remaking us thereby.[34] In a treatise on the Eucharist, Luther paints the picture this way: "Perishable food is transformed into the body which eats it; this food, however, transforms the person who eats it into itself, and makes him like itself, spiritual, alive, and eternal. . . . It is as if a wolf devoured a sheep and the sheep were so powerful a food that it transformed the wolf and turned him into a sheep."[35]

Whatever our theology of the Lord's Supper may be, passages such as John 6 leave no doubt that our ability to experience the exceedingly abundant life of God is integrally related to our participation in Christ's body, which the Father gives directly from the storehouses of heaven and which Jesus himself gives for the very life of the world. Whoever eats his flesh-and-blood self, Jesus tells the crowds, will live forever (John 6:51). Or as Tertullian once put it, "the flesh is fed by Christ's body and blood that the soul may fatten on God."[36] Anything less amounts to death, whether literal or figurative or both. We simply cannot have God's Son apart from his body.[37]

What does all of this have to do with corporate worship? At the very least, it means that we can never think of our physical bodies as objects that we possess, like property, or as *mere things* that we carry in and out of the space of worship so that the real work of worship can be done by hearts, minds, and wills. Far from it. Our bodies belong to Christ—intimately, integrally, viscerally even—and we handle them with the same care that Christ's own body is cared for by the women at the tomb. And yet, miraculously, our bodies are also ours to do with as we please in a qualified sense. The Spirit not only incorporates us in Christ; the Spirit also grants us the freedom to offer our bodies wholly to God in worship or to hide and withhold our bodies. It is a risky freedom that the Spirit entrusts to us, which we should steward with great care.

A Temple Body

Directly related to this work of incorporation is the Spirit's work of enabling our bodies to function as temples, or holy sites, of God's felt presence. In 1 Corinthians 3:16, Paul asks the believers, "Do you not know that you are God's temple and that God's Spirit dwells in you?" The pronoun here is plural (you all), and what once described the physical Jerusalem temple now describes the people of God. But it is not just the new community that is a temple, it is also our physical bodies. Paul writes in 1 Corinthians 6:19, "Do you not know that your body is a temple of the Holy Spirit within you?" The corporate (again, "y'all") is now seen to be inseparable from the corporeal.

Why does this matter? As we have mentioned already in our biblical exposition of the body, our physical body as a temple of the Spirit experiences now the "Spirit-ed" power of the age to come, and because our bodies belong to Christ, they should also be consecrated to Christ. The fact that our bodies are betrayed by advanced age, disappoint us repeatedly, unexpectedly fall ill, frequently break down, or fail to live up to our expectations is no reason for the Christian to yield to despair or to give in to acts of bodily sabotage when we gather in corporate worship. Instead, we must remember that the Spirit wishes always and ever to shelter and to sustain our bodies in our darkest hours, in addition to giving us a taste of the new creation in our present bodily acts of worship.

A Mortified and Vivified Body

Last, knowing how regularly our bodies succumb to the damaging forces of sin and entropy, the Spirit has thankfully not left us to our own devices. Instead, the Spirit gives to us the power of heaven and earth to mortify all the destructive powers that get lodged in our bodies, so that our bodies might be freed to worship God faithfully and fully—without fear. The remedy for the debilitating frailty and corruption that mark our bodies in this fallen world, therefore, is not excessive worry or faithless rejection. The remedy is more of the Spirit's empowering presence. Any anxiety that we may experience around the possibility of misuse or abuse of the body in worship ought not to dominate our thinking. Instead, we ought to remain confident in the power of the Spirit of God to mortify and to vivify our bodies, so that they might be freed to fulfill their good creaturely purposes.

And whenever and however our bodies bring us low, or break down, or betray us in some fashion, the Spirit not only gives strength in our hours of need, the Spirit also suffers with us. Meeting us in "the depths," as Psalm 130 puts it, the Spirit enables us to persevere in the face of chronic pain or the palpable burden of unanswered prayer that conspires to bring us into dark and oppressive places. The Spirit shows us the Suffering Servant near at hand, bearing with and for us, who offers his own body as medicine for our broken bodies that fail to mend on any timetable that makes sense.[38] And the Spirit makes it possible for us to experience profound comfort in the gentle hand of another member of Christ's Body, resting on our body, in an act of prayer that makes tangible the groaning of the Spirit interceding within our own hearts (Rom. 8:26 ESV). For it is not just rescue and restoration that make the Spirit known to us but also sympathetic care and intimate companionship when we are in the depths.

The Fullness of the Body

In the beginning, God breathes the breath of life into our earthy selves and we became a living thing, a *nephesh hayah*, all of which receives the divine benediction. In Christ, the whole of our humanity is again blessed and consecrated for the holistic work of bearing the image of God in the world. We become flesh of Christ's flesh, so that all flesh might become whole and wholly given over to God in praise and prayer. And because of the indwelling presence of the Spirit, every square inch of our humanity is colonized by the sanctifying power of God. Nothing is left untouched by the healing and re-creative touch of the Spirit.

What, then, should a trinitarian theology of the physical body result in? It should result in a positively expansive vision for the body at worship. There should be nothing penny-pinching or higgledy-piggledy about it. The question for the Christian is not, "What is the *least* offering of my body to God?" The question rather is, "How might I offer *all* of my body to God, yielding it, along with all of my anxieties and limitations and self-absorptions, wholly over to God in worship?" For the embodied nature of our prayer and praise is never neutral. It is always caught up in the inertia of Christ's own body and in the Spirit's work to enable our bodies to offer faithful praise to the Father, to give honor to whom honor is due. This is our body's glory: to participate in the fullness of God's own glory and in the fullness of creation's glorious praise.

7

The Nature of the Body

Scientific Perspectives on the Body in Worship

The liturgical year is the year that sets out to attune the life of the Christian to the life of Jesus, the Christ. It proposes, year after year, to immerse us over and over again into the sense and substance of the Christian life until, eventually, we become what we say we are—followers of Jesus all the way to the heart of God.

—Joan Chittister, The Liturgical Year

Are you hurting? Pray. Do you feel great? Sing. Are you sick? Call the church leaders together to pray and anoint you with oil in the name of the Master.

—James 5:13–14 (The Message)

Scent of a Human

When our adopted son, Sebastian, arrived on the afternoon of March 28, 2017, at the Woman's Hospital of Texas, in downtown Houston, the nurses handed his small body, still slick with the amniotic fluid of his birth mother, to my wife and me. Our social worker, Sara, who had walked with us through the long journey of adoption, urged us to hold him skin to skin (often called "kangaroo care") without delay. Such skin-to-skin contact, she explained, would cause a release of oxytocin, known as the love hormone, and would forge a crucial emotional bond between us.[1] It was important, she stressed, that he learn what we smelled like in these first few hours of his life outside the womb, since this would ensure healthy physical development over time.

This is, of course, what scientists have known for a good while. Neurobiologist Lise Eliot writes in her book, *What's Going On in There?*, "For newborns, whose 'long-distance' senses of vision and hearing are still poorly developed, the more immediate senses of smell, taste, and touch are far more important in assuring adequate growth and parental protection." Known as the chemical or proximal senses, the senses of smell and touch "begin with neural excitation in response to specific molecules in the environment."[2] It is this near-at-hand aspect of smell in particular that plays a decisive role in our survival as a species. Good smells correlate to life-giving things, such as "safe" humans and edible foods, while bad smells often signal danger and the possibility of death.

> **Let us see those things [God] does for us every day!**
> **How many tastes for the mouth!**
> **How many beauties for the eye!**
> **How many melodies for the ear!**
> **How many scents for the nostrils!**
> **Who is sufficient in comparison to the goodness of these little things!?**
> —Ephrem the Syrian, Hymns on Virginity

It is also the case that each of us has a one-of-a-kind smell.[3] Each human being, writes Eliot, is believed "to carry a unique olfactory signature resulting from his or her exact combination of genes."[4] The sense of smell likewise creates strong attachments to specific places and to particular memories. As Matthew Cobb, a professor of zoology, explains in his introduction to the science of smell and the role that it plays in culture and history, the frontal areas of the brain, which are involved in both olfactory processing and spatial learning, account for the close link between high olfactory abilities and spatial memory.[5] In the case of our son, Sebastian, the scent of our skin would become a way for him to know what "home," with us, smells like.

The Odor of God

Something similar is at work, I think, when God decides to link the smell of the tabernacle—the place of concentrated divine presence that functioned for Israel as "the house of the Lord" (Exod. 23:19; 1 Kings 6:1; Pss. 27:4; 122:1)—to a specific cocktail of spices:

> The LORD said to Moses: Take sweet spices, stacte, and onycha, and galbanum, sweet spices with pure frankincense (an equal part of each), and make an incense blended as by the perfumer, seasoned with salt, pure and holy; and you shall beat some of it into powder, and put part of it before the covenant in the tent of meeting where I shall meet with you; it shall be for you most holy. When you make incense according to this composition, you shall not make it for yourselves; it shall be regarded by you as holy to the LORD. Whoever makes any like it to use as perfume shall be cut off from the people. (Exod. 30:34–38)

To put it another way, God commissions Moses to create a specific incense and then trademarks it.

One of my contentions here is that Israel participates in a liturgical sensorium whose purpose is to evoke a desire for God and wherein the sense of smell plays a decisive role. Specific scents serve to signal the "odor of God," such as anointing oils (1 Sam. 10:1), fragrant incense (Exod. 30:1–8), lamps with olive oil (Exod. 25:6), the sweet smell of roasted beef (Lev. 1:9), and the use of aromatic spices in burial practices (2 Chron. 16:14; Jer. 34:5; Mark 16:1). All such liturgical accessories activate the unique sense of smell in the worship of Yahweh.

There is also a more figurative use of smell language in the Bible. Christ both gives himself up as a fragrant offering to God (Eph. 5:2) and invites us to become an aromatic means by which others might experience the true knowledge of God (2 Cor. 2:14). In church history, certain people are said to exude a particularly potent "odor of sanctity," while all believers are charged to avoid the foul odor of Satan and the stink of sin. But none of these figurative smells abrogate the use of actual physical smells in worship. They simply serve as spiritual analogues for the physical media through which we acquire a sense of God through our nose.[6]

Here I focus not so much on specifically biblical or theological arguments for the senses, but rather on the insights that the sciences might offer to the active role that our senses play in worship. I explore three specific senses: smell, sound, and sight. First, I show how particular smells can turn our hearts toward God; second, how singing together in a common physical space involves specific neural dynamics; and third, how a color-coded liturgical calendar includes a powerful psychological value for corporate worship.

Scratch-and-Sniff Worship

Having already identified some of the scientific insights on the sense of smell, I will simply say here that there is plenty of good reason why God prescribed the use of scent-inducing materials in Israel's worship and why Christians throughout history have continued to make use of those same materials in worship. I focus in this first section on three materials: oil, incense, and flowers. With the case of anointing oils, such olfactory materials function as media through which we experience the curative power of God; the use of incense serves to enrich our activities of prayer and to intensify our sense of God's dwelling place; and with the inclusion of aromatic flowers, we find ourselves aroused with a desire to be at home in the sweet-scented presence of God.

The use of *anointing oil* appears throughout Scripture: in Leviticus 8 with Aaron; in 1 Samuel 10 with Samuel; in Mark 6:13, where the disciples are said to anoint the sick with oil in order to cure them; in James 5:14–15, where the apostle encourages the elders to anoint any in the church who wish to be healed; and in John 12, where Mary of Bethany anoints Jesus's feet with oil. In church history, practices of anointing have usually accompanied liturgies of baptism and healing, rituals for the burial of the dead, and ordination ceremonies. In certain practices of baptism, such as Eastern Orthodox, the whole body is involved in such anointings: ears, eyes, hands, forehead, and feet.

Ambrose once described the experience of anointing at baptism as the attunement of the senses to God, so that the initiate "may receive the good odor of eternal piety . . . and that there may be in you the full fragrance of faith and devotion."[7] Such uses of consecrating and anointing oils have served not only to signal the power of God to enable us to fulfill our true calling and to make us whole, but they also may participate themselves in that healing work. Serapion of Thmuis, a fourth-century bishop in the Nile Delta and a friend of the desert father St. Anthony, includes this prayer for the Egyptian Christians of the time in his *Prayer Book*, written around AD 350:

> We invoke thee who has all authority and power, the Saviour of all men, father of our Lord and Saviour Jesus Christ, and pray thee to send healing power of the only-begotten from heaven upon this oil, that it may become to those who are being anointed (with it) or are partaking of these thy creatures, for a throwing off of every sickness and every infirmity, for a charm against every demon, for a separation of every unclean spirit, for an expulsion of every evil spirit, for a driving out of all fever and ague and every infirmity, for good grace and remission of sins, for a medicine of life and salvation, for health and soundness of soul, body, spirit, for perfect strengthening.[8]

As a liquid emblem placed on our bodies, anointing oils enable us to smell like our true selves, and as a salve they become a sacramental means by which the Spirit of God effects the repair of our whole selves, both body and soul.

With *incense*, Christians have generally taken the idea of incense-as-prayer in either literal or figurative terms. For those who take it figuratively, Psalm 141:2 has served as a primary text: "Let my prayer be counted as incense before you." For those who take it literally, the text of Malachi 1:11 is often determinative: "For from the rising of the sun to its setting my name is great among the nations, and in every place incense is offered to my name, and a pure offering." For all Christians, the idea that our prayers can be represented in the billowing smoke of incense is firmly rooted in the biblical imagination. In Revelation 5:8, for instance, the seer writes, "When he had taken the scroll, the four living creatures and the twenty-four elders fell before the Lamb, each holding a harp and golden bowls full of incense, which are the prayers of the saints."

In church history, the use of incense in liturgical contexts has taken its cue from a wide variety of biblical narratives. In some cases, incense has functioned mimetically, serving to re-image the myrrh-bearing women at the tomb. In other cases, it has played an exorcistic role as a way to embody and to continue the healing ministry of Jesus. It has been used in honorific fashion, such as at the reading of the gospel in an imitation of the temple practices in Israel; as intercessory, as in the morning hours, echoing the psalmists; and as penitential, as in the evening hours, in a mirror of the priestly activities of Leviticus 16.[9]

All contemporary uses of incense in worship might be reduced to three purposes: consecratory, purificatory, and representational. In its use during the entrance procession, for example, incense serves to consecrate the space of worship to God. In censing the priests and people, such as is done in Roman Catholic settings, incense serves to symbolically purify the congregation that enters into an encounter with the presence of a holy God. During a funeral service, a priest might cense the coffin of the dead as a sign of honor to the body of the deceased who lived as a temple of the Spirit during their life on earth. And in a special gathering of the congregation for prayer, incense rising upward might be used to represent a people's desire to offer acceptable prayers to God.

However it may be used in a liturgical context, I suggest that incense offers our noses firsthand knowledge of the presence of Christ, and it cultivates in us a longing for the awe-filled mystery of God. In contrast to the idea that our experience of God's presence will take place "in the sweet by and by," many years into the future, the use of incense in worship for many Christians today is a way to experience *here and now* a real whiff of that beautiful place where God dwells in glory (Exod. 31:11; Ps. 84:1).

Last, the use of *flowers* in many ways represents the most universal and least controversial deployment of the sense of smell in worship. Flowers may visually decorate a space, infuse it with a pleasant smell, or serve to symbolize the journey of faith (say, from the garden of Eden in Gen. 2 to the implied garden of the new creation in Rev. 22). In some cases, flowers will tie the church's worship to the natural rhythms of the immediate environment. Certain churches, for example, will use only flowers that are in season, while flowers that remain out of season or out of region, such as hothouse flowers and expensive imports, will be refused for ethical reasons. Other churches might reject artificial flowers for similar reasons and choose dried flowers, ferns, and sprays instead, preferring the spare organic beauty of the latter over the synthetic beauty of the former.[10]

Whether it is poinsettia flowers at Christmas or lilies at Easter or the purposeful absence of flowers during Lent, flowers have historically played a decorative and symbolic role in worship. Augustine, for example, is believed to have preferred the use of cherry flowers during Lent, because its red pulp serves as a powerful symbol of Christ's passion, while the pit recalls the wood of his cross. And for many Christians in so-called liturgical traditions, the anemone flower often symbolizes the Trinity, while the calendula may be employed in order to symbolize faith and loyalty.[11] In certain Protestant Korean churches, flowers are often used to decorate the pulpit, where the Word of God is proclaimed, and thus to visually represent the holiest place in the sanctuary.[12]

However scents are used, the idea is that the physical stuff of oil, incense, and flowers have an active role to play in the worship of the church and that the nose has something to do in worship, something that only it can uniquely do. While the possibility of misuse or abuse of such things in worship is one to which church leaders should always remain alert,[13] and although the New Testament remains devoid of explicit instruction regarding the use of these specifically physical aids to worship, with Basil the Great we can affirm the peculiar benefits that such aids bring to our prayers and praises.[14]

In the end, the use of flowers in worship serves to give sensory meaning to the idea that our encounter with God has a fragrant, perhaps even holy intoxicating, quality to it. Incense becomes a way for us to know—not just as an idea in our heads but as a reality that we experience in our bodies—that our prayers transit back and forth between heaven and earth. And with the use of oil, we are reminded of the integral work of God to transform our whole selves: body and soul.[15] We breathe in these scents and receive their healing gifts, trusting that God is in the business of using all the good gifts of creation to secure in us the remembrance of our salvation, deepen the true knowledge of God in our lives, and arouse in us a desire for God to become our truest dwelling place.

Hardwired to Sing

What insights might the sciences offer to our experience of communal song in corporate worship? I suggest that science makes good sense of the acute experience of loss that many of us felt during the lockdown period that COVID-19 demanded of us in 2020.[16] There is, in fact, a scientific explanation for why the experience of exclusively digitally mediated singing left so many of us deeply dissatisfied. Working in harmony with the witness of Scripture, the sciences underscore the value of singing together *in* our bodies, *near* the bodies of others, *as* the Body of Christ.[17] The phenomena of entrainment and interactional synchrony are specifically helpful on this account.

In technical terms, ***entrainment*** describes "the synchronization of one rhythmic process with another."[18] In practical terms, entrainment is what happens when a congregation at praise experiences a synchronization of their bodies in such a way that they become rhythmically coordinated to one another.[19] A particularly catchy hymn, for instance, may cause one's feet to start tapping unconsciously. A rousing rendition of a hip-hop worship song may find a group of people bobbing their heads in a metronomically synced way. Or a massive congregation may find itself clapping at the exact same tempo without consciously intending it. This is called mutual or interpersonal entrainment. Ethnomusicologist Nathan Myrick explains: "In this scenario, people entrain to one another, with music acting as a coupling factor: independent rhythmic processes create shared experiences of sensory data. Our brains and bodies become coupled to others. We do not have the same thoughts or feelings, but have our thoughts and feelings together, at the same time, with those around us."[20]

The notion of ***interactional synchrony*** sheds further light on what happens to our brains when we do things together with our bodies in a common physical space. In the simplest terms, interactional synchrony describes the experience of two people mirroring each other in terms of their bodily (and vocal) movements (cf. mirror neurons).[21] One of the most common instances of interactional synchrony can be witnessed in the exchange between mother and baby: a mother smiles, her baby smiles; a mother frowns, her baby frowns; a mother's voice softens, her baby becomes still; and so on. As it relates to communal music making, writes cognitive scientist William Benzon, "Human beings create a uniquely human social space when their nervous systems are coupled through interactional synchrony."[22] Benzon continues,

> When two people are making music together, and really listening to what each is doing, they are sharing in the same pattern of neural activity. . . . If the whole village is listening and dancing, then the whole village is enacting a single pattern of musical activity, even though they are physically distinct individuals with distinct nervous systems. What makes this sonic communion possible is that all these physically distinct nervous systems are cut from the same mold, and all are attuned to the same patterns of sound.[23]

Scientists have also shown how certain forms of music, such as a choral performance of Mozart or a congregation that sings the doxology at full volume, evoke "neural activation that is shared among listeners in key emotion areas such as the amygdala, insula and caudate nucleus."[24] Such experiences, which often involve a surge of endorphins and a release of oxytocin, result in a heightening of "fellow feeling," a deepening of "social bonds," a loss of self-protective "boundaries," and an increased sense of "feeling felt by another," which is to say an increased sense of mutual empathy.[25]

It is likewise the case that friends synchronize more readily than strangers, and strangers will do so more easily with people with whom they feel a sense of kinship.[26] In terms of "Hebb's axiom," neurons that fire together wire together.[27] They become, in short, tethered to one another in neurological and physiological ways, not just in affective or relational ways.[28] For congregations that sing together in dynamically physical ways, there is also the possibility of *muscular bonding*, which University of Chicago historian William McNeill defines in *Keeping Together in Time* as the "euphoric feeling that prolonged and rhythmic muscular movement arouses among nearly all participants."[29] Rob Moll, in *What Your Body Knows about God*, argues a similar line of thought when he writes that bodies that move together are particularly apt to stay together.[30]

To put the point of this section on sound in plain language, it pleases God to make a world where human bodies and brains perform such marvelous functions in the context of corporate worship.[31] Over against the notion that the Spirit works in exclusively immaterial ways in the singing ministry of the church, binding the people of God through principally "soulish" means, scientists help us understand how the Spirit produces the "one body" life not *despite* our bodies but rather *in* and *through* our bodies. The Spirit's work, in short, is not *extra*-physical but *pro*-physical, gracing our bodies to become the means by which we are united to other members of Christ's Body.[32] Science simply helps us to understand what happens to our bodies at the neural, chemical, and biological level in a way that complements, rather than competes with, the witness of Scripture about the goodness of singing together in a common corporeal place.[33]

The Color of a Story

Lastly, how might the psychology of color enable us to inhabit more viscerally the christological story that the church calendar tells through tint and tone and shade?[34] Color has undoubtedly fascinated humans for centuries. Colors have served to separate people by race (brown skin vs. white skin), politics (red state vs. blue state), and class (redneck vs. blue blood).[35] They have served to distinguish emotional states, like happiness (tickled pink) and sadness (feeling blue). And they have served to reinforce social hierarchies, which the sumptuary laws did in the High Middle Ages by controlling what colors commoners and aristocrats could wear in public.[36]

While color is certainly rooted in the microphysical properties of colored objects and in the eye's photoreceptors,[37] psychological factors invariably come into play.[38] The color red, for example, is frequently used by advertisers to express ideas of power (think "power tie") or desire (as with Coca-Cola cans). This is not surprising, given its physiological links to increased heart rates and flushed faces. Orange, by contrast, often nicknamed the color of the uninhibited by virtue of its association with breezy sunny days, is commonly used to convey notions of youthfulness and sociability, as the soft drink Fanta does in its purposeful targeting of teenagers.

Context, of course, always proves decisive for our experience of color. A blue ribbon, for instance, is a positive thing at a dog show, while blue on a piece of meat is an unwanted thing, revealing the meat to be rotten. In cultures influenced by Christianity, black is the color that properly tells the story of a funeral,[39] whereas in modern Korea and Iran it is blue that narrates the experience of heartache in the face of death.[40] The point here is that color always tells a story.[41] Or, as German artist Josef Albers once put it, seeing is always coupled with imagination.[42]

The Story of Time

It is in this sense also that the liturgical calendar tells a particular story through color and invites us to imagine ourselves into Christ's own story by way of a particular sequence of colors. In doing so, it reconfigures our identity as Christ's Body so that we might live in the world in Christocentric fashion.⁴³ And while I recognize that not all congregations tie their corporate worship to the church calendar, my hope is that this brief study of color and time, christologically construed, might inspire readers to enter more deeply into the church calendar as a way to partake more fully of Christ's sufferings and the power of his resurrection.

The story of the liturgical calendar begins with **Advent**. Often nicknamed a "Little Lent" because of its invitation to repentance in preparation for Christmas, Advent is a season in which we anticipate the coming of God in Christ. From the Latin *adventus*—which is the Latin translation of the Greek word *parousia*, a word frequently used to refer to the second coming of Christ—Advent challenges us to consider the following: How does the original coming of God to earth and the future coming of God inform our experience of God's coming here and now? Instead of seeing God's coming as a distant idea, fossilized in the past or far-flung in a perpetually receding future, Advent reorients our sense of God's coming in our own day and time.

Following the four darkening weeks of Advent is **Christmas**, which historically has been celebrated as a twelve-day feast rather than as a one-off day of gifts and gustatory delights. What is the story of Christmas? It is the story of fantastic encounters with angels who announce the word of God to people very much like ourselves. It is a story of pain and hardship—of infertility, social stigma, and the massacre of innocents. It is a multigenerational and multicultural story. It is also a story of spontaneous songs that serve as the only suitable vehicle for the expression of astonishment. And with the ending of Christmastide the church celebrates the Feast of the **Epiphany**, whereby Christ is manifested to the world.

In a mirror to this trilogy of light, the celebration of Lent, Easter, and Pentecost involves a triad of stories that bring us into an intensive experience of the triune life. At **Lent**, which in early Christianity involved a time of preparation for baptismal candidates, we are invited on a forty-day pilgrimage through the passion of the Christ—stemming from Israel's forty-year exodus through the desert, which Jesus himself recapitulates in his forty-day sojourn in the wilderness. Aided by penitential exercises of self-abnegation and self-giving, like fasting and service, Lent's aim is to conform us to the life of Christ. Through such exercises, the Spirit mortifies all that is bent against God in us so that we might become agents of Christ's life in the world.

Following the Paschal Triduum, which includes the liturgies for Maundy Thursday, Good Friday, Holy Saturday, and the Easter vigil, the church enters the season of **Eastertide**. This includes the forty days that run up to the Feast of the Ascension, then another ten days until the Feast of **Pentecost**, on which we celebrate the descent of the Holy Spirit. In this season Christians seek to make tangible the love of God in Christ in all spheres of life. Between Trinity Sunday and Christ the King Sunday, which lands on the Sunday before Advent, the church seeks to fulfill the mission of God in the ordinary circumstances of life.[44] Observes Bobby Gross, "This is the extended season to walk in Christ's light, to grow in Christ's life and to embody Christ's love."[45]

The Story of a Color

What role, then, does color play in our ability to enter meaningfully into the story of the liturgical calendar? It offers to us visual cues that serve to symbolize the plot-point of Christ's life and to evoke in us a desire to immerse ourselves in such a story within the context our own individual and common lives. The colors of the calendar can also be said to function like visual metaphors. As metaphors, they include the possibility of multiple associations. With purple, for example, both royalty and penitence can be represented in the liturgical paraphernalia of the church.[46] Or with the color red, the ardent life of the Spirit or the blood-spilt death of Christian martyrs could be evoked, depending on the time of year.

While it was not until the twelfth century, during the reign of Pope Innocent III (1198–1216), that a specific set of colors (violet, white, black, red, green) was prescribed for the church's liturgy (in this case, the Roman Rite), and while "a complete standardization of colors in the Roman church was not attempted until the nineteenth century," as J. Barrington Bates helpfully explains, color has never been absent from the church's public worship.[47] White, for example, functioned as the dominant color up to at least the fourth century, while "popinjay," "tawny," and "crane" seemed to have been popular in the medieval era. In contemporary churches across the globe, color often serves to beautify the gathering space of worship through natural, painterly, and digital means, including the use of environmental projection, which immerses a congregation in a visually saturated space.[48]

The liturgical calendar begins properly with the color **purple**.[49] As a symbol for both heavenly majesty and human contrition, purple is commonly used during Advent and Lent. Like black, it is a penitential color, in contrast to a festive one, and Christians have used it in order to reinforce the penitential posture of somberness and solemnity that befits a time of preparation for Christ's coming. It also serves to depict Christ's sovereignty. In some cases the color **blue**, evocative of heaven and hope, is used to distinguish the season of Advent from Lent. As the color of the sky above, blue symbolizes the One who comes to us as the "Dayspring" and who will return from that same blue sky where he ascended to the right hand of the Father.[50]

White, which brings to mind images of holiness and purity for Christians, is used principally at Christmas and Easter. It is also used for Trinity Sunday, All Saints' Day, and the Last Sunday after the Epiphany, also known as Transfiguration Sunday, as well as for baptismal liturgies and for weddings. It is likewise the suggested color for the last Sunday in the church year, called Christ the King Sunday. The color white includes rich associations with the experience of being cleansed by God (Ps. 51:7), with the dazzling white clothes of Jesus that his disciples witness at his transfiguration (Matt. 17:2), and with the multitude of saints in heaven, who are clad in robes made white by the red blood of the Lamb (Rev. 7:9). **Gold** is, for some traditions, the optional color for Easter Sunday.

Red, the color of blood and fire, marks the activities of Holy Week, specifically from Palm Sunday through Maundy Thursday. Yet it is also employed on Pentecost Sunday, the day on which Christians commemorate the descent of the Spirit-like tongues of fire that rested upon the heads of the disciples. Evoking the imagery of the "beloved" in Song of Songs 5:10 and of Yahweh's wine-soaked garment in Isaiah 63:2, the color red—which like all the other colors that mark altar and table, lectern and ambo, vestments and banners and walls—involves a surplus of meaning for the church at worship. This includes the desire of the faithful to have their hearts kindled with the fire of the Spirit and the remembrance of the bloody death of martyred saints.

The color **black** suggests ideas of death, illness, mourning, and loss. The calendar usually calls for its use only twice: on Ash Wednesday and on Good Friday. In some traditions it is used during the weekdays in Lent. It is also, of course, a primary color for funerals. In contrast to this color that symbolizes the diminishment and destruction of life, the color **green** symbolizes the explosion and expansion of life. Used chiefly during Ordinary Time, which might be regarded as the "green meadow" of the church's life, the color green is closely associated with ideas of bounty, growth, and the triumph of life over death.[51] And like the "green plants" of Genesis 1:30 and the "green pastures" of Psalm 23:2, the use of green over the long stretch of Ordinary Time is meant to foster in Christians a desire for God's kingdom to come in fullness, everywhere and always.

The End of Color

While it is always important to remain sensitive to those who experience color blindness in some fashion,[52] and while we must never forget the contextual nature of color, in which people and cultures experience the same color in radically different ways, the role that color plays in the liturgical calendar should never be reduced to *mere* visual sign (such as a traffic light) nor to a *mere* decorative touch (such as hotel flowers). As a visual metaphor, each color of the church year narrates for us the complex story of Christ's life. Purple signals not simply Christ's royalty but that such royalty is marked by wounded vulnerability and self-sacrificial love, rather than by brute power and privileged birthrights. Or the color red, for Christians, signifies not chocolate, wine, and sentimental acts of courtly love, but rather the irruption of heavenly fire and a love that does not cling to life in the face of death.

And as with the sense of smell and sound, the sense of sight here serves to give the body an active role to play in corporate worship. Nose, ear, and eye participate in their God-given purposes and draw the whole of our humanity into a holistic offering of praise and prayer to God. Do incense and communal song and the colors of the year perform these liturgical goods magically or automatically? No, they do not. How our senses form us in worship is always a complex and complicated business, requiring wise pastoral care and disciplined effort. But like the scents that we smell and the sounds that we hear, the sight of colors can help us to live more deeply into the story of God—a God who is both color coordinated and color profligate in all his works—and of a story that envelopes, explains, and invests all our individual stories with ultimate purpose. The service that scientists perform on this account is simply to bear witness to the marvels of God's book of nature in our physical bodies themselves.

8

The Art of the Body

Artistic Perspectives on the Body in Worship

Come old and young, come great and small,
There's love and union free for all.
And everyone that will obey
Has now a right to dance and play.
For dancing is a sweet employ
It fills the soul with heav'nly joy,
It makes our love and union flow
While round and round and round we go.
—Shaker hymn

Praise with a blast on the trumpet,
 praise by strumming soft strings;
Praise him with castanets and dance,
 praise him with banjo and flute;
Praise him with cymbals and a big bass drum,
 praise him with fiddles and mandolin.
—Psalm 150:3–5 (The Message)

The aim of this chapter is to explore the gifts that the arts bring to the experience of the body in corporate worship. My argument here is that the arts bring us into an *intentional and intensive participation in the aesthetic aspect of our humanity*.[1] The arts engender a way to grasp the world through our senses; they give us a feel for things that we might not be able otherwise to articulate; they enable us to imagine what, at first glance, may seem improbable or even impossible; and they immerse us in a sphere of metaphors by which we as humans make sense of our personal and social lives.

The arts, in short, foreground our sensory, affective, and imaginative experience of the world, and they traffic richly in metaphors, enabling us thereby *to figure out* the world through *figurative* means. After briefly explicating the distinctively aesthetic aspects of artistic media, I explore at greater length three examples from the arts—painting, dance, and architecture—in order to draw attention to the unique ways in which the arts might form the bodily dimension of our communal worship. Plenty of other artistic media could, of course, have been considered here, such as poetry, music, drama, film, and so on. But my hope is that this treatment of visual, kinetic, and spatial works of art might serve to illumine what is possible with *any* work of art in the formation of Christlikeness in and through our physical bodies.

Aesthetic Media

The first thing to say about the aesthetic character of the arts is that they make their primary appeal to our five **senses**. In *Heart of Darkness*, Polish-British novelist Joseph Conrad observes that "All art appeals primarily to the senses."[2] A beautifully illustrated Bible, for instance, appeals directly to my eyes. Bach's *St John Passion*, written during his first year as director of church music at St. Thomas Church, in Leipzig, Germany, and originally intended for use in a Good Friday service, appeals directly to my ear's love of melody, symmetry, rhythm, and repetition. Or the frankincense and myrrh-scented oil with which I anoint the broken of body and of soul in our congregation appeals to my nose and what it knows about a Spirit-revitalized life.[3]

In this appeal to our senses, the arts invite us to inhabit our bodies and, through them, to get a grasp of the world. When we sit for the hearing of Scripture, for example, our bodily posture trains us to be attentive to the word of God so that we may remain attentive to God's voice throughout the week. Or when we cross ourselves on entering a place of worship, such a gesture serves to inscribe in our bodies a desire to live a cruciform life at home and at work. And to gaze at length on a painting of the resurrected Christ can become a way to resensitize ourselves to a sense of God's presence in the mortal and mundane circumstances of our lives.

As it is with the physical senses, so it is with the **emotions**: the arts foreground them.[4] It is through the arts that we often find our hearts *moved*, for better and for worse.[5] The arts can both name and manipulate our emotions, as the exquisite performance of an organ sonata by Felix Mendelssohn might do in a prelude to the liturgy or as an equally exquisite rock anthem might do in the middle of a musical set performed by a worship band in a large auditorium. The arts can elicit empathy, as a dramatic reading of the good Samaritan parable might do, and they can incite anger, as a similarly dramatic reading of Matthew 27 might accomplish.

The arts can also shape our emotional lives so that they might become more finely attuned to the heart of Jesus. Jeremy Begbie writes, "Music can help us discover something that we *could* feel, that we have not felt before. And, we might add, we can also be educated emotionally: we might discover what we *should* feel in particular situations."[6] This is especially true, for example, with the singing of the psalms. As sung poems, the psalms invite us to sing the joys and heartaches of our neighbors, whether or not we feel those things ourselves. On other days, they invite us to sing our own joys and heartaches. To sing in both ways, over time, is to cultivate what Begbie calls "faithful feelings," which involves the capacity to feel what God feels, so that we might love our neighbors in emotionally in-tuned ways, among other things.[7]

> **The life of faith does not go in a straight line but turns, falls, sinks, pulls, pushes, releases, clings, pauses, leaps, and dances.**
> —Celeste Snowber, lecture on "The Christian Imagination"

As it is with the senses and the emotions, so it is with the **imagination**: the arts bring us into a concentrated experience of it. With the imagination, we are able to see things that are not immediately present or as yet actual; we imagine what might have been and what yet may be.[8] Such is the case, for instance, with the playful architecture of Antoni Gaudí's *Sagrada Familia*, with its joyful vision of a world renewed by the resurrected Christ.⁹ Such also is the case with Jesus's parables of the kingdom, Michelangelo's painterly glimpse of God's justice in the "Last Judgment," and the Asian, Latino, and African hymns that a congregation might sing on All Saints' Day as a way to imagine that final day when song from every tongue and tribe shall be lifted up to the Lamb on his throne.

A similar dynamic, I suggest, is at work with Eastern Orthodox worship. Worship in such a liturgical context correlates faithful worship to a sensory richness. A fecundity of aesthetic data—fragrant incense, chanted music, endlessly burning candles, ornamented vestments, icons both portable and permanent, things tasted and touched, along with a symbolically rich kinetic activity—trains the worshiper to see the world as God sees it, *through* and not despite these artistic artifacts. Said otherwise, the "festal muchness" that distinguishes the distinctly aesthetic character of Orthodox worship serves to form the imagination of worshipers, training them to imagine something true about "heaven and earth" so that they may fulfill God's will, on earth as it is in heaven.¹⁰

A last aspect that comprises a distinctly aesthetic understanding of the arts is the element of **metaphor**.¹¹ A metaphor is the understanding of one thing in terms of an unexpected other, such as "Jesus is a vine," "the church is a temple," and "Miles Davis is the Picasso of jazz."¹² For artists, metaphors are the "breakfast of champions," as writer Ray Bradbury once quipped.¹³ In their deployment of metaphors, furthermore, artists say things about the world that could not be said in any other way but that, in the saying, disclose for us something true about the world.¹⁴

What does sorrow sound like, for example? It could sound like Verdi's "Requiem" or like The Porter's Gate's "O Sacred Neck, Now Wounded." It sounds as dramatic and terrifying as Verdi's music or as haunting and plaintive as the Porter's Gate song, depending on who it is that requires such music to name the experience of sorrow faithfully. Does joy literally sound like Beethoven's "Ode to Joy" or like Aretha Franklin's rendition of "Oh Happy Day"? *In a manner of speaking*, yes—and no. Joy may sound exultant and ebullient, but it may also sound like many other things. However sorrow and joy may sound on any given day, each of these musical works suggests something true about the nature of sorrow and joy, but they do so in metaphorical form.

Pixilated Bodies

A similar thing is at work in the metaphor of Christians as the "hands and feet of Jesus." What does it mean to live into the reality that Jesus preaches in Matthew 25, where the feeding, clothing, tending, and welcoming of a stranger become the occasion to love Jesus himself in like fashion? What does it look like to love "the least of these," whether or not they belong to the family of faith? How do we become a people who love—with our own hands and feet—our distant and despised neighbors as the good Samaritan does in Jesus's parable in Luke 10? And how might the visual arts train our bodies to embody the love of Jesus in such a radical way? An exhibit that appeared in a church in Austin, Texas, trained the congregants in such a manner.

In 2007, Hope Chapel, a nondenominational, moderately charismatic congregation where I once served as a pastor, invited Laura Jennings, one of its members, to exhibit her paintings in the sanctuary. When her art first appeared in the sanctuary, I explained to the congregation that, as with all the visual art that hung there, Jennings's work was not intended to merely ornament the space. It was there to help us to see the gospel afresh through distinctly visual media and to inspire us to live out the gospel afresh. I suggested that in the same way that Jesus repeatedly directed his disciples to notice things that society ignored, so Jennings's work drew our attention to groups that we frequently overlooked—in this case, the Dalits ("untouchables") of India and victims of war violence.

With respect to the materiality of the work, there are two things to note. First, the paintings were hung in the sanctuary space, along the two walls that ran horizontally from back to front. As such, the paintings remained *physically present* to the congregation. Unlike the singing of a song, which occurs "through time," these paintings were fixed "in time." And they did not "expire," as a musical note might; they stayed put. In this way, Jennings's hyper-colored paintings fixed before our eyes a set of images that profoundly shaped the visual character of our sanctuary. Second, Jennings's artwork foregrounded the experience of physical things such as pigment, color, canvas, texture, frame, and so on. While they did not invite actual touch, the primary experience for the viewer was not of an abstract idea but of a physical object: a painting.

How did these paintings foreground the emotions? The scenes that Jennings's work depicted included issues related to suffering, slavery, racism, injustice, and death. The kinds of emotions that these images provoked in viewers over the course of weeks included sadness, anger, guilt, fear, helplessness, and an awareness of apathy. But more than a permission to feel certain things, the art purposefully aimed to train the congregation in "faithful feelings." The systemic exclusion of Dalits and the random experiences of mass destruction: these were things that one *should* feel sad or angry about. Further, unlike the daily news that floats in and out of our minds as we scroll through our digital screens, the *material fixity* of the art refused to let people turn off these tragic aspects of our world. They invited people to remain present to their emotional responses to such tragedies—to keep looking and to keep feeling.

Jennings's work not only represented a truthful way to perceive the love of the poor and needy, it also informed how we imagined ourselves loving such people. Over against the temptation to view public suffering as a spectator sport, resulting in a tragic indifference, or to give in to a feeling of fatalism because such things seem impossible to solve, Jennings's work invited us to imagine the unimaginable: that something could in fact be done to redress the suffering of the world and that Jesus might in fact choose us to be his hands and feet.[15] Jennings's artwork challenged our impoverished imaginations and invited us to imagine things that, for God and thus also for us, were fully possible.

But are human beings *literally* pixilated dots, as they appeared in Jennings's work? Do they *actually* occupy abstract spaces that defy the laws of gravity? Do they *really* float faceless in swirls of color? No. But the point of the artwork was not to produce physiologically realistic representations of human bodies. The point was to represent them in the form of a true metaphor. By showing us pixilated bodies rather than solid ones, Jennings's art reminded us that we do not see people rightly simply by looking at them; our sight is damaged and needs mending. In depicting fragmented bodies, the art also reminded us of our fragmented perceptions of the bodies of others, including those nearby. And in showing us only the outline of bodies, the art reminded us of our own tendencies to "erase" others' bodies, through neglect or injury, thereby making it all too easy for us to demean the dignity of those bodies that have become "invisible" to us.

Dancing Bodies

An extraordinary reform movement that sought to make the body more *visible*—in particular, the bodies of women and of people of color—and thus more consequential to corporate worship took place among a people called the Shakers.[16] Founded in England in 1747 and nicknamed the "Shaking Quakers," the Shakers, who established a presence in the American colonies in the 1770s, were famous for two things: they practiced celibacy, along with a radical commitment to gender and racial equality, and, unlike the vast majority of Christians in eighteenth-century America, they danced.[17] They danced, they said, in order to achieve closeness to God and to fulfill their earthly vocation in anticipation of their heavenly future. Writes J. G. Davies: "The Shakers danced not only because they believed the Holy Spirit was inspiring them, nor simply because they found authority for it in the Old Testament; they danced because they wanted their worship to involve them totally."[18] In their own words: "To worship God is my delight / With hands and feet in motion."[19]

What began, however, as a charismatic practice, involving "an involuntary emotion" and resulting in zealous dancing, hand clapping, foot stamping, and violent "quakings," eventually transitioned to "a voluntary duty."[20] Spontaneous movement became organized movement. Explains Davies, "They had shuffle dances, a forward-and-backward square order dance, marches, round and ring dances, wheel dances, etc."[21]

What exactly did their dances involve, physically speaking? While Shakers originally allowed the Holy Spirit to move them as the Spirit willed, around the late 1700s they began to ritualize their movements, and they gave specific names to such movements. A few of these include the Holy Order, the Regular Step, and the Hollow Square. Typical gestures would include a rhythm of hands facing up and facing down. Hands might be waved around or they might be shaken around or they might be waved back and forth in front of the body. Bowing at the waist was common as well as marching forward and backward while tapping the toes on wooden floors with force and purpose.[22] Men and women frequently faced each other, sometimes in large numbers.

Writer James Fenimore Cooper once visited a Shaker worship service and noted the following observation in his journal: "At the commencement of the song, the dancers moved forward, in a body, about three feet each, turned, shuffled, and kept repeating the same evolutions the whole time of this remarkable service."[23] During a trip to Kentucky in the fall of 1817, Baptist minister Andrew Broaddus of Virginia wrote a firsthand account of a typical Shaker dance, which is worth quoting at length as it shows how Shaker dances foregrounded the physical dimension of worship.

> The men formed in rows, making a solid column in one room; the women facing them in the same manner in the other; and the communication was opened. They stood in silence two or three minutes, and then broke forth in a loud and melodious manner in singing an anthem, which might last ten minutes. Then changing their position, they stood in readiness for the sacred dance; the men in rows facing their row of singers, and the women in a similar attitude. The musick [sic] began with a lively air, animating the pleasing tone, and the dance went on in complete unison with the time. Words composed for the occasion, in lively rhyme, soon followed. The ... singers grew more animated, keeping time by stamping with the foot; while the dancers went on with answerable animation, traversing the room up and down backwards and forwards, and sometimes facing about, with a simultaneous motion. At certain quick parts of the time the singers strike the time by several loud clappings. Presently a pause was made, and all stood still for nearly a minute. A new tune was struck up, verse soon followed, and the same kind of exercise went on.[24]

What role did these dances play in the emotions of the faithful? For many Shakers, dancing served to give expression to an effusion of joy. They danced in imitation of the joyful victory dances of the Old Testament, and they danced to realize the victory of God in their own day. In the words of an early nineteenth-century observer: "These people rejoice in the dance because they have experienced a deliverance from a more potent and powerful enemy, even him who hath reigned and ruled in the hearts of all the children of men ever since the fall of Adam."[25] But the Shakers danced not only to express an emotional response to God; they also danced in order to grow joy in their hearts. Dancing in this way served to cultivate an emotional disposition, so that the heart might be attuned to the joy of God.

Lillian Phelps, a mid-twentieth-century Shaker, summarizes the emotional, or psychological, dimension of Shaker dance this way: "If one could have been present, as I was, and could have seen the perfect spiritual union that was produced when a soul combined the physical motions, the singing voice and the dedicated heart, in giving praise and thanks to God—I'm sure you would have agreed that the physical motions added a still greater dimension to the expression of Prayer."[26]

But the purpose of dancing, for Shakers, was not simply to foster the joy or the unity of God's people here on earth. Its purpose was also to anticipate and to realize the common life that was promised with the second coming of Christ. Its purpose, that is, was to help them imagine what seemed impossible to many Christians of the era. It is in this sense, we might say, that their dances were eschatologically inflected; they served as a foretaste of what was to come for the faithful. "They danced in the ecstasy of a chosen and exalted people," observes Davies, "performing now what many Christian writers had referred to the distant future and to heaven, viz. the mystic dance of the blessed."[27]

Their dancing reflected in this way an inaugurated eschatology. The kingdom of Christ had already come, they believed, and their dancing simply served to participate in the fullness of Christ's kingdom that yet awaited them. Again, their songs routinely served to articulate what their bodies aimed to incarnate, what their hearts sought to experience, and what their imaginations longed to realize.

> The work which God had promis'd long,
> Hath now appear'd at last so strong,
> 'Tis verify'd with a new song,
> With dancing and with shaking.[28]

Because the year of jubilee had already come, they argued, the bond of love between men and women, and White and Black, became imaginable in the dances that forged Spirit-fashioned relational bonds through kinetic means. Their dancing, in sum, both signified and actualized that which it envisioned: God's gift of universal brotherhood, which for many Christians of the day remained foreign or anathema.

It is in this sense that we can say that typical Shaker dance practices of the late eighteenth and early nineteenth centuries served as a corporeal metaphor for a particular idea of Christian unity. While music has historically been given a privileged place in the church's pursuit of artistically mediated unity within the context of corporate worship—and while debates about the relative value of melody over harmony, or metrical over syncopated rhythms, to forge "true" unity among Christians at worship have ebbed and flowed throughout the centuries—dance has typically played a marginal or excluded role in this work. But for the Shakers, dance served as a primary artistic medium for the experience of genuine unity.

In dances that involved forward and backward movement, with men and women facing one another, the Shakers symbolized the relational nature of faith that involved a mutual give-and-take, as Paul articulates it in 1 Corinthians 12. In movements that were at times highly individual while at other times highly choreographed, the Shakers made sense of the idea that God had given to each a manifestation of the Spirit for the common and coordinated good. With hands that were shaken around and with feet that stamped hard on the wooden floors, the Shakers embodied the "shaking off of sins" that prevented the unity of the Spirit and caused division among the saints. And with both frenzied movement and scripted movement, the Shakers bore witness in their bodies to the work of the Spirit in both 1 Samuel 19:24 and 1 Corinthians 14:40.

What the Shakers did with dance in their corporate worship is far from unique, however, even if it might be unusual for its time.[29] In a way that is similar, for example, to the Shakers' embrace of whirling dance, or "Estatick Fits," as a way to enact with the body a complete self-surrender to God, the use of electronic dance music in certain free church worship contexts aims to free worshipers to get outside of themselves (from the Greek *ekstasis*) in order to get over themselves, so that they might be entirely yielded to God at all times and places.[30] Or much like the eruptions of joy that occur in some Black churches in the form of praise dances, whether scripted or spontaneous, so Shaker worship sought to reflect and to cultivate the emotion of joy in their communal worship.[31] And akin to the whole-bodied worship that takes place in the Anglican Church of Uganda or in the Catholic Church in Zaire, so Shaker worship believed "that every faculty should be used in the worship of God."[32]

On the other side of such spontaneous movement, the Shaker practice of pre-scripted movement in worship closely resembles the highly choreographed motions of contemporary ballet groups as well as of the modern liturgical movement that swept through the Roman Catholic Church in the twentieth century.[33] Similar to the deliberate incorporation of physical movement that takes place within many mainline churches, the highly participatory movement in Shaker worship sought to break down socioeconomic and racial dividing walls among Christians.[34] And like the purposeful welcome of kinetic activity in worship that certain "Bapticostals" (Baptist + Pentecostal) believe is warranted by the Bible, so too Shakers appealed repeatedly to the Bible as the basis for their dance in worship. Their appeal to Scripture also subverted any lingering notion that dance belonged to the exclusive domain of women.

Finally, the practice of Shaker dances may also forge a sense of kinship with many praise and liturgical dancers today, who might find themselves on the margins of liturgical life.[35] And in the same way that nondenominational churches have often built multipurpose spaces in order to accommodate the free movement of bodies, so too Shaker Christians built meeting houses with moveable pews in order to facilitate uninhibited communal dance.[36] In creating such architectural structures, they believed that the body had something decisive to do in corporate worship. The body played an *active*, not a passive, role.

Coordinated Bodies

In Shaker worship we witness acutely how both architecture and interior design open up and close down possibilities to form our bodies at worship.[37] This is another way of saying that no building is neutral, no design is neutral, and no seating arrangement in a worship space is ever neutral. Every seating arrangement reinforces certain ideas about ecclesial identity by the manner in which our physical bodies are oriented to one another. Three seating arrangements, I suggest, have functioned as most determinative for the church's worship throughout history and each activates our physical bodies in distinctive ways, with concrete implications for how we understand ourselves as Christ's Body.

One determinative seating arrangement is what might be termed *side by side*. Such a physical arrangement of bodies might evoke a general association with public processions and marches. For Christians, it might recall the marches of Israel (Ps. 68:24–27) or the processions of saints on pilgrimage that the Psalms of Ascent describe for us (Pss. 120–34). In such processions human beings usually walk side by side, shoulder to shoulder, eyes facing forward, while moving toward a common endpoint. It may invite Christians to imagine life as it is lived now in this present age in relation to life in the age to come: as pilgrims on a pilgrimage.[38] Translated to liturgical spaces, like the Gothic style of Salisbury Cathedral, in England, a longitudinal architectural plan invites the physical body to move from back to front, and from outside ("world") to inside ("sanctuary").[39]

A second determinative seating arrangement is what might be called *circling up*. This includes both actual circle arrangements, like the central-plan design that characterizes much of Byzantine architecture, or half-circle arrangements, such as St John's Abbey, in Collegeville, Minnesota, where the monks gather daily for worship.[40] Here the primary association might be one of camaraderie. Human bodies stand side by side but slightly angled toward other bodies. We are together in this way, we might say, tuned in toward several "one anothers." Jean N. Kidula describes the common experience of distinctively African worship this way: "Creating a circle means that members of the performance group are visible to everybody, but each member can really be seen properly by the few that are close by, especially when there is a big group performing. This rather ambiguous placement ensures community and anonymity while promoting individuality and particularity."[41]

In such an artful arrangement of human bodies the experience of congregational song has a quality of companionship about it. Here we *glimpse* the eyes of others; here we *sense* that we are not alone in our song, and the faces around us inspire our own song; here bodies *lean into* each other and gather around a commonly perceived center; here we *imagine* ourselves as the friends of Jesus, gathered in half-moon fashion around a common table. Our gathering in this way, with an opening on the other side of our semicircular space, does not close off the possibility that Christ—by his Spirit—may wish to enter, or even to interrupt, our worship. We keep that space open in symbolic fashion to remind us that our worship never masters God. We feel keenly our dependence upon one another in the presence of a God who encircles us.

A third determinative seating arrangement is *face-to-face*. Here human bodies exist in close proximity; direct attention is given to the bodies of others; the expressiveness of the face is consequential. Sitting across from one another—as parishioners do at St. Gregory's Episcopal Church in San Francisco or as individuals may do in the choir stalls of large cathedrals or, as is common with the persecuted church, in house churches—means that what is done with one's physical body affects others in the most immediate fashion. How might such an artful arrangement form our bodies at worship?

For starters, it creates a strong resonance with the biblical promise of a face-to-face encounter with God in glory (1 Cor. 13:12) and perhaps also the idea that we behold that glory in one another's faces (cf. 2 Cor. 3:18). A face-to-face arrangement may also evoke echoes of the disciples gathered around the Lord's Table and enable us to imagine worship as the experience of table fellowship with Christ himself. We are together in this way, we might say, as we gather in this intimate manner. In such an arrangement the experience of congregational song involves singing one to another, whereby we know in our bodies what it means *really* to address one another with psalms, hymns, and "Spirit-ed" songs (Eph. 5:19). Last, our bodily actions may evoke immediate emotional responses in one another. We exchange knowing glances and share our feelings openly as we imagine ourselves sitting at the marriage supper of the Lamb (Rev. 19).[42]

While most congregations may not be able to easily rearrange their seating patterns, it is important to understand how the design of our primary space of worship is never neutral. No one seating arrangement can form in us the richly biblical imagery of the church, with its kaleidoscope of mutually enhancing metaphors. This begs a sober reflection from church leaders about the ways in which their people may fail to feel what it means, for example, to be the Bride of Christ, a temple of the Spirit, or God's royal priesthood, as the case may be, in any way that makes a decisive difference for how they embody their faith at church and beyond the church. The hope, of course, is that a congregation might be able to make changes, even if only minor ones, in order to explore the fullness of their calling as God's people, gathered in their bodies as the Body of Christ. But, as always, these will need to be undertaken with wise care.

The Aesthetic Body

In the end, we could preach about Spirit-saturated, baptized imaginations, but we might also give our eyes something to look at, such as He Qi's painting *The Risen Lord*, and trust that this experience of seeing will help us to imagine the singular power of Christ's resurrection.[43] We could talk about humility, but we might also invite our bodies to get a sense firsthand for a self-surrendered life through bent knees and hands raised high. We could read books about lament, but we might also give our people a chance to feel sadness by singing a psalm of lament and thereby acquire a capacity to feel for our neighbor with the empathy of God.[44] And we could think about God's majesty, but we might also invite our people to inhabit a majestic space, such as a work of Gothic architecture, as a way to figuratively proclaim the lofty and exalted character of God to all who pass by.

This, in short, is the good news of the arts to the body at worship.

9

The Way of the Body

Ethical Perspectives on the Body in Worship

[Black Roman Catholic worship creates] a concert or orchestration in which the ear sees, the eye hears, and where one both smells and tastes color; wherein all the senses, unmuted, engage in every experience.

—Clarence Rivers, Plenty Good Room: The Spirit and Truth
of African American Catholic Worship

I looked again. I saw a huge crowd, too huge to count. Everyone was there—all nations and tribes, all races and languages. And they were standing, dressed in white robes and waving palm branches, standing before the Throne and the Lamb and heartily singing: Salvation to our God on his Throne! Salvation to the Lamb!

—Revelation 7:9–10 (The Message)

What a Body Must Do

Henri Van Allen is six years old and a delightful member of my church in Austin, Texas. He is affectionate toward adults, joyful in his play with kids his own age, and liberal in the hugs he doles out to newcomers. He also has Down syndrome. Though he is high functioning and has a speech level that surpasses his thirteen-year-old sister, Layla, who is intellectually disabled and a SWAN (an acronym for someone with a syndrome without a name), Henri's experience of our liturgy is limited. The verbally rich elements, like the sermon, the prayers, and the creed, remain largely inaccessible to him, as they do also to Layla.

Their parents, Paul and Lisa, have told me that Layla's primary entryway to the liturgy is through the music. She also gladly joins in bodily wherever she can, kneeling, bowing, and, with difficulty, signing herself with the cross. Recently, Layla was asked to be a crucifer and was thrilled to play this role in the official worship of our church. The first time she served in this capacity, she struggled to carry the heavy metal cross that our congregation routinely uses. "As she labored under the cross, leaning it against her shoulder," her father told me, "I thought of Jesus and Simon of Cyrene laboring under an actual cross."[1] The second time she acted in this capacity, she was given a lighter wooden cross that she reverently bore down the nave toward the altar, placing it in its stand with wobbly care.

Their parents have observed over time that what makes worship meaningful for Henri and Layla is the combination of embodied rhythms, infused by a charismatic spirit, and the richly aesthetic character of our liturgy. These qualities make space for the Spirit to communicate beyond their intellects, through their bodies, directly to their hearts. What worries their parents, however, is how their two children will fit in as they grow older and possibly more self-conscious about their disabilities. While Henri and Layla's public schools have put a great deal of effort into fostering inclusion and helped the kids around them to "see" and to involve them, the members at our church largely lack this training and may, down the road, unwittingly cause harm, resulting in a painful experience of worship for the two.[2]

For many disabled persons, regardless of tradition, the experience of pain in corporate worship is a present reality, not a future concern. Because their bodies cannot do what other bodies might do easily in worship, they often find themselves on the margins of worship, misunderstood and dismissed in a way that causes deep hurt. Instead of finding the Body of Christ to be a welcoming place for bodies that do not conform to societal norms, people with disabilities find Christ's Body to be an exclusive Body. As Nancy Eiesland summarizes things in her book *The Disabled God*, "For many disabled persons, the church has been a 'city on a hill'—physically inaccessible and socially inhospitable."[3] What, then, must the

Body of Christ do to welcome all who find themselves unseen, ignored, unwelcome, or outright rejected in corporate worship?

In this chapter I argue that because the church's worship is caught up in God's desire to restore all things in creation, our practices of corporate worship must reckon not only with the very broken ways that we gather bodily as the church but also with the Spirit's desire to reconcile all things bodily in Christ. This chapter, then, considers the ethical implications of the body at worship with a focus on three specific issues: the bodies of those with disabilities, the bodies of the unseen, and digital bodies. As with other topics covered, a proper treatment of this matter lies beyond the scope of this book. My hope, however, is that what readers find here will encourage them to learn more in order to discern God's good purposes for them in their own distinctive, concrete contexts.

Disabled Bodies

First, then, with respect to the experience of disabled persons, I wish particularly to explore the unique gifts that they might bring to our common uses of the body in corporate worship.[4] Although I cannot suggest all possible solutions for a deeply meaningful experience of worship for disabled persons—which includes people with physical, psychological, or cognitive impairments, such as deafness, post-traumatic stress disorder, and Down syndrome, as well as those who suffer from chronic illness or a debilitating disease, such as Epstein-Barr virus and Alzheimer's disease—my hope is that readers might feel both challenged and inspired to embrace a bodily form of worship that more fully includes persons with disabilities and that is enriched by

> *If you have never been to a gathering of people with disabilities when praise songs and dancing breaks out, I am not certain you have ever seen true worship.*
>
> —Amy E. Jacober, Redefining Perfect: The Interplay between Theology and Disability

their unique perspectives on and experiences of embodied worship. Four gifts of the disabled body deserve our attention here.

First, the disabled body enables us to see the true *body of the crucified and resurrected Christ as, in fact, a disabled body. In seeing Christ's body truly, our assumptions about a "perfect" body are questioned.* In what sense specifically is Christ's body disabled? On the usual terms of discussion around disability, Jesus's body is disabled in the following ways. In his life and ministry, his is a despised, needy, jeered, rejected, misperceived, and misunderstood body. On the cross, it is a broken, incapacitated, and disfigured body. In his resurrected body, Christ retains his "rich wounds, . . . in beauty glorified," to borrow language from Matthew Bridges's 1851 hymn "Crown Him with Many Crowns," and he takes his scars up into the very life of the Godhead. In the Eucharist, Christ's body is broken again by a Body of very broken people who turn against one another in desperately broken ways. Who is the God we worship? In Christ, he is a God whose body is broken and blemished, not "perfect."[5]

What might we conclude from this? For starters, we might assert that his blemished body does not represent a disappointing outcome for the resurrected body; it represents instead an icon of our true humanity. His is not a "perfect skin"; his is a perfected skin, perfected by the Spirit of God. His is not a "flawless complexion"; his is a radiant complexion, "the flawless expression of the nature of God," as Hebrews 1:3 (J. B. Phillips) describes it. His is not a "pure anatomy" or an "immaculate beauty"; his is a scarred and stigmatized body that now includes a "beauty mark." His, finally, is not a "display case" body, distant and untouchable; his is rather a breakable body, a body that will break every time that the Body of Christ handles it. Eiesland observes:

> Here is the resurrected Christ making good on the incarnational proclamation that God would be with us, embodied as we are. . . . In presenting his impaired hands and feet to his startled friends, the resurrected Jesus is revealed as the disabled God. Jesus, the resurrected Savior, calls for his frightened companions to recognize in the marks of impairment their own connection with God, their own salvation. In so doing, this disabled God is also the revealer of a new humanity.[6]

Second, the disabled body offers to us a true image of all human bodies this side of the eschaton. Put otherwise, the disabled body disrupts our ideas about "normal" bodies, or what has often been termed a "cult of normalcy." The concept of a normal body, as Sara Hendren points out in her book, *What Can a Body Do?*, is a relatively recent phenomenon, dating to around 1840 in European languages. "Prior to that time," she writes, "*normal* referred to being perpendicular or *square*, a technical term that would have been used, for example, by a carpenter."[7] In time, the idea of normal began to be seen as what was natural, and that in turn became what was right, not just for some but for all human bodies. In certain cases, at state fairs in the Midwest of the 1920s, this led to Better Babies and Fitter Families contests, based on their relative heritable qualities.

But the gift of a disabled body is a reminder not only that all our bodies are far from normal but that our abnormal bodies are primary sites for God's manifest grace. This includes the experience of limitation (for instance, of relative athletic or mathematical ability), of neediness (especially, e.g., in infancy and old age), of brokenness (whether literal in the case of multiple sclerosis or figurative in the sense of "a broken spirit"), of weakness (which God is pleased to work through, as 2 Corinthians 12:9 resoundingly affirms), and of disabling conditions of any sort, whether that involves a disease like polio, the experience of trauma, or an incapacitating event such as a stroke. When life is seen under the light of disability, writes Thomas Reynolds, a more holistic picture emerges of what it means to be a truly human person.[8]

Third, the disabled body opens up a space for bodily hospitality that, in turn, makes possible the experience of a deepened relational hospitality. Paul's experience of the "thorn" in his flesh, for example, causes him to become not only more dependent on God but also more dependent on the people of God. This is, of course, the only natural result of being a many-membered Body of Christ (1 Cor. 12). In the story of Moses's profound speech impediment in Exodus 4:1–17, God refuses to heal Moses's disability so that he can get the job done. God instead makes Moses *more* dependent on the power of God and *more* needful of others around him, including his brother Aaron.[9] "Within God's providence," observes John Swinton, "disability has deep meaning. Disabilities do not prevent one from having a powerful ministry within God's coming kingdom."[10]

The New Testament teaches us that we are integrally and pneumatologically dependent on one another. The experience of disability simply makes this God-given reality obvious. Writes Eiesland, "Unwilling and unable to take our bodies for granted, we [as people with disabilities] attend to the kinesis of knowledge. That is, we become keenly aware that our physical selves determine our perceptions of the social and physical world."[11] Whether one feels it presently or not, in old age all of us will experience a certain diminishment of our bodies and minds. On that day, neediness will not be optional; it will be unavoidable. The experience of disability simply foregrounds this reality and brings to light the goodness of a corporeal *we*, or what Hendren calls "shared bodily vulnerability."[12] In specifically theological terms, such mutual need is central to the *imago Dei*. Stanley Hauerwas offers this noteworthy observation on mutually vulnerable friendship: "As Christians we know we have not been created to be 'our own authors,' to be autonomous. We are creatures. Dependency, not autonomy, is one of the ontological characteristics of our lives. That we are creatures, moreover, is but a reminder that we are created with and for one another. We are not just accidentally communal, but we are such by necessity. We are not created to be alone."[13]

Fourth, the disabled body offers itself as an invitation to richly multisensory and holistic worship. Over against the tendency to compartmentalize our senses or to privilege the cognitive dimension of worship over against the kinesthetic, affective, imaginative, and relational dimensions, worship that keeps the bodies of disabled persons in mind is worship that invites all our senses and that provides entry points to prayer and praise through every aspect of our humanity. In Amos Yong's reading of Luke's Gospel in *The Bible, Disability, and the Church*, for example, Jesus's ministry is seen to involve a multisensory epistemology and a holistic spirituality that prioritizes *both* cognitive reason *and* embodied cognition, that is, ways that Jesus is known *through* palpable, sensory means. Because of this, Yong argues, "the church should be a haven specifically for people with intellectual disabilities."[14]

Because God in Christ, moreover, is in the business of touching human bodies, healing human psyches, reviving human hearts, repairing human imaginations, and restoring the sick and infirm to community, we as the Body of Christ ought to be in the business of making it possible for people to worship God with every part of their humanity, not just one part.[15] Yong acknowledges that although it may be true that the profoundly disabled may never experience worship in the same way as others, "this doesn't mean that they are excluded from the fellowship and communion of the Spirit. It just means that the church needs to be sensitive to the workings of embodied and affective reason, and to nurture the capacities of each of its members."[16]

In drawing attention to this particular gift, my point is not chiefly how we make worship more accessible to disabled persons, though that certainly remains our responsibility and a serious need for many congregations. My point is that disabled persons bring to our attention things to which we remain blind or ignorant but that are primary to Yahweh's dealings with Israel, central to Jesus's ministry, and a distinguishing feature of the Spirit's work in our lives—namely, that all humanity is invited into the true knowledge and love of God. The point here, again, is not inclusion for inclusion's sake but rather inclusion for the sake of holistic worship that many of us may be failing to enact, precisely because we have gotten the triune God wrong.[17]

How do these four gifts relate to the body in worship? All of us, no matter our physical condition, bring to worship broken bodies. As I have already pointed out in the introduction to this book, we bring bodies that are infected with self-hatred, oppressed by sickness, pierced by loneliness, haunted by aging, fearful of rejection, and terrified of being out of control. We bring bodies that have been scarred by touch and bodies that have been starved of touch. We bring to worship broken perceptions of our own bodies and broken dynamics toward others' bodies. We bring, in short, vulnerable bodies. Such bodies are intimately familiar to persons with disabilities. But we ought not be ashamed about our vulnerable bodies, they might tell us, or pretend that all is "normal," or be embarrassed by our "needy" bodies, or to privilege our souls over our bodies in corporate worship. We ought instead to offer them humbly to God just as they are.

Although Christians have often regarded disabled persons as objects of pity and paternalism, and while churches have frequently treated them as hindrances to corporate worship, the disabled bodies of people like Henri and Layla Van Allen remind us of the extraordinary gifts that they bring to us, without which we could not be the fullness of Christ's Body at worship. With Henri, we give and receive the care-filled touch of others in worship as sacramental signs of God's tangible care for us. With Layla, we offer up to God the gift of our "moan-full" song, as her mother describes it, confident that God receives all our embodied gifts of praise, no matter how "imperfect" they may be. And mindful that each of us comes to worship disabled in some fashion, we trust that the Spirit of God gladly meets us in the scarred body of the Son in order to make grace palpable to us in the hour of our need.[18]

Unseen Bodies

A second ethical issue that deserves careful consideration is the matter of what I am calling "unseen bodies." By this I mean bodies that remain invisible to a particular congregation at worship but that ought *not* to be invisible. Which bodies, for example, show up in the stained glass windows or in the paintings that hang permanently in a sanctuary? Which bodies appear most frequently in the videoed testimonies that get aired on a Sunday morning? Which bodies occupy center stage—and which ones remain stage right or offstage altogether? And which bodies gain easy access to the main space of worship, and which ones are forced by architectural design reasons to remain at the boundaries of the space? Is the answer to these questions the "best, the brightest, and most beautiful" bodies? Or is it all bodies?

One of the ways that bodies might become invisible is in the permanent works of art that mark the primary space of a congregation's worship. One of the powers that permanent artworks possess, barring the sale or destruction of a church building, is their capacity to singularly define a church's identity over time—for better and for worse. The stained-glass windows that belong to the congregation that meets at Duke Chapel, for example, vividly illustrate the potentially "worse" side of things.[19] Depicting various biblical characters and stories, the seventy-seven windows installed after the initial dedication of the space in 1935 took nearly three years to complete and used more than one million pieces of glass. The windows include representations of the usual biblical characters, like patriarchs and prophets, in addition to less usual characters such as Rebekah and Hagar.

When examined closely, however, the figures depicted in these windows have a European cast about them. What is problematic about this is the idea, unconsciously inferred perhaps, that Duke Chapel belongs principally to White people and that White people bear the most "obvious" resemblance to the people of the Bible (who themselves more likely looked like people of Middle Eastern and African origin). This may be the story that non-White Christians hear most loudly when they gather in the sanctuary. When combined with the Caucasian images of Jesus that frequently appear in devotional literature and the light-skinned biblical characters that routinely show up in children's Sunday school material, the message communicated—consciously or unconsciously—is that Christ's Body is principally White. This is a false and pernicious message.

Such a story can be mitigated, however, by occasional works of art. Occasional artworks allow a congregation to tell other equally important stories about Christ's Body. When Duke Chapel, for instance, installed an exhibit of Japanese artist Sadao Watanabe's prints on the walls of the sanctuary in early 2018, these prints offered the congregation an opportunity to see scriptural narratives that have been set within distinctly Japanese settings.[20] While the permanent stained-glass windows tell one story of God's people, this temporary exhibit tells another story that serves both to complement and to counter the story told in the windows. Other exhibits that represent biblical characters in their true physiognomic nature or that show a globally diverse body of believers may, over time, as Duke Chapel has done, enable a congregation to see the true character of the church as a body of believers from every tongue, tribe, and nation (see Rev. 7).

Another ethical issue related to unseen bodies involves the experience of multiethnic worship. In a piece for Religion News Service, Adelle Banks writes that between 1998 and 2019, "mainline Protestant multiracial congregations rose from 1% to 11%; their Catholic counterparts rose from 17% to 24%; and evangelical Protestant multiracial congregations rose from 7% to 23%."[21] Although the percentage of multiracial or multiethnic congregations in the United States is relatively small, and while a more complicated story lies behind the statistics—which itself demands a sober and clear-headed analysis—the challenges that such congregations face deserve a care-filled hearing by all congregations, no matter where they find themselves on planet Earth.[22]

One specific challenge related to visibility in multiethnic worship relates to who stands center stage, that is, who leads the worship of the congregation, whether it involves the music, the prayers, or the preaching and reading of Scripture.[23] What does it mean, for instance, when a congregation not only *sings* a Black gospel song but also *sees* a Black woman lead such a song, and, more crucially, for their participation in that song to be an integral thing rather than just a token display? This is the difference, I suggest, between multiethnic worship as ethnic *curio* and as comprehensive *cultural practice*. One of the specific challenges that multiethnic worship faces is the need to learn how to be together in our own physical bodies alongside the bodies of others in a fundamentally new way, in such a way that they see each other in mutually responsive, Spirit-capacitated ways.[24]

This involves, among other things, the ability to truly see one another in humility and love. This kind of seeing is not the kind that characterizes a spectator sport, in which the spectator is essentially separate from the action on the field. It is the kind of seeing that a jazz band or a pair of ballroom dancers experience firsthand. While each member has a distinctive role to play, the goal is to become mutually attuned to one another—to really see each other. The bodies of individuals become synced up and tuned in, rather than autonomous and out of sync. In the case of multiethnic worship, the individual members of a congregation must allow their bodies to become attuned to one another in order to learn how to be a new Body of believers.[25]

In the end, however, it is never really about the songs or the prayers or the preaching. It is always about relationship. For a congregation to become truly multiethnic in its worship, the experience of mutual self-giving must mark its diverse members. "Music alone is not sufficient," writes Gerardo Marti in *Worship across the Racial Divide*, "it is relationships and a sense of belonging that bind people to their church."[26] While visible and diverse ethnic presence up front is critical to accomplish such worship, Marti argues that equally important is a congregation's ability to truly see one another as equal participants in worship. Seeing what happens up front enables a church to reimagine itself over time.[27] Seeing what happens in the quality of relationships that mark a church at all times is what enables a church to become altogether new members of Christ's Body. And although not all congregations around the world will feel called or able to become multiethnic in their worship ethos, all congregations can intentionally look for ways to make visible the richly diverse global Body of Christ.

Digital Bodies

A final ethical issue that we cannot escape in our contemporary age is the issue of digital technology in corporate worship. Like the two issues that we have explored already, this issue comes with plenty of heated passion and fiery dispute.[28] On one side stand churches like Capitol Hill Baptist Church (CHBC), which filed a lawsuit against the District of Columbia on September 22, 2020, arguing that DC's coronavirus restrictions had violated their First Amendment rights to gather physically for worship.[29] For specifically theological reasons, CHBC's pastor Mark Dever insisted that live-streamed worship was not a viable liturgical option for them.[30] This stands in contrast to churches like Life.Church, based in Edmond, Oklahoma, which has an online campus featuring ninety services per week.[31] On the weekend of March 20–22, 2020, a week after the world shut down on account of COVID-19, Life.Church streamed its worship to more than seven million devices.[32]

While one side of this issue involves a debate over the theological viability and liturgical benefit of digitally mediated worship, another side involves an argument around what exactly counts as "embodied" worship. In a *New York Times* opinion piece written by Tish Harrison Warren around the time that the Omicron variant had been waning and the CDC had begun to relax its restrictions for indoor gatherings, she argued that it was time to drop virtual worship. "Online church," she wrote, "while it was necessary for a season, diminishes worship and us as people. We seek to worship wholly . . . and embodiment is an irreducible part of that wholeness."[33] Arguing against this view were people like Samir Knego, a disability/accessibility advocate, who offered this as a counterpoint:

> There's something deeply condescending . . . about the idea that proponents of online church options don't believe that "bodies . . . are part of our deepest humanity, not obstacles to be transcended through digitization." . . . Bodies that require assistance are still bodies, and accepting assistance comes from a place of understanding one's body and its limits—not a belief in transcending/rejecting/abandoning embodiment. I am human over Zoom and human in my wheelchair—these pieces of technology enable me to engage with the world around me physically and socially. To deny me, then, would not make me more human, just more isolated.[34]

It goes without saying that equal parts undiluted enthusiasm and visceral antipathy, along with a great deal of talking past one another, have marked Christian discussion of technologies such as live-streaming, Zoom, and broadcast television, among others, in relation to corporate worship.[35] For some, the preservation of virtual worship amounts to the death of our embodied liturgical life. For others, such technologies not only serve the missional purposes of corporate worship but also make it possible for people on the margins—such as the homebound, the immunocompromised, and those who face persecution if they worship publicly—to enter meaningfully into worship. It is a tension between what we might call incorporated bodies and distributed bodies, or between what physicist Michio Kaku calls a "High Touch" and "High Tech" experience of public worship.[36] How shall we then live?

I suggest that, first, we must reckon soberly with the losses that the use of digital technologies entails for physical bodies in corporate worship and that we embrace with faith, hope, and love all the good that they might bring to our liturgical experience.

One loss involved in virtual worship is the loss of serendipity, which occurs uniquely in a gathering of people in a common physical room. Serendipity within such a context, whether in the passing of the peace or in an extended time of communal song, opens space for the Spirit to interrupt the activities of worship with a word for the moment or a work of healing sensed in real time. Jon Tyson, the lead pastor of Church of the City New York, for example, remarked how during the early weeks of the global pandemic he missed the spontaneous laughter that took place during a sermon and the need to linger in prayer, discerned by reading the room intuitively.[37] This is a loss that was shared by many pastors and worship leaders at the time.

Such things are exceedingly difficult to replicate on Zoom or during a live-streamed worship service. Similarly difficult to replicate in an online space is the experience of nonverbal communication. Psychiatrist Curt Thompson says this about the power of nonverbal communication: "Human beings use our bodies, vis-à-vis our actual words, to communicate upwards to 85–90% of everything we 'say.' These nonverbal cues—eye contact, tone of voice, facial expression, body language, gestures, timing and intensity of responses—are the body's portion of what it means to 'be' with others and ourselves—to communicate what we are experiencing."[38] Worship without nonverbal communication is like playing basketball on the video game *NBA Live*, which lacks the possibility of *on-the-court* moments of serendipitous play, facilitated by *real-time* nonverbal cues between jostling, juking, sweaty bodies, with senses that remain responsive to the total physical environment.[39]

While it is extraordinarily difficult for worship leaders to get a feel for the room in the experience of digitally mediated corporate worship, either because it is unfeasible to see everyone at the same time on a Zoom screen or because they are on the other side of a digital camera, unseen and unheard, it is impossible in a virtual context to sing seamlessly in four-part harmony, or to smell incense, or to anoint bodies with oil, or to partake of a common cup, or to share silence in a meaningful fashion.[40] For liturgical traditions, shared bodily worship fundamentally involves the experience of bodies "marching in time," as William McNeill describes it, whereas for charismatic traditions the experience of bodies "improvising in time" is central to their common worship.[41] All such things not only define true worship for many, they also represent what bodies *must* do in a shared physical space in their corporate worship.[42]

But are digitally mediated experiences of worship not truly embodied, or even real, as many on one side of the divide might allege?[43] This depends on how we define our terms and frame the discussion. Teresa Berger, in her book *@Worship: Liturgical Practices in Digital Worlds*, challenges the assumption of many within her Roman Catholic context who argue that online worship is a contradiction in terms. In defense of a more expansive notion of embodied worship, Berger insists that "rather than being fundamentally dis-embodied, digitally mediated worship entails its own specific bodily properties."[44] All digitally mediated experiences of worship are necessarily bodily and, in some cases, as with members of a hospice care center or a family sick at home, a *shared* bodily experience.[45] "In digitally mediated worship," Berger concludes, "'perceived co-presence' rather than 'physical co-location' becomes a defining feature."[46]

While Berger's argument may feel like stating the obvious ("*Of course* everybody who worships online has a body"), the obvious sometimes needs stating.[47] The pain that many in the disabled community experience on account of the persistent rejection of their unique needs and perspectives on corporate worship by the able-bodied deserves to be acknowledged. A similar pain marks the experience of the elderly, the terminally sick and their caregivers, the shut-ins, the homeless, and those who suffer from types of autism, among other conditions that cause people to experience acute anxiety in social spaces. Such people, who perpetually find themselves on the margins of a church's liturgical life, are often made to feel that they are a problem to be solved or to be simply ignored. Put bluntly: this is wrong.

For them, digitally mediated worship opens extraordinary opportunities for relationship, discipleship, and mission. Douglas Estes, in his book *SimChurch*, shows how for many people today the experience of worship in a virtual world is attractive because of the transparency and diversity that they find there.[48] David Bourgeois, in *Ministry in the Digital Age*, makes a similar point, grounding his argument in Jesus's ministry to draw those on the margins into community.[49] And the authors of the book *Mobile Persuasion* add that mobile ministry is much less about technology and much more about connectedness.[50] Not only does digital worship become an occasion to be salt and light in the digital spaces that increasingly mark worship in our contemporary age, it also becomes an occasion to offer hospitality to those who earnestly wish to stay "in touch" liturgically rather than "out of touch" with Christ's Body.[51]

The Way of Bodies

As with the Sabbath, it is always important to remember that technology is made for humans, not humans for technology. However we may use digital technologies to facilitate corporate worship, then, it must always be done for the sake of deepened relationships and formation in Christlikeness. Naturally, there will be no one-size-fits-all approach. And we may get it wrong the first, second, or even third time around, but we get to try again—together. In doing it together, we aim to invite *all* members of Christ's Body into the discernment and decision-making process, rather than treating any one member as a passive observer, without agency, or as a mere recipient, without insight. We especially invite those who may find themselves on the margins, trusting that Jesus has entrusted to them, too, wisdom that the Body of Christ sorely needs for our worship to be faithful.

"To try to heal the body alone," writes Wendell Berry, "is to collaborate in the destruction of the body. Healing is impossible in loneliness; it is the opposite of loneliness. Conviviality is healing."[52] What Berry says here applies not just to the ethics of digital worship but also to every matter that remains part of our ethical responsibility as followers of Jesus. The way forward, *together*, is the way of true, embodied corporate worship. Anything less betrays our truest convictions as Christ's Body, showing such convictions to be hollow or false. How we treat one another in worship, moreover, is a reflection of how we might treat one another outside of worship. "Liturgy of the neighbor," writes Nathan Mitchell, "verifies liturgy of the church," by which he means that if we fail to love our neighbor well in life, it is because we have failed to worship God in the sanctuary.[53] The hope, of course, is that our liturgical life will remain integral to our ethical life, lest we betray in our bodies what we confess with our lips.

10

The Discipline of the Body

The Prescriptive Body in Worship

For those united to Christ in the Holy Spirit, the body is a living, mobile location of prayer, a living monstrance for Christ.

—Mary Timothy Prokes, Toward a Theology of the Body

> *Because your steadfast love is better than life,*
> *my lips will praise you.*
> *So I will bless you as long as I live;*
> *I will lift up my hands and call on your name.*
> —Psalm 63:3–4

Ambulatory Worship

Public worship in fourth-century Jerusalem was dynamically ambulatory. On any given holiday, Christians would walk across the city, tracing the steps of Jesus's life, death, and resurrection in order to commemorate his earthly pilgrimage as well as to inhabit his life "from the inside."[1] It was a way for Christians of this time to take literally the words of 1 Peter 2:21 and follow in Christ's steps. "Where he walked," we might imagine them saying, "we shall walk too and know something of his life that we cannot know any other way—seeing what he saw, hearing what he heard, feeling and smelling and touching what he himself experienced."

Lester Ruth, Carrie Steenwyk, and John D. Witvliet, the authors of *Walking Where Jesus Walked*, describe this public and communal ritual as *worship on the move*. "This people ranged across the whole city and its environs, sometimes celebrating in one building and sometimes in another."[2] The female pilgrim Egeria chronicles the experience in the diary that she kept of her visit to Jerusalem, somewhere around the early 380s. On Palm Sunday Christians would gather at the Eleona Church, located on the Mount of Olives, and begin a lengthy procession through the streets of Jerusalem. She recalls the experience this way:

> The babies and the ones too young to walk are carried on their parents' shoulders. Everyone is carrying branches, either palm or olive, and they accompany the bishop in the very way the people did when once they went down with the Lord. They go on foot down the Mount to the city and all through the city to the Anastasis, but they have to go pretty gentle on account of the older women and men among them who might get tired. So it is already late when they reach the Anastasis (that is, the building around the cave where Jesus had been buried and raised again).[3]

While certain holy days involved short walks and limited circuits, other holidays, like Holy Week, involved movement that "seemed to encompass the whole city."[4] A similar organized event was taken up by the March for Jesus movement. This involves processions of Christians, often singing, frequently praying, carrying festive banners, or other insignia of the faith, through the streets of a given city. In 1994, over ten million Christians from 170 nations covered every time zone on the planet with a planned march to celebrate the life of Jesus.[5]

These contemporary processions, I suggest, function as a kind of analog to the processions that took place in fourth-century Jerusalem. They give Christians an opportunity to "walk the talk" in both deliberate and prescriptive ways. They offer men and women, children and elderly, friends and strangers, a chance to discover things about the communal nature of Christian faith *on the go*. Such processions offer an occasion to discover things about God at three miles an hour, as Kosuke Koyama describes it in his book *Three Mile an Hour God*.[6]

"Walking returns the body to its original limits again," writes Rebecca Solnit in her book, *Wanderlust: A History of Walking*, "to something supple, sensitive, and vulnerable." Walking affords us in this way a form "of knowing the world through the body and the body through the world."[7] And while there is plenty of benefit to the experience of leisurely ambling through nature or to spontaneous marches through a city street—like the kind that may occur in the aftermath of an athletic victory—there is a particular good that results for human beings in the practice of planned, purposeful, and prescriptive movement.

This might be the case, for example, with walking the Stations of the Cross, which grew out of the desire of Christians who lived impossibly far from Jerusalem in the Late Middle Ages to recreate the *via dolorosa* of Jesus in miniature in their own villages and cities and eventually in their own churches. I contend that a similar thing is at work in walking a labyrinth, which, Solnit writes, "were sometimes called *chemins à Jerusalem*, 'roads to Jerusalem,' and the center was Jerusalem or heaven itself."[8]

Both of these ritualized forms of walking afford us an invaluable opportunity to inhabit a story through the body, a story that we can trace out with our feet as we seek to walk faithfully according to the example that Jesus set for us.[9] Such prescriptive uses of the body, along with others like them—such as spiritual pilgrimages, Palm Sunday processions, and neighborhood prayer walks—remind us in both actual and symbolic fashion that the *way* of our faith is just as important as the *end* of our faith. The *how* of our spiritual walk shapes us just as much as the *culmination* of our walk, and the people *with whom* we sojourn in this earthly pilgrimage inevitably form what we imagine is desirable for those who *walk in the way of the Lord* in anticipation of our heavenly journey (Deut. 10:12).[10]

The relevant point is this: the corporate worship of the people of God has always had a processional dimension to it.[11] From the journey to Jerusalem commemorated in the Psalms of Ascent to the design of the fourth-century city of Constantinople, which aimed to facilitate liturgical processions across the boulevards of this "new Rome,"[12] the physical body of Christians is not only for sitting, standing, and singing. The body is also for walking in prescriptive ways, as befits a people who are called to walk by the Spirit of God, so that they might fulfill their vocation to walk in the love of God.

The more general point as it relates to the task of this chapter is that the prescriptive use of our body in worship, through formalized postures, gestures, and movements, positively contributes to our discipleship and offers good news to both sides of the liturgical aisle—to "liturgical" and "free church" folk alike. When we do such things in heartfelt but also habitual ways, I suggest that we acquire a *feel* for the ways of God that we can know in no other fashion.[13] And although I am not able to describe all possible prescriptive uses of the body in a corporate worship context, and while I treat here uses that may be more familiar to the "historic" liturgy, my hope is that readers might be inspired to give themselves more fully to their existing prescriptive uses of the body and perhaps welcome new ones too.[14]

We begin with standing, the original posture of Christians in the early centuries of the church.

Standing

As Christians we stand in worship for many different reasons. We stand to confess our faith, as baptismal candidates did in the early church to confess the creed for the first time, with consequences that involved the possibility of persecution or martyrdom. We stand to praise God and to pray to God. We stand to hear the gospel in honor of the One who stands among us, sovereign and supreme. In certain liturgical contexts, we also turn our bodies to the gospel reader who stands in the middle of the sanctuary to remind ourselves of our desire to make Christ's life and words central to our lives. We likewise stand to bear witness to marriage and ordination vows as well as to solemnly vow to support those who have entered the household of faith through baptism.

To what purpose do we stand in worship, and what does such a posture signify? In biblical terms, we stand in order to properly encounter the awe-filled presence of God (Pss. 22:23; 33:8). We stand "at the ready," in respectful attention of God's word to us (1 Tim. 4:13). We stand as we recite the creed in order to remind ourselves of the story that defines all our individual stories (1 Cor. 16:13; Phil. 2:1–11). We stand at times facing east, *ad orientem*, as a reminder that we have been "raised with Christ," the Light of the world, who shall rise like a new sunrise to new life (Col. 3:1–4). We stand, finally, with open and empty hands as a way to say to

God, "I have nothing that I have not received from you, nothing that you have not placed in my empty hands."[15]

In historical perspective, one of the oldest and most persistent postures of prayer was standing with hands open wide, often called the *orante*.[16] In *De Oratione*, a treatise on prayer written sometime between 232 and 235, Origen of Alexandria makes this observation: "For there can be no doubt that among a thousand possible positions of the body, outstretched hands and uplifted eyes are to be preferred above all others, so imaging forth in the body those directions of the soul which are fitting to prayer."[17]

Augustine felt that the only proper posture of prayer during the season of Easter was standing, which for him functioned as an image of the resurrection. Clement of Alexandria argued that we ought to stand in prayer to mirror the movement of the rising sun, which symbolized for him the triumph of light over darkness and of new life over death. We stand, writes Antonio Donghi, "because we are before the one who determines and defines our life, who gives strength to our existence and makes it full."[18] We stand, finally, fully alert and with arms open wide in renunciation of all self-sufficiency and in imitation of Christ on the cross.

Kneeling

Like the posture of standing, kneeling is a common bodily posture for Christians at worship, though it may surprise many to know that kneeling is a latecomer to corporate worship. Standing in worship served as the default liturgical posture for Christians throughout the first millennium of the church. Kneeling was the exception. A completely open space without any sign of chair or pew, expressly designed for standing and moving around, defined the usual spaces of public worship. It was only in the Middle Ages "that the posture of kneeling, combined with the gesture of folded hands resting at the breast, became decisively the attitude of the Christian at prayer."[19]

Compared to the ancient "opening out" gesture of the *orante*, "this new practice of kneeling with folded hands indicates a 'closing in' of the person bodily. This gesture thus reveals a tendency from the twelfth and thirteenth centuries to seek individual interiorized devotion."[20] But though it arrived late, it came with plenty of biblical backing and sufficient historical precedent in Israel's worship. Psalm 95:6 says, "O come, let us worship and bow down, let us kneel before the LORD, our Maker!" And Psalm 22:29 proclaims that "all the earth's powerful will worship him; all who are descending to the dust will kneel before him" (CEB).

Why do we kneel in worship? We kneel most fundamentally to signify humility and to cultivate humility.[21] More concretely, we kneel to present our prayers to God and to gratefully receive the prayers of others. We kneel in our confession of sin. We kneel in the blessing of a marriage. We kneel in an image "of our own poverty as creatures and of our weakness as sinners," in order to remind ourselves, vulnerable creatures that we are, that it is Christ, at whose name one day every knee shall bow, who alone can deliver us from our captivity to sin.[22] And in kneeling, finally, we affirm with our bodies the reality that our hearts seek to believe daily, that the Lord is the One who gladly lifts up the humble (James 4:10).

The Sign of the Cross

With the sign of the cross we enter into territory that will be familiar to so-called liturgical Christians and that may perhaps make many who grew up in nonliturgical churches decidedly nervous or possibly suspicious. Though there are good reasons for this suspicion, there are plenty more reasons why Christians across ecclesial lines should wish to cross themselves physically in order to confess Christ crucified and to mark their head, heart, and hand with the sign of the Holy Trinity.[23] Very early in the church's liturgical history, the sign of the cross became a gesture fit for every creation. Tertullian wrote: "In all our travels and movements, in all our coming in and going out, in putting on our shoes, at the bath, at the table, in lighting our candles, in lying down, in sitting down, whatever employment occupies us, we mark our foreheads with the sign of the cross."[24]

As the central concern of New Testament writers and as the emblem that served historically to identify Jesus's followers, the cross has functioned as the theologically determinative lens for faithful Christian living (1 Cor. 1:23). "May I never boast of anything except the cross of our Lord Jesus Christ," writes Paul in Galatians 6:14, "by which the world has been crucified to me, and I to the world." Donghi adds, "From the cross, we see the world with the heart and the eyes of Christ, and we rejoice in that divine intimacy that is the unique source of the meaning of our lives."[25]

The Prescriptive Body in Worship

John Stott bluntly states that "if the cross is not central to our religion, ours is not the religion of Jesus."[26]

It is for this reason that Christians throughout history have sought to embrace this reality in their bodily acts of worship and devotion.[27] John Chrysostom encouraged the Christians of his day to "never leave your house without making the sign of the cross."[28] Martin Luther urged believers similarly: "As soon as you get out of bed in the morning, you should bless yourself with the sign of the Holy Cross and say, 'May the will of God, the Father, the Son and the Holy Spirit be done! Amen.'"[29] With this sign we declare bodily our faith in the Trinity. Our hands descend from head to heart in a mirror of the descent that Christ makes from heaven to earth, they cross over from shoulder to shoulder to represent our whole selves in summary form, and they remind a frequently forgetful mind and an often fickle heart that the Trinity is the true origin and end of our lives.[30]

> *To seal oneself with the sign of the Cross is a visible and public Yes to him who suffered for us; to him who in the body has made God's love visible, even to the utmost; to the God who reigns not by destruction but by the humility of suffering and love, which is stronger than all the power of the world and wiser than all the calculating intelligence of men.*
> —Joseph Cardinal Ratzinger,
> **The Spirit of the Liturgy**

When would we make the sign of the cross during worship? The answer, of course, will depend on one's liturgical context. In some cases, we will cross ourselves after dipping our fingers in the waters of the baptismal font or bowl to remind ourselves of our essential identity (which is ecclesial, not biological). We will cross ourselves at the mention of the "resurrection from the dead" in the creeds to signify our hope of one day seeing our Lord face-to-face. We will cross ourselves three times prior to the reading of the Gospel: first on our foreheads to symbolize our desire for Christ to reign in our minds, then over our mouths to show our need for Christ to tame our tongues, and finally over our hearts to represent our desire for Christ to rule at the center of our being. We cross ourselves when the priest asks God to "sanctify us by your Spirit," and we cross ourselves before and after receiving the bread and the wine.

Is there a danger of crossing ourselves too much? Not really—that is, not if crossing oneself becomes a way to willingly offer up every square inch of one's life to the Trinity. Is there a danger that such a sign might become rote or superstitiously employed, as perhaps was the case with my Roman Catholic friends while on the soccer fields of my childhood in Guatemala? Yes, that is certainly a real danger.[31] But it is not a danger that remains unique to the sign of the cross. It is a danger that haunts *any* bodily activity in worship, whether that of Quakers or Messianic Jews or Latino Pentecostals. It is for this reason that it must be done with all of one's heart and mind, even if it may often be done in a purposefully unselfconscious manner. Scott Hahn offers to us this good word of encouragement: "It's no small thing we do when we make the Sign of the Cross. It should take our breath away—but only so that we can be filled up with another wind, another breath: the Spirit of God."[32]

As with all such signs, the purpose of the sign of the cross is not only to remind us of our true identity in the triune God but also to spur us to *want* to live more fully into our true identity. It is a sign that remains commensurate with our calling to imitate Jesus in all that we say and do as well as a sign that invites our physical bodies to participate in that very calling.

Hands

"Next to the face," writes Romano Guardini, "the part of the body fullest of mind is the hand."[33] The hands, as the saying goes, are always talking. With our hands we bless and comfort, but it is also with our hands that we wound and withhold the care that our neighbor requires. Our hands are never neutral, even hidden in the pockets of our pants, as they often are when we gather liturgically. And what we do with our hands in worship will always be meaningful in context. A closed fist may signify a tightfisted spirit or a moment of exultant joy. The hand of another may be held willingly or begrudgingly. And the decision to raise one's hands may come naturally to certain congregational cultures but require a great deal of courage in others.

To what ends do we use our hands in corporate worship? Among other ways, we open our hands to signify a willing reception of God's mercy in response to the words of pardon. At the offering of our monies, we lift our hands in thanksgiving to the God who is our constant provision, regardless of our present financial condition. In prayer, such as the Collect for Purity, we open our hands to express our utter need of God. At the *Sursum Corda*, we lift our hands to show visibly the desire of our hearts, that they be offered up to God without hesitation or qualification. In our words of hosanna, such as at the *Sanctus*, when we join in the praise of the company of heaven, we lift our hands in a reminder of Christ's triumph over sin and death. With hands open, we *receive* rather than *take* the elements of the Lord's Supper.[34] With our hands we wash the feet of others in fulfillment of the command of Jesus in John 13. We may strike our breast in order to open our hardened hearts to God, so that the love of God may flow freely again.[35] And in sharing the peace of Christ, a handshake becomes a tangible sign of true reconciliation that only the Spirit of God makes possible.

The laying on of hands is another way that we use our bodies prescriptively, and it is one that goes back to the early church (1 Tim. 4:14; 2 Tim. 1:6). It was part of the ministry of Jesus (Luke 4:40) as well as the pastoral care of Moses before him (Num. 27:18). We lay hands on the newly married, ordained, confirmed, and baptized. We lay hands on the little children in order to bless the work of God in their lives. We lay hands on the sick and the dying. To lay hands on another's head, moreover, as the Bible reminds us repeatedly, is a way to communicate both tender affection (Mark 10:16) and divine power (Acts 8:17; 28:8). In doing such things, we become the hands of Jesus to others. Yet it is not our power but God's that accomplishes the work of blessing in another's life. "It is God who lets power, by the sign of the laying on of hands by the minister," writes Donghi, "descend upon the heads of the people so that everyone may rejoice in the truth of divine life."[36]

Bowing

Every instance of bowing in worship, much like kneeling, both illustrates humility and trains us in humility. It is a physical gesture that speaks across human cultures and that most naturally depicts a disposition of respect for another or submissiveness to an honored one. Such is the case with Abraham's encounter with the three mysterious men of Genesis 18 and as in the case of the four living creatures of Revelation 19. With bowing, we assume a vulnerable posture. In lowering our heads and eyes, we put ourselves at the mercy of another, risking the possibility of harm against our person. We risk also, of course, the gift of a blessing.

In worship we bow at the mention of the name of Christ. We bow to a physical cross as if we were bowing to Christ himself, standing with us in the flesh.[37] We bow our heads at the *Sanctus* in order to join the praise of the heavenly company. We bow at the mention of Christ's descent to earth in our confession of the Nicene Creed in order to join our bodies and hearts to the one who emptied himself and took the form of a slave so that he might recover our truest identity as sons and daughters of God.[38] We bow to the table/altar in honor of Christ's sacrifice. We bow with angels and archangels before the triune Name in the *Gloria Patri*. We bow in rapturous adoration of the everlasting desire of nations. We bow our bodies in all these ways, not only because it is "meet and right" that we should do so but also because the Lord eagerly wishes to lift up those who are bowed down (Ps. 146:8).

Passing the Peace

"The sign of peace," writes Aidan Kavanagh, "was originally a full kiss on the lips, men with men, women with women. The kiss was perhaps the liturgy's most intimate gesture next to baptismal washing and anointing, so intimate indeed that the early church writers emphasize the need for it to be kept 'pure,' but kept nonetheless."[39] While this may shock some of us in the Anglo-American world, it would not be seen as strange in Middle Eastern or Slavic cultural contexts, or in South Africa, where a quick kiss on the lips with a closed mouth is a common practice. In certain parts of Afghanistan, in fact, a formal greeting will involve no less than eight kisses on the cheek.

For Origen, Tertullian, Justin Martyr, and others in the early centuries of the church, the act of kissing was perceived as a common, and decidedly remarkable, practice among Christians. The exchange of a kiss, which involves an intimate physical proximity, would have taken place at baptisms and ordinations, after prayers, or following acts of reconciliation.[40] Exchanging a kiss of peace was remarkable specifically for the way in which people across allegedly unbreachable divides—master and slave, rich and poor, Jew and gentile, male and female, ruler and the ruled—set aside social barriers as a sign of the unity that Christ had brought them.[41]

These days, the holy lip-to-lip kiss is usually replaced with a hug, a handshake, a bow, or a kiss on the cheek (once, twice, or thrice, depending on one's culture). Such offerings of peace function as an embodied sign of the reconciliation that God achieves on our behalf, with all our sharp elbows, idiosyncratic differences, and strange ways of being in the world. The act of passing the peace fundamentally signifies a gift offered and received: the objective peace that Christ wins for us on the cross and the subjective experience of peace that we sense in the exchange of words and physical contact. For just as we sow discord with our lips and hands, so too we embrace peace with our lips and our hands.

Anointing the Body

While the exchange of a holy kiss on the lips may seem strange to many Christians, the experience of anointing may be a far more familiar practice. Examples of this convention are common in Scripture. Throughout the Old Testament, priests, kings, and prophets are set apart for their vocation by a ritual anointing. Such is the case with the prophet Elisha (1 Kings 19:16), King David (1 Sam. 16:12–13), and the priest Aaron (Exod. 28:41). Jesus anoints the sick in Mark 6:13. Mary of Bethany anoints Jesus's feet in Mark 14. The elders of a church are encouraged to anoint the sick with oil so that they might be healed (James 5:14). And while the Bible includes plenty of figurative instances of anointing (e.g., 2 Cor. 1:21–22; Heb. 1:9), the physical act of anointing is as commonplace in the Bible as it is ubiquitous throughout church history.

What the practices of anointing with oil and holy water have in common is their physical power to animate and to revitalize the body. As anyone who has ever used oils for curative reasons knows firsthand, when the right oil infuses a room with a fragrant scent it can accelerate the healing powers of the body, cleanse a noxious atmosphere, enliven the senses, clear the mind, facilitate rest and relaxation, and protect against infection. Each of these physical or natural benefits finds a corresponding symbolic analog in the liturgical practices of Christians. Whenever an anointing takes place, the hope is that the Spirit of God will sacramentally bless the person with vitality to fulfill a specific vocation or with divine health to restore the body.[42]

Most commonly, Christians anoint the bodies of others during ordination ceremonies, at baptisms, for the last rites and the burial of the dead, in the blessing of a home, and in the healing ministries that mark distinctly charismatic worship. In doing such things, Christians testify to the integration of their humanity and to the desire of God to care for the whole person—body and soul, heart and mind, personal and social, private and public. Donghi remarks, "The history of salvation, with respect to this sign, gives particular significance to the gesture of anointing: the person is put in the position of docility before God."[43]

Other Prescriptive Uses of the Body

While space does not permit me to deal at length with every single prescriptive use of the body in worship, I wish briefly to mention a few additional actions, starting with sitting. For many in the Western church, sitting is a default posture of worship.[44] Sitting supports the work of attentive listening to God's word, a quiet consideration of God's work, a restful welcome of God's presence, a pliant reception of God's Spirit, and a reverent reckoning with the One who is seated at the right hand of God—and who invites us to be seated with him in the heavenly places. In sitting we take on the posture of the disciples at the Sermon on the Mount and of Mary of Bethany in Luke 10:39.

In addition to sitting, when we enter and exit a church building we might consciously reflect on our physical entrance into the presence of God and our return to the world by the empowering presence of the Spirit. If there are bells that can be rung, they might be rung to summon all within earshot to public worship. On Ash Wednesday, we may mark our foreheads with ashes in order to symbolically disfigure our faces. This will serve as a reminder of our mortal condition and prepare us for the scorching practices of repentance, including the practice of fasting that may mark the Lenten season, and in anticipation of the adornment of our lives with the radiant beauty of Christ at Easter.[45]

At the start of the Lord's Supper, the elements of bread and wine might be carried from the back to front to symbolize our desire to give God thanks for the gifts of the earth and of our human labor as we approach in gratitude for the supreme gift of Christ's body and blood. We may do so also asking that, just as God has accepted our gifts, he might also distribute us as the hands and feet of Jesus in service of our neighbors.[46] In sharing this symbolic meal, or in an actual meal that we might share with one another in the aftermath of worship, we might do so in anticipation of the heavenly banquet that one day awaits us.

The Silent Body

It bears mentioning, in conclusion, that the true purpose of all prescriptive uses of the body in worship is formation in Christlikeness. Whenever and however they fail to form us in the life of Jesus, we must pause and ask ourselves the hard questions.[47] Have we failed to properly instruct our people in the meaning of their corporeal activities in worship? Have we succumbed to mindless rote behaviors? Have we begun to regard our bodily actions superstitiously? Have we given rigorous attention to the body at the expense of a rigorous attention to the heart? Have we come to love our visible deeds for the sake of being seen and praised by others, as Jesus charged the hypocrites in Matthew 6?

If we begin to detect any of these tendencies, we should eagerly ask for the Spirit's help to recover the true purpose of all our bodily practices. One of the ways that we might make space for the Spirit's help is through silence in our corporate worship.[48] Silence, in this case, is not to be seen as a negative thing: the absence of speech, the omission of sound, or the refusal to act. It is to be seen as a positive thing. Much like Mary's "Let it be," uttered in response to the divine word in Luke 1:38, silence is a kind of active passivity that creates a space for God to speak, to convict, to heal, and to draw us back to a holy way of life.

"To be silent," writes Donghi, "is to recognize ourselves as needy creatures in the presence of the divine."[49] In choosing silence as an act of hospitality to God, we welcome a voice that we may drown out for fear of being found out by God.[50] In choosing silence, our desperate need to fill our lives with activity that makes us feel useful is set aside. In choosing silence, we learn that we are not ultimately in control but are weak and vulnerable creatures, desperately in need of God's grace. It is in this sense that liturgical silence, as Kavanagh writes, is both purposeful and pregnant.[51]

I argue here that we ought to welcome silence in worship, not simply because we wish to be faithful to God (Hab. 2:20) but because our very lives depend on it. We choose to quiet our bodies because it is the still small voice of God that we hunger for in the midst of a world that is ruled by "the dictatorship of noise," as Cardinal Robert Sarah expresses it.[52] We choose to quiet our mouths and our ears in a recognition that God must get the first word in the work of worship rather than any human being. And we choose to quiet our instruments and our microphones—along with the spectacles that fill up our screens and the visual data that crowds our sanctuaries—in order to counter what C. S. Lewis describes as the dehumanizing and diabolical power of noise.[53]

"If you bear on your forehead the sign of the humility of Jesus Christ," wrote Augustine, "bear in your heart the imitation of the humility of Jesus Christ."[54] This is a helpful reminder of the purpose of all our prescriptive uses of the body in worship. They are not an end in themselves. They do not automatically produce a virtuous life. They should not be undertaken in lazy or perfunctory fashion, and they should not be engaged in a way that is disconnected from the activities of the hands and feet that reflect and represent the image of God throughout the work week.[55] They should be engaged instead in a way that increases the love of Christ in us so that we might love God, neighbor, and self, as Christ himself loves such as these.

11

The Freedom of the Body

The Spontaneous Body in Worship

The more I raise my hands, the more liberating it feels.
—Sarah Park, "How Lifting My Hands
in Worship Became My Protest to God"

In God's presence I'll dance all I want! He chose me over your father and the rest of our family and made me prince over God's people, over Israel. Oh yes, I'll dance to God's glory—more recklessly even than this. And as far as I'm concerned . . . I'll gladly look like a fool.

—2 Samuel 6:21–22 (The Message)

The Dancing Man

During my years as a pastor in Austin, there was a young man whose story stands out in my memory. And while I have written about him elsewhere, his story bears retelling for our purposes here.[1] At the time that I knew him, Tim Diehl was an MBA student at the University of Texas and had joined our congregation during his sojourn in college. As I remember him, Tim was the perfect image of the conservative business student: khaki pants, button-down dress shirt, soft spoken, polite, measured, a clean haircut, smart as a whip.

But Tim was also a complete wonder of a human being. While our church was theologically Pentecostal, we were practically a moderate charismatic bunch. Hand raising and the occasional holler of praise to God would not be uncommon. We were not, however, the typical tongues-speaking, miracle-generating, Spirit-slaying, two-stepping congregation.[2] People rarely, if ever, danced. Tim did—and extravagantly so.

At a certain point during our extended time of congregational song, Tim, usually standing at the end of a pew, would launch out into what can only be described as part hopscotch, part hand windmill movement, part Maria von Trapp-singing-her-heart-out-that-the-hills-were-alive-with-the-sound-of-music. It was an utterly unselfconscious expression that, to the untrained eye, might be perceived as outlandish. For Tim, however, the words of Psalm 150 were to be taken literally: praise the Lord with dancing.

I would often watch Tim's uninhibited dancing with a combination of delight and envy. I never once joined him, however, much to my regret today. But I did eventually ask him why he danced. His answer surprised me. He danced, he said, not because it came naturally to his personality. Nor did he dance because an overflow of emotions demanded a corresponding physical response. He danced instead out of obedience. For Tim, dancing in this way represented a sacrifice of praise to God.

"In singing praise," writes Old Testament scholar Walter Brueggemann, "all claims for the self are given up as the self is ceded over to God."[3] Such is the nature of self-abandonment that an encounter with the very presence of God demands. Psalm 63:1–4, as John Goldingay translates it, captures this sense of divine encounter that invites a total bodily response:

> God, you are my God, I search for you;
>   my whole person thirsts for you.
> *My body aches* for you,
>   in a land that is dry and faint, without water.
> So I have seen you in the sanctuary,
>   *beholding* your power and honor.
> For your commitment is better than life;
>   my *lips* glorify you.
> So I will worship you *throughout my life;*
>   in your name I will *lift my hands.*[4]

As the psalmist sees it, the experience of theophany evokes a desire, acutely felt in the form of a physical ache, to worship God with the whole self. There is also a continuous sense implied in verse 4. The decision to worship God involves not just the whole person, it also involves the *ongoing* act of embodied worship. Hand raising, in this instance, is what might occur at any given point in time or place, as the moment demands it. For the psalmist, as for Tim, the experience of worship includes a deliberate choice to offer up one's physical body to God as well as the possibility of spontaneity in that gift, a gift that has an uncalculated, "purposeless" quality about it.

Such is the character of worship that one finds all throughout the psalms. Like a pattern of weather, bodily worship within the context of the Psalter involves a predictability about it, in the sense that one can count on it. With predictable patterns of weather, for example, it will rain or shine because such a thing occurs naturally in a particular environment. Likewise with the worship of the psalmist: we can count on his commitment to lift his hands—or to shout, revel, exult, cry out, and dance. "Of course he will lift his hands to Yahweh," we might say, because it is his nature to do such a thing. And "Of course Tim will dance at some point in the Sunday worship," we might say, because he has purposed to be such a worshiper by nature of his consistent behavior.

But like the patterns of weather that one might experience in Chicago or in Vancouver, faithful worship is never quite the same. One can never predict *exactly* when it will start raining in Vancouver, and one need only wait the proverbial five minutes in Chicago for the weather to shift from stormy to balmy. Such weather, in short, will always have a spontaneous quality about it. In similar fashion, Tim's dancing had an extempore aspect about it, which is to say, it was "of the moment" and "for the moment." It was from the heart, but it also served to train the heart. It was purposeful but never coordinated to a precise point in the liturgy. It originated in a resolve of the will, but it always occurred spontaneously. And while few of us joined in his extravagant gift of embodied worship, it was always welcomed by the congregation because it fit our liturgical culture.[5]

Worship Extempore

Spontaneous expressions of bodily worship such as Tim's are, of course, far from foreign to the world of Holy Scripture. In Exodus 15:20–21, for example, Miriam performs a spontaneous dance with other women in response to Yahweh's deliverance from Pharaoh's hand. In 1 Samuel 10, Samuel anoints Saul as king over Israel. On his way to Gibeah immediately following, Saul meets a band of prophets. The text tells us that the Spirit of God possesses him, causing him to fall "into a prophetic frenzy along with them" (v. 10).[6] In 2 Kings 3:14–15, the power of the Lord comes upon the prophet Elisha "while the musician was playing," the text tells us. The musical performance becomes the context for God's sudden visitation.

Additionally, Mary, in Luke 1, like Hannah before her in 1 Samuel 2, breaks out into spontaneous song in response to Elizabeth's Spirit-prompted word. In Mark 7, the Syrophoenician woman bows down on the spot before Jesus. In John 12, Mary of Bethany pours over Jesus a precious nard without any external prompting, and, in Luke 7, a "sinful woman" bathes Jesus's feet with her tears in a lavish act of unrehearsed devotion. In Acts 2, the Spirit descends on the disciples, who instantly break out into tongues. In 1 Corinthians 14, Paul encourages the Corinthian believers to be eager to prophesy. In Ephesians 5, Christians are charged to be filled with the Spirit *while* they sing to one another. And in Revelation 1, on seeing the Son of Man in all his glory, John immediately falls down at his feet.

> **My heart was so full that I could not confine myself to the forms of prayer which we were accustomed to use.**
> —John Wesley, Journals and Diaries I (1735–1738)

In 2 Samuel 6, King David famously engages in an effusive act of spontaneous dance in a way that embarrasses both family and political elite. The text says twice that David dances before the Lord "with great abandon." Afterward his wife Michal upbraids him for doing something so "vulgar." In response, David tells her that he "will become even more undignified than this" (v. 22 NIV). The Message puts it this way: "In God's presence I'll dance all I want!" David Toshio Tsumura comments, "The mood and intent of the celebration is one of unfettered, unashamed extravagance."[7] What takes place in the streets of Jerusalem, Tsumura continues, is a public liturgy involving endless burnt offerings, peace offerings, and communal meals. Within the context of this public and festive worship, we witness a response to God as the moment seems to demand it.[8]

Nothing is held back in David's self-abandoned behavior, "leaping and dancing before the Lord" (2 Sam. 6:16), so much so that he risks being judged a mindless fool. The text tells us that while Michal feels embarrassed by how he has conducted himself in "the eyes of his servants' maids" (v. 20), David chooses to be humiliated "in his own eyes" (v. 22). Key here, as elsewhere, is the statement that David dances "before the Lord" (v. 21). Such, again, is the natural result of a genuine encounter with God. Love for God *wants* such a thing; the heart *compels* it; the body *needs* it; the occasion *demands* it. As with Tim's dancing, King David's actions have a playful aspect. In dancing, he engages in the serious business of play that requires that he take himself unseriously. In yielding himself fully to God, he cedes control of his reputation to the judgment of bystanders. And in giving himself wholly to this spontaneous act of embodied worship, he makes himself vulnerable to failure and ridicule.

A Body at the Ready

It is important to stress that most instances of spontaneous worship in the Bible occur outside the official context of public worship. If a case is to be made, then, for spontaneous uses of the body in corporate worship, we should avoid cobbling the pieces together in an exegetically careless fashion. Attention to the details of each instance is crucial. What befits one context of worship—such as the one-off, half-naked worship of David on the road to Jerusalem—may not serve the worship that takes place at the Jerusalem temple in the usual course of things. In contemporary terms, what works for worship that takes place at a retreat or summer camp may not fit the worship that occurs during the regular gathering of corporate worship.

This is not to say that a biblical case cannot be made for spontaneous uses of the body in such a context. It is simply to say that one must proceed with care. Two things, however, may be asserted with relative confidence.

First, expressions of spontaneous worship in Holy Scripture are positively commended to the reader as a fitting response to the character and presence of God. The presence of God exercises an irresistibly attracting force on worshipers and frequently involves spontaneous responses of worship—freely, gladly, willingly offered. As with the example of Abraham in Genesis 17 or of the "multitudes" of heaven in Revelation 7, the adoption of unscripted postures of reverence for God is normative. It is, as it were, what a body must do.

Likewise, the power of God that leads to the rescue of his people invariably provokes unpremeditated expressions of thanksgiving and praise for God. As with the leper in Luke 5 who bows before Jesus, impromptu bodily responses to God represent a physical disposition at the ready. The body in this instance is readily available to Jesus himself. It needs no preparation or persuasion to bow low; it does so in an unrehearsed manner. Similarly, the redemptive purposes of God revealed definitively in the ministry of Jesus, which he announces in Luke 4, elicit extemporaneous physical demonstrations of affection and honor. We witness this, for example, in Luke 17:16 and Matthew 28:9.

Second, in light of this conviction about the character of God, I suggest that a theology of spontaneity may open a way for us to perceive the singular benefits of the spontaneous use of the body at worship. Said otherwise, a spontaneous expression of bodily worship is warranted by the character of the God whom we worship as Christians. Although I can offer only a rough sketch of such a theology, and while I will focus my study on the person and work of the Holy Spirit, my hope is that such a theology may clarify our understanding of spontaneous bodily worship, deepen our practices of it, illumine its unique work of Christlike formation, and perhaps inspire some among us to embrace the possibility of spontaneous worship for the first time ever.

A Theology of Spontaneity

My argument, in sum, is that the Holy Spirit authors spontaneous uses of the body in worship by being (1) the Spirit of the Moment, (2) the Personalizing Spirit, and (3) the Spirit Who Plays Jazz. While the focus of my argument is on the Spirit, it is important to stress that the Spirit's work is not a solitary venture. It is the work of the "Two Hands" of the Father, as Irenaeus described the joint efforts of Christ and the Spirit.[9] In Christ, we might say, the worship of the church is a given, while in the Spirit not everything is given in advance. In Christ, the church discerns the fundamental structures of worship, but it is the Spirit who supplies the worship's dynamism. And in Christ, the church experiences the reality of the form of corporate worship, while "the Spirit is active 'to enable new possibilities [and] to empower freedom to live in the abundance that is given.'"[10]

The Spirit of the Moment

One of the things that we discover in the New Testament is not just instructions about the kind of normative worship that befits the people of God in light of the coming of Christ and the descent of the Spirit. We also discover the manner in which God is "living and active," to borrow the language of Hebrews 12, within the context of corporate worship. We witness a way in which the Spirit is living and active in both immediate and mediated fashion, working through established forms of worship as well as through serendipitous moments of encounter with God—capable of surprising with fresh gifts of grace and always near at hand to a particular people in a particular time and place. The key text here is 1 Corinthians 14.

In this passage, Paul offers instruction to the Corinthian believers about the proper use of Spirit-given gifts.[11] These are, we might say, gifts of the moment that a believer might bring to the gathered worship. While the role of such gifts in corporate worship may be disputed by Christians today, what cannot be disputed is that Paul assumes not *whether* but *how* such gifts might bear witness to the immediate presence of the Spirit in the liturgical life of the church. On this view, the Spirit speaks through both scripted sermons and unscripted "prophecies." The Spirit reveals through both Scripture (1 Tim. 3:16) and a revelation of the moment (1 Cor. 14:26). The Spirit authors both the witness of the disciples (2 Thess. 2:15) and the tongues that bear witness to the purposes of God (Acts 2). The Spirit ministers through both traditional prayers, such as the psalms, and through the extemporaneous intercession of the saints (Rom. 8:26–27; Jude 1:20).

These spontaneous activities of the Spirit are ad hoc and extempore, which is to say that they serve the purposes of a particular community in the moment that could not have been foreseen or prescribed in advance from a human vantage point. In welcoming such Spirit-ed activities, the church cedes its Spirit-inspired order of worship to the Spirit's sovereign will over the church's established forms of worship. In welcoming such interventions, the church at worship is rescued from the notion that the Spirit of God can be contained by a given order of worship or sufficiently explained by any number of liturgical texts and prescribed words. I am not arguing, of course, that the Spirit's work stands in contrast to regularity or routine. Far from it. In biblical perspective, the Spirit is the author not only of freedom but *also* of order, not only of serendipity but *also* of structure, not only of newness but *also* of tradition.

It is equally important to stress that for Paul disorder does not stand in contrast to order, or to propriety and restraint (1 Cor. 14:33). Disorder stands in contrast to *peace*.[12] Harmony in this context stands over against a willy-nilly approach to worship and to the individual who occupies the liturgical space in a self-determining, idiosyncratic fashion. It also stands over against an inflexible structuring of worship that precludes all possibility of extemporaneous activity or the possibility of being interrupted by the Spirit. It is in this sense, we might say, that the order-loving Spirit is in the business of interrupting the uninterruptible in our liturgical gatherings in order to surprise us with an in-the-moment gift of God's word or mighty deed.

What might it look like to welcome the in-the-moment work of the Spirit in corporate worship? Among other things, it might involve giving oneself permission to pause at any one point in the liturgy to pray in response to the Spirit's prompting. This might occur in complementary fashion to the regularly scheduled prayers, or it might occur in surprising ways. It might involve a petition for healing or an invitation to silent prayer. One may also feel compelled to kneel immediately after the reception of Communion. One could choose to lie prostrate during the confession of sin. One might "talk back" to the preacher in a joyous affirmation of God's good word to the community. Or one may wish to holler one's alleluias, as Catholic theologian Balthasar Fischer describes it here:

> Our Alleluia, especially in developed musical form, is like the yodeling of an Alpine shepherd, who at daybreak sees the morning sun touch the snowy peak with the first delicate tint of rose. The feelings in the shepherd's heart at this moment cannot be expressed in well-chosen words he may have learned in school; he must yodel his feelings. That is how it is with us Christians: As we gaze at the Sun that has risen high over the darkness and cold of our Good Friday, all well-chosen words are useless. We can only stammer out our Alleluia of wonder and jubilation.[13]

The Personalizing Spirit

In addition to addressing the Body of Christ in the moment, the Spirit also deepens the *personal* dimension of worship, freeing us thereby to be fully ourselves before God. In being fully ourselves in worship, we become acutely present to the state of our own hearts and minds as well as to the community that surrounds us in real time. In being fully ourselves, we choose to be attuned to the voice of the Spirit and to be pliable to the work of the Spirit. Yet we must not confuse this idea of being fully ourselves with popular ideas around being "true to yourself" or understanding this in the sense of "you do you," which privilege the uncontested sovereignty of the self. Vigilance against the tyranny of the self is always required. Also required is a clear-headed pneumatological account of personhood.

I find Karl Barth especially helpful here. Barth argues that the Spirit is in the business of opening a space for the human creature to be its truest self. According to Barth, God takes a "sporting joy" in giving the creature this space "to be itself" to "its very depths."[14] In fact, it goes against the character of God to deny the creature the freedom to be just what it is in its unique human life. In the Spirit there is a place for each person in creation; this place is a gift, and it is a grace. And it is a place for the creature to go of itself rather than to be governed by irresistible deterministic forces. It is a place for the creature to go anew, more fully and richly itself. This is our true end as humans.[15] This too, I suggest, is the Spirit's work to secure our "heart language" in worship.[16]

Reworking Barth's language, this Spirit-established freedom is to be seen as a *bounded* rather than an *unbounded* freedom.[17] It is a freedom to be a *certain* kind of person, not *any* kind of person. It is to be a person within our limits rather than free of limits.[18] It is to be free from selfish ambition so that we might zealously love our neighbor as ourself. It is a freedom not to do as we please but to do as God pleases, and it pleases God immensely to free us to be our truest self—*in Christ*.[19] Under this light, the result of an increase of Christ's life in us is not a diminishment of ourselves but, by the Spirit's power, a freedom from the imprisoning walls of absolute self-reliance, so that we might become truly at home in ourselves, for God's sake and others' sake too.[20]

With this in mind, what are ways that we might be fully ourselves in spontaneous moments of corporate worship? This might involve the simple act of holding one's hands open during the prayers of the people or during reception of the final word of blessing. It might involve holding one's hands high above in a gesture of acclamation to God or in earnest pleading for God's redemptive intervention. It might involve the gentle touch on the shoulder of a fellow member in order to communicate God's comforting presence. It might involve a courageous act of seeking the forgiveness of a fellow member with whom there may be "ought," as the King James Version translates Mark 11:25. Or it might involve, finally, a willingness to dance before God in praise, whether in a small or extravagant manner.

The Spirit Who Plays Jazz

A final aspect of a theology of spontaneity is captured in the language of the Spirit as jazz player. While this particular metaphor is widely used in theological writings about the Holy Spirit, it remains useful for our purposes here too. Jeremy Begbie helpfully unpacks the meaning of the metaphor as it relates to the context of corporate worship. Over against the presumption that only order and disorder might characterize our experience of worship, Begbie proposes a third mode, non-order, and uses laughter as an example. "It is not order (predictably patterned)," he writes, "but nor is it disorder (destructive)." It is instead what might be called non-order or the jazz-factor. Begbie explains at length:

> Those who crave regular order often assume that the only alternative is detrimental disorder. (This is probably why dictators tend to be humorless.) Some church pastors are adept at ordering all the non-order out of life, like Harold Crick in *Stranger Than Fiction*. Worship becomes cleansed of anything remotely spontaneous; church meetings are impeccably prepared and entirely devoid of surprise. Project this onto God, and he becomes the embodiment of order *ad infinitum*, lifeless and dull (as many outside the church believe). But the New Testament opens up to us another dimension of goodness, another dimension of living which exploded into the world on the day of Pentecost, the kind of life we will see in the world to come—the life of the Holy Spirit.[21]

The life that the Spirit makes possible, Begbie argues, is a kind that involves the interplay between order and non-order. By this he means a dynamic relationship "between the given chords and the improvised riff, between the faithful bass of God's grace and the novel whirls of the Spirit."[22] As it relates to worship specifically, this means giving space to the Spirit to improvise in our midst in order to cause something surprisingly novel to occur.

In his book *Beyond Pentecostalism*, Wolfgang Vondey brings a theology of play into conversation with a theology of spontaneity in a way that further clarifies our metaphor of Spirit as jazz player.[23] Much like the performance of jazz music, Vondey contends, the Spirit invites God's people into a mode of active listening. In worship we listen not only for the voice of the Spirit, we listen also for the voice of the Spirit *in* one another. We incline our ears to hear what the Spirit might be saying *to* us and *through* us. And when we hear something, we respond. Such a response does not, of course, presume upon either the Spirit or one's neighbor. An invitation is always required. We ask, "What *might* the Spirit be doing among us in this moment?" We wonder, "What *could* the Spirit be saying to us, here and now?" We inquire of one another: "How do you hear the Spirit's voice?" Just as active listening is a hallmark of jazz music played well, then, so too a Spirit-enabled active listening is a hallmark of the practice of spontaneity in worship.

A last facet of this metaphor is illumined by way of the idea of an "aesthetic of surrender." This is a phrase Frank Barrett uses to describe the willingness of jazz musicians, whether alone or in jam sessions with others, to explore things that take them out of their comfort zones, which involve risk and the possibility of failure. Musicians practice spontaneity by engaging in deliberate improvisational exercises, no matter how stretching or scary they may feel, in order to open up new possibilities in the music. The goal of such exercises, as Barrett explains, is to nurture an aesthetic of surrender. By this he means the removal of the familiar from the equation, so that the musicians are forced to attend to the music "of the moment," within which something truly new might be discovered. Barrett writes,

> Musicians must *surrender* their conscious striving. They prepare to be spontaneous by practicing, mastering, and then letting go: by deliberately facing unfamiliar challenges, by developing provocative learning relationships and by creating incremental disruptions that demand experimentation and risk. . . . Cultivating an aesthetic of surrender invites openness and wonderment to what unfolds, enhancing the self-organizing potential of the system by preparing players to respond in unpredictable, novel ways.[24]

Within a liturgical context this involves the practice of surrender to the initiative of the Spirit and to the members of Christ's Body. It is done not for its own sake but for the sake of love, as Paul sees it in 1 Corinthians

14:1. Spontaneous worship may have a deeply personal aspect to it, but it is never inattentive or insensitive to the community. In other words, spontaneous worship aims at an experience that is shared *with* others, rather than a performance *for* others, even if one may be the only one engaged in the spontaneous act. Like the rules of a game set in place to facilitate creativity and surprise, the order of worship might be seen to function like rules that aim to free worshipers, not to constrain them. The order of worship, on this account, will be less like the "perfect" performance of a piece of classical music and more like the "faithful" performance of a piece of jazz music, which makes space for both individual and communal improvisation.

This might include, among other things, a moment of purposeful quiet after the sermon in order to give space to people to truly listen to the voice of the Spirit through the words of the preacher. It may involve allowing the music to go longer at a certain point in the service, because the worship leader has heard the voice of the Spirit through the voice of the singing congregation. It may involve the "cultivation of spontaneity," as strange as this phrase may sound, as a way to develop the muscle of responsive listening in real time. It may involve teaching the community about the importance of spontaneous worship, as I experienced firsthand in my senior year of high school, while attending an Assembly of God youth group. Having grown up in a card-carrying dispensationalist church culture, I knew nobody who raised their hands in worship "for no reason." But here, at this small church, a youth pastor taught from Scripture about the significance of such worship, and slowly I began not only to understand but also to embrace the practice of such spontaneous worship.

Infectious Worship

What is the proper end of spontaneous worship? As the New Testament sees it, the goal should always be the edification of the Body (1 Cor. 14:26) as well as the common good of the congregation (1 Cor. 12:7). The goal is not idiosyncratic expression, nor is it a straitjacketed communalism. In making space for spontaneous uses of the body in worship, we must always resist tendencies to naturalism (dissolving the object of worship), institutionalism (shackling the worship of the community), formalism (narrowing worship to liturgical externals), traditionalism (idolizing the heritage of worship), and pragmatism (reducing worship to its efficiency and measurable productivity).[25] We must embrace instead both the ordered and non-ordered work of the Spirit in our midst.

One of the understandable concerns around spontaneity is the possibility of manipulation, often expressed in the form of negative peer pressure, and of idiosyncratic self-indulgence on the part of one member that undermines the unity of the whole community. These no doubt represent real dangers to a purposeful welcome of spontaneity in worship. Church and worship leaders should always remain alert to these dangers. Yet while the dangers are real, they do not represent a legitimate reason to exclude spontaneous uses of the body in worship altogether.

With respect to the fear of manipulation, one might look to the world of sports for help. When at a sporting event, such as a soccer match or baseball game, there will be moments when the crowd finds itself acting as one. They might be doing the wave, or singing a chant, or clapping and shouting. While the possibility of being manipulated by the crowd is always real, there is a kind of group logic that makes such spontaneous acts normal to all in attendance, even if any given spectator may refrain from such activities at any point. More likely, however, there is a willing surrender to the infectious joy of the group, which is what we might call positive peer pressure.

Regarding the possibility of self-indulgent behavior in worship, this is certainly a reality that I have witnessed firsthand. While one should always count to ten before judging the actions of another, the likelihood of self-indulgent behavior that detracts or distracts from the common worship is endemic to liturgical cultures that place a high value on spontaneity in corporate worship. Some may regard the risk of such behavior not worth it and preclude spontaneity altogether. Others will believe that the risk is worthwhile and that God will not only give the community grace to absorb it in the moment but also the wisdom to discern how such behaviors might be addressed in pastorally judicious ways after the fact.

One last thing should be said here. Spontaneous and prescribed activities perform their own distinctive role in forming Christlikeness in God's people in corporate worship. With the first kind, our bodies are often led by our minds and hearts to offer our whole self to God in worship; with the second kind, our bodies may lead our hearts and minds in the way of faithful discipleship. With the first, it might be an outflow of the emotions; with the second, it might be a sacrifice of praise, often despite our emotions. In both cases, however, we wish to affirm the integrity of our lives and to offer whole bodies in humility to God.[26] This, among other things, represents the true end of our bodies in worship.

12

The End of the Body

A Conclusion to the Body in Worship

One cannot be faithful to Jesus without tending to the bodies of his sisters and brothers.

—Kimberly Bracken Long, The Worshiping Body:
The Art of Leading Worship

Let every living, breathing creature praise God! Hallelujah!
—Psalm 150:6 (The Message)

To what end do we offer to God our bodies in worship? We offer our bodies to God so that the life of Jesus might be made manifest in our often very broken bodies (2 Cor. 4:10). We offer our bodies to God so that all of it—hand and foot, eye and ear, breath and brain, touch and taste, skin and sinew—might be given over fully to Jesus in Spirit-ed service of our neighbor. And we offer our bodies to God in anticipation of that day when we shall stand before our risen Lord in our gloriously resurrected bodies, finally and truly at home in our own skin, in love-filled wonder. We offer them, in short, so that we might become like Christ, serve like Christ, and love like Christ.

The Training of the Body

First, we offer our bodies wholly to God in worship so that they might be trained in Christlikeness. Over against the prevailing assumption of our contemporary world, our bodies are not ours to do with as we please. Our bodies are not, as chef Anthony Bourdain once quipped, an amusement park, subject to our idiosyncratic whims.[1] Our bodies belong to Christ's flesh, and his flesh belongs to us. They belong to Christ's flesh, not in the way that professional athletes belong to a sporting team, which they are free to join or to leave as they wish, contract issues notwithstanding. Our relationship to Christ's body is not a contractually binding one—it is an *ontologically* binding one.

Our body likewise belongs to Christ not simply as an act of the will. Our body, that is, does not belong to Christ because we have volunteered our tangible services on his behalf. While there is certainly a volitional dimension to our Christian life, our participation in Christ's bodily life is not fundamentally a voluntary affair. It is a *pneumatological* affair. Our body belongs to Christ because God's Spirit has incorporated us in Christ.[2] In worship, writes Joseph Cardinal Ratzinger, "we are laid hold of by the Logos and for the Logos in our very bodies," and it is the Spirit of God who makes this seemingly impossible conjoining possible through myriad sacramental and liturgical means.[3]

Last, our bodies belong to Christ not just because he has ransomed us at a costly price. To be sure, Christ redeems us from slavery to sin so that we might live in our bodies as "slaves to Christ" (Eph. 6:6), now and evermore. And this surely is reason enough to live for Christ in the corporeal circumstances of our lives. In Paul's words from 1 Corinthians 6:20, we glorify God in our bodies because we have been bought at a considerable price. But we belong to Christ in a greater sense than the commercial metaphor that inheres in this vocabulary of ransom. We belong to Christ as a temple (*naos*) of the Spirit, and it is this temple language that brings into sharp relief the intimate relationship between corporate worship and corporeal worship.

If our human body discovers its right orientation by being conformed to the *body* of Christ, as I have argued throughout this book, it is within the context of the corporate worship of Christ's *Body* that training in Christlikeness becomes central and all-encompassing. In worship we offer "not only our skin and bones," as John Calvin once wrote, "but the totality of which we are composed."[4] It is our whole selves and thus also our whole bodily selves that we offer up to God as a living sacrifice. A sacrifice, significantly, is something that is not only used but also used up. Yet here in corporate worship the body remains living, not dead, and in being consumed by the Spirit, it becomes alive with the life of Christ, not diminished in any way.[5]

In order to properly offer up our whole bodies to Christ, however, we must adopt the disciplines of a Christlike disciple. In adopting such disciplines, we become habituated through repeated exercise to the kinds of things that Christ might do *in* and *with* and *through* our own bodies, were he our hands and feet, eyes and ears. We do things in and with our bodies in worship so that our bodies might become instinctually oriented to the resurrected body of Christ, not just on Sunday but throughout the week. To put it otherwise, we use our bodies in worship so that they might become "capable of the resurrection," oriented toward the sacrificial love that marks Christ's own life.[6] This is what it means, in short, to say that the physical disciplines that we take on in worship enable us to become disciples of Christ.

This is also what we might call the work of *askesis*, or self-discipline. By this I do not mean ascetic in the monastic sense of the term, and even less so in the stereotypical connotations that often accompany it, such as emaciation or self-flagellation, or even worse, a hatred of the body. I mean rather the kind of training that an athlete engages in to hone his or her body for a specific purpose—gymnastics, martial arts, or long-distance running, for example. Eugene Peterson explains askesis this way: "No one becomes more spiritual by becoming less material. No one becomes exalted by ascending in a gloriously colored hot-air balloon. Mature spirituality requires *askesis*, a training program custom-designed for each

> *Thy gifts, O God, alone I'll prize,*
> *My tongue, my eyes,*
> *My cheeks, my lips, my ears,*
> *my hands, my feet;*
> *Their harmony is far more sweet;*
> *Their beauty true.*
> *And these in all my ways*
> *Shall themes become*
> *and organs of Thy praise.*
>
> —Thomas Traherne, "The Person," *in* **Selected Poems and Prose**

individual-in-community, and then continuously monitored and adapted as development takes place and conditions vary."[7]

In practice, this means that most Sundays our bodily worship will involve things that we do repeatedly for the good of the body, regardless of temperament or our feelings of the moment. It also means that what we do with our bodies in worship contributes positively to the Spirit's therapeutic work: countering the idols of the mind, correcting our defective memories, restoring a will that is bent against God, healing affections that suffer the warping effects of sin, and delivering us from distorted passions that get embedded within our bodies themselves. It is in this sense that we might say that the Christian in corporate worship is *informed* in Christ, *transformed* by the Spirit, and *reformed* by embodied practices, whether of the spontaneous or prescriptive sort.[8]

On this account, it is difficult to overestimate the value of regular teaching and encouragement by the senior leadership of a given congregation around the good use of our bodies in worship. Plenty is learned, of course, through the routinized practice of our bodies over time, which one hopes will generate Christlike habits and instincts that enable us to be in the world in faith, hope, and love. But reflective thinking on our embodied practices of worship is nonnegotiable for the long-term health of a congregation. James K. A. Smith helpfully remarks, "For the sake of the community of practitioners, worship planners and leaders need to take on the responsibility of reflexive evaluation of our practices in order to ensure that the imaginative coherences of worship are consistent with the vision of God's kingdom to which we are being habituated."[9]

Church and worship leaders would do well to remind those under their care of very basic things, like the fact that our bodily worship should never be marked by legalism of any sort. As Christians we do not live under an oppressive law; we live under a law of love. Sustained and surrounded by such a love, we offer our bodies as a sacrifice to God, in glad obedience to his good, pleasing, and perfect will for our bodies. To affirm the role of our bodies in the liturgy is likewise not about automaticity. The act of bowing to the cross does not automatically make us humble, nor does the act of raised hands in itself indicate maturity. Both might be egregiously absent from the heart of such a person. But perhaps a heartfelt habit of bowing and hand raising might, by God's grace, inculcate humility and maturity in us over time.

Congregants also need to be reminded that embodied worship is not a matter of personality type. It is not for extroverts only, or solely for the charismatic and emotionally expressive in our midst.[10] While we aim to worship God authentically, our personalities do not have the last word in our worship—the gospel does. And over against the fear that the actions of others in worship may feel pressuring, perhaps the context of a sporting event may offer a reassuring word here (as I have similarly suggested in the previous chapter). When we experience the enthusiasm of others in an athletic stadium, we often call that enthusiasm socially infectious. We get caught up in it and feel ourselves willingly drawn into physical expressions of joy and surprise. Similarly, when we witness the fulsome praise of others in our congregation, perhaps we might see such expressions as a form of invitation, drawing us into an infectious love for God, rather than as a burdensome demand.

The hope, of course, is that however we use our bodies in worship, they might form in us a deeper sense of our fellowship in Christ's broken body and of our participation in the power of his resurrected body. The hope is that our bodies might always bear witness to the enfleshed Word wherever they may find themselves—that they might become mobile shrines that take "the triune God out and about in the world," conveying God's blessings to others, as John Kleinig vividly puts it.[11] My body, like yours, bears the privilege of functioning as the temple of the Spirit. My body, in fact, *houses* the Lord; the Lord is its inhabitant, and his radiance willingly shines from it. Ambulatory as it usually is, my body carries the Lord around with me wherever I go. Paul Griffiths remarks,

> Christians are glued to Jesus's flesh, stuck on it, brought into it, made participant in it. They are in it and it is in them. . . . What they do with them is what he does with his. What he does with his, which now include theirs and them, is partly constituted by what they do with theirs. Their fleshly agency and his are no longer cleanly separable. They, now, should glorify God in their own bodies (*glorificate ergo deum in corpore vestro*): the verb is imperative, which is to say that they're being asked (demanded, encouraged, required) to do this, to carry Jesus around with, in, and as, their flesh.[12]

What Griffiths says here about the integral relation between ontological and missiological dimensions of our participation in Christ's bodily life is crucial to the work of Christlike love. To be bound *to* Christ's body is to be bound *up* in Christ's own loves. It is to love *what* he loves and to love *how* he loves. To cleave to his body, moreover, is to find ourselves, like him, no longer clinging to our bodies self-protectively but rather, by the Spirit's help, offering them over to others in vulnerable love. And in relinquishing self-absorption, we find ourselves freed to love the bodies of the hungry and the thirsty, the naked and the sick, the deserving and the undeserving, the friend and the stranger, as if we were loving Christ's own body (cf. Matt. 25).

The Touch-and-Go Business of the Body

This, then, leads to a second major hope for our bodies in worship: that our training in Christlikeness might always result in deeper Christlike service of our neighbors.[13] From Romans 12:1 we discover a close link between divine service and neighbor service. In the thinking of Romans, as elsewhere throughout the New Testament, the true worship of God does not exist hermetically sealed off from the mission of God. The body that we offer up to God as a living sacrifice is the same body that gets deployed in sacrificial service of both saint and sinner. This, Paul argues, is our "spiritual" (*logikos*) worship, which is to say, the most logical outcome of our common worship of God.

"No worship is pleasing to God," writes John Stott in his commentary on Romans 12, "which is purely inward, abstract and mystical; it must express itself in concrete acts of service performed by our bodies."[14] A body rightly oriented to God, as Paul sees it, is a body that willingly orients itself to hospitality, not just to fellow brothers and sisters in Christ but also to outsiders to the family of faith, even if that outsider is an enemy (Rom. 12:13, 20).[15] Kleinig adds that "we have a kind of circuit in which we offer our bodies and minds to God in the divine service, so that we can serve him better in our bodily dealings with others in our daily lives and be thereby equipped for our fuller participation with our bodies in the service of worship."[16]

The Christians of the third century understood this fact well and embodied it fully in their practices of baptism and of service. An imaginative exercise might help to illumine this second point well.[17] Imagine with me, if you will, that you live in the ancient city of Carthage, in what is today the

North African city of Tunis, in Tunisia. The year is AD 220. The emperor Antonius sits on the throne, while the great African theologian, Tertullian, a local, has just died, and the memory of the martyrdom of Felicitas and Perpetua seventeen years earlier is still fresh for your community. You have prepared for three years to be baptized. Over the past forty days you have fasted from meat and wine, you have kept all-night vigils, and you have visited the poor, the widows, the orphans. The night before your baptism your bishop breathed upon your face as a sign against the devil. He anointed you with oil on your forehead, your ears, and your nostrils. And he placed salt on your tongue to remind you that you are the salt of the earth.

Today is Easter morning, the day of your baptism. Standing in the antechamber with members of the same gender, you remove your clothes and wait for the deacon to call you to the stone font that has been carved into the ground. In stripping off your clothes, you are symbolizing the removal of your "old self" in order to receive the "new self" promised to you in Jesus's resurrection. If you are a woman, a female deacon will then perform the entire rite in the place of your pastor. Standing in the water, naked like Jesus on the cross, your pastor asks whether you renounce the devil and all his schemes. You proclaim yes, with vigor. Your pastor now immerses you three times in the waters, each time asking if you believe in each person of the Trinity. The font has become both your tomb and your womb, signifying your death and rebirth.

Having been baptized, you step out of the font and your pastor anoints you again with oil. He also makes the sign of the cross over you. Laying his hands on you, he prays that the Spirit might empower you for new life, and you are given a new set of clothes, a white garment that symbolizes your life now as a child of the light. Your new brothers and sisters in Christ embrace you, each giving you a kiss on the cheek as a sign of welcome into the family of God. Your pastor then offers you a cup that includes a mix of milk and honey as a token of your symbolic entrance into the promised land, and for the first time ever you share the eucharistic bread and wine with the whole church.

Every sense in your body has been included in your baptism—sight, smell, sound, touch, and taste—because there is no part of your body that does not get consecrated to Jesus.

For the Christians of the early church era, worship was a fundamentally sacramental thing. It was not simply about what one thought or felt; it was about what one did with one's body. In giving their bodies wholly to God in baptism, these Christians became freed to offer their bodies wholly to others in love: in the care of the members of Christ's Body, in the service of the poor and needy, and in sacrificial charity to strangers and enemies of the gospel—including those who might send them to prison or have them killed.

Sociologist Rodney Starks shows in his book *The Rise of Christianity* how the Christians of this era did what their pagan neighbors were unwilling to do.[18] In AD 251 a horrific plague swept across the Roman Empire. Historians speculate that about a quarter of the population died as a result. In equivalent terms, it would amount to a pandemic in our current time causing the deaths of eighty million Americans. Cyprian, the bishop of Carthage at the time, recounts his experience of seeing human carcasses lying in the streets, untouched and rotting. His pagan neighbors, he observed, ran away or exposed their own friends to the plague, hoping that this might keep death at bay. But the Christians stayed.

They stayed in order care for plague victims. They stayed because they knew that death did not have the last word. They stayed because they had been baptized with Jesus. They stayed because this was the Jesus way. Dionysius of Alexandria (248–264), a bishop at the time in another region of the empire, writes about how Christians loved the diseased bodies of their neighbors. They nursed them, embraced them, and washed them. They closed their eyes and mouths. They carried them. They wrapped them in graveclothes and buried them, and soon enough the same service was performed for them.

In all these ways they manifested the tender love of Jesus in the burial of the dead—in a ritual that both honors the body and serves the heart's need to grieve, both of which my family never experienced in the instance of my aunt Grace's death in the spring of 2020. The Christians of this time did these things because they had encountered a Spirit-ed power that had freed them *from* sin-distorting passions and had received a Spirit-ed grace that had freed them *for* a life of embodied service to others. This is, of course, a power that belongs to every member of Christ's Body. We too have in our veins the power that raised Jesus from the dead. We too give away our bodies to others who need to experience the healing touch of God. We too get to offer our bodies as "instruments of righteousness" (Rom. 6:13).

And in doing any number of such things, in Christ, we will without a doubt make ourselves, like Christ, vulnerable: vulnerable to rejection, to misunderstanding, to loss and injury and death. There is no way to escape the vulnerability that lies at the heart of Christlike service, just as it also lies at the heart of true worship. And while it is natural to weary of this "long struggle to be at home in the body, this difficult friendship," as American poet Jane Kenyon puts it in her poem "Cages,"[19] and though we may neglect or reject the vulnerability that remains central to our bodily experience of the world, we must not fear such vulnerability, as tempting as it may feel to do so.

Like Jesus, we must see such vulnerability as a sign of our true embodied glory and a way to become like Jesus himself. In vulnerability, the Second Person of the Trinity becomes incarnate in the form of fragile infant flesh. In vulnerability, the Christ child permits his body to be handled, carried, and caressed by family and friends, among others. In vulnerability, this little Human One grows into adulthood and, yet again, allows himself to be handled and *manhandled*, to be carried and *seized*, to be caressed and *wounded*, to be tended to by angels and women, among others, and to be *abandoned* by friend and *crucified* by foe.

On the cross, this Truly Human One hangs physically naked at the hands of brutish soldiers and dies spiritually open-armed, in a willing embrace of the violence of human sin. In his resurrected body, our Lord offers his wounded hands and feet as evidence of his fully human, albeit glorified, body, so that the disciples might "handle" his flesh. And prior to his ascension, the enfleshed Word leaves his disciples, and us along with them, three gifts: the gift of the Spirit to empower us to be Christ's body in the world, the gift of his body and blood to nourish our bodies with "living food," and the gift of his Body—the fellowship of saints—to sustain us in the work of vulnerable love in anticipation of that day when we shall behold our risen Lord in an intimate face-to-face encounter (1 Cor. 13:12).

In all these ways, our own physical bodies find themselves caught up in something bigger than themselves: the very movement of heaven and earth in responsive love to its Creator. *This, in turn, represents a third hope for our bodies in worship, that, however we may use them, they will grow in us a wondrous love for our Maker, akin to the love that Christ has for his Father* (John 14:31; 15:10).

The Telos of the Body

In *The Trinitarian Faith*, Scottish theologian Thomas Torrance writes that, "far from God being inactive in his inner being, it belongs to the essential and eternal nature of his being to move and energise and act."[20] This movement that occurs within the triune Godhead continues on the stage of human history and throughout the entire cosmos. In the beginning, there is movement (Gen. 1:1); in the end, there is movement (Rev. 22:17, 20); and in between, the Holy Trinity is dynamically at work drawing all things in creation to their true end.

In the story of the incarnation, the Father sends the Son, the Spirit hovers over Mary's womb, and the good news is cast abroad by angels. At the baptism of Jesus, the Spirit alights on the Son and the sound of the Father's voice breaks through the cloud. Throughout his earthly ministry, Jesus stretches out his hand to the sick and he touches the untouchable, he lifts the oppressed and restores them to the community, and he sends the disciples out into the world so that they might be his visible, tangible, and reconciling presence, both announcing and embodying the good news of the new creation (2 Cor. 5:17).

In the story of ascension and Pentecost, the Son rises to the Father "like fire into the heavens," as Eugene Rogers puts it, while the Spirit descends like a gale force on the disciples in the upper room.[21] In the story of the Lord's Supper, Christ descends to us by his Spirit in our partaking of the body and blood, so that we might ascend in faith by that selfsame Spirit into fellowship with the Father. We *too* participate in the dynamic movement of the Trinity in our own unique creaturely ways and contexts.

With our bodies we join the upward movement of creation's praise; we participate in the outward movement of God's re-creative and redemptive purposes for the world; and we experience bodily the inward movement of our souls, and discover, thereby, all the ways that we might cling to God and release to God, stretch out to God and retreat from God, turn and return to a God who reaches out to us in grace in order to turn our tentative gestures of faith into full-fledged movements of love.

In so doing, we experience a foretaste of the dynamic praise of the host of heaven (Rev. 5:11). In Dante's reimagining of this scene in his fourteenth-century epic poem, *Paradiso*, a circle of angels swirls in perpetual movement around the divine light:

> The other host, which, flying, sees and sings
> the glory of the One who draws its love,
> and that goodness which granted it such glory,
> just like a swarm of bees that, at one moment,
> enters the flowers and, at another, turns
> back to that labor which yields such sweet savor,
> descended into that vast flower graced
> with many petals, then again rose up
> to the eternal dwelling of its love.[22]

Dante's vision, albeit fictional, reminds us of something central about our bodies in worship—namely, that we do not offer them to God for the body's sake alone. We offer our bodies to God because we wish to be caught up in something bigger than ourselves. What is this bigger something? It is the movement of angels who bend their gaze before the ascended Christ. It is the movement of saints drawn irresistibly to the Lord of heaven and earth. It is the movement of rivers that clap their hands and of mountains that skip for joy. And it is the movement of stars in their heavenly course and of the entire cosmos that assumes an orbit of love around the Lamb, in whom all things are held together.[23]

Poet Samuel Taylor Coleridge once remarked that all philosophy begins in wonder and ends in wonder. While "the first Wonder is the offspring of Ignorance," he writes, "the last is the parent of Adoration."[24] Much the same can be said about worship. In Genesis, worship begins in wonder, just as in the book of Revelation, we see how wonder is the end of our worship. In Coleridge's terms, wonder sustains, precedes, and results in adoration. J. B. Phillips's translation of 2 Thessalonians 1:10 captures this sense of wonder, when he writes that our experience of the radiance of the face of our Lord will be marked by "breath-taking wonder."

Just as our bodies in their original creation are wonderfully made (Ps. 139:14–15), then, so too our resurrected bodies, in the new creation, shall find themselves caught up in the wonder-filled praise of all creation, caught up in the "heart-whelming wonder" of being made new in the presence of the One who makes all things new.[25] According to Charles Wesley, in witnessing "the glorious joy unspeakable, the beatific sight" of the risen Lord himself,[26] we shall find ourselves there a new creation, charged with the weight of glory, "lost in wonder, love and praise."[27]

In the end, in our encounter with our risen Lord, nothing will be held back. Everything will be willingly and joyfully yielded over to the "wonder of the mighty Architect, who loves His work so inwardly, His eye doth ever watch it."[28] Trust in the One who has done "all things well" (Mark 7:37) will replace any faithlessness that we may feel toward our present bodies. Hope in the One who has promised to us a resurrected body will replace any despair that we may feel today about our bodies. And love in the One who fashions us in love will replace any loveless feeling that we may feel toward the bodies of others. And it is to that end that we worship the Holy Trinity with the totality of our bodies today, for that is the true end of all our bodies.

Notes

Chapter 1 The Glory of the Body

1. The Book of Common Prayer, "The Burial of the Dead: Rite One," https://www.bcponline.org/PastoralOffices/BurialI.html.

2. Bessel van der Kolk, *The Body Keeps the Score: Brain, Mind, and Body in the Healing of Trauma* (New York: Viking, 2014), 101–3.

3. Julianne Holt-Lunstad, Timothy B. Smith, Mark Baker, Tyler Harris, and David Stephenson, "Loneliness and Social Isolation as Risk Factors for Mortality: A Meta-Analytic Review," *Perspectives on Psychological Science* 10, no. 2 (March 2015): 227–37.

4. Louise C. Hawkley and John P. Capitanio, "Perceived Social Isolation, Evolutionary Fitness and Health Outcomes: A Lifespan Approach," *Philosophical Transactions B* 370, no. 1669 (May 26, 2015), https://royalsocietypublishing.org/doi/10.1098/rstb.2014.0114.

5. Lois M. Collins, "Losing Touch: What 6 Feet of Safety Costs Us," *Deseret News* (May 12, 2020), https://www.deseret.com/indepth/2020/5/12/21246611/coronavirus-utah-covid-physical-touch-hugs-hand-shakes-affection-distancing-effects. See also Sirin Kale, "Skin Hunger Helps Explain Your Desperate Longing for Human Touch," *Wired UK* (May 29, 2020), https://www.wired.co.uk/article/skin-hunger-coronavirus-human-touch. See also Paul Brand and Philip Yancey, *Fearfully and Wonderfully: The Marvel of Bearing God's Image* (Downers Grove, IL: InterVarsity Press, 2019), esp. chap. 7, "Skin: The Organ of Sensitivity."

6. According to Scott Hahn, "In the liturgy we contemplate the Gospel, but that's not all. We hear it, see it, feel it, taste it, and smell it as well." *Signs of Life: 20 Catholic Customs and Their Biblical Roots* (New York: Image, 2018), 85.

7. Nathan D. Mitchell, *Meeting Mystery: Liturgy, Worship, Sacraments* (Maryknoll, NY: Orbis Books, 2006), 149.

8. Irenaeus, *Against Heresies*, 4.20.7, available at https://ccel.org/ccel/irenaeus/against_heresies_iv/anf01.ix.vi.xxi.html.

9. John Calvin writes this in a preface for the 1534 French translation of the New Testament by his cousin Pierre Robert Olivetan. *Calvin: Commentaries*, trans. Joseph Haroutunian (Philadelphia: Westminster, 1958), 60.

10. Cited in Peter A. Levine, *In an Unspoken Voice: How the Body Releases Trauma and Restores Goodness* (Berkeley: North Atlantic Books, 2010), 135.

11. See Louis Weil, *Liturgical Sense: The Logic of Rite* (New York: Seabury, 2013), 111.

12. Maxine Sheets-Johnstone, "Charting the Interdisciplinary Course," in *Giving the Body Its Due*, ed. Maxine Sheets-Johnstone (Albany: SUNY Press, 1992), 2.

13. Mayra Rivera, *Poetics of the Flesh* (Durham, NC: Duke University Press, 2013), 113.

14. Helpful resources on this account include Paul J. Griffiths, *Christian Flesh* (Stanford, CA: Stanford University Press, 2018); Ola Sigurdson, *Heavenly Bodies: Incarnation, the Gaze, and Embodiment in Christian Theology*, trans. Carl Olsen (Grand Rapids: Eerdmans, 2016); Ian A. McFarland, *The Word Made Flesh: A Theology of the Incarnation* (Louisville: Westminster John Knox, 2019); Colin Gunton, *The Triune Creator: A Historical and Systematic Study* (Grand Rapids: Eerdmans, 1998); Gerald Hiestand and Todd Wilson, eds., *Creation and Doxology: The Beginning and End of God's Good World* (Downers Grove, IL: IVP Academic, 2018); Mark Johnson, *The Body in the Mind: The Bodily Basis of Meaning, Imagination, and Reason* (Chicago: University of Chicago Press, 1990); Joel B. Green, *In Search of the Soul: Perspectives on the Mind-Body Problem*, 2nd ed. (Eugene, OR: Wipf & Stock, 2010); Gordon Lathrop, *Holy Ground: A Liturgical Cosmology* (Minneapolis: Augsburg Fortress, 2003); John W. Kleinig, *Wonderfully Made: A Protestant Theology of the Body* (Bellingham, WA: Lexham, 2021); and Mary Timothy Prokes, *Toward a Theology of the Body* (Grand Rapids: Eerdmans, 1996).

15. Such is the case, e.g., with Kimberly Bracken Long, *The Worshiping Body: The Art of Leading Worship* (Louisville: Westminster John Knox, 2009); Ronald Gagne, Thomas Kane, and Robert VerEecke, *Introducing Dance in Christian Worship* (Washington, DC: The Pastoral Press, 1984); Aidan Kavanagh, *Elements of Rite: A Handbook of Liturgical Style* (Collegeville, MN: Liturgical Press, 1990); and Antonio Donghi, *Words and Gestures in the Liturgy* (Collegeville, MN: Liturgical Press, 2007).

16. While my social location involves bringing a set of blind spots and biases to this topic, it also opens up unique vistas. Being a White, American, highly educated man, among other things, requires in humility that I depend on the insights of others in social locations different from my own for wisdom about the proper use of the body in worship. But being a "third culture kid" means that I also bring distinctive perspectives on the body in worship that hopefully serve other members of Christ's global Body. Such is the promise and challenge for every reader, I believe.

17. Augustine, *Sermon* 126.6 in the Angelo Mai collection, *Miscellanea Agostiniana*, quoted in *The Essential Augustine*, ed. and trans. Vernon J. Bourke (Indianapolis: Hackett, 1974), 123. Cf. Alexander W. Hall, "Natural Theology in the Middle Ages," in *The Oxford Handbook of Natural Theology*, ed. John Hedley Brooke, Russell Re Manning, and Fraser Watts (Oxford: Oxford University Press, 2013), 58–60; Oskari Juurikkala, "The Two Books of God: The Metaphor of the Book of Nature in Augustine," *Augustinianum* 61, no. 2 (2021): 479–98.

18. John Chrysostom, *Homilies on the Statues to the People of Antioch* IX.5, available at https://www.newadvent.org/fathers/190109.htm.

19. John Calvin, *Institutes of the Christian Religion*, ed. John T. McNeill, trans. Ford Lewis Battles (Philadelphia: Westminster, 1960), I.14.20; cf. I.5.1–12; see also his "Sermon on Job 9:7–15," in *Sermons on Job*, trans. Douglas Kelly (Edinburgh: Banner of Truth, 1993).

20. John Calvin, "Commentary on Psalm 19:3," in *Calvin's Old Testament Commentaries*, trans. T. H. L. Parker (Edinburgh: T&T Clark, 1986). The Belgic Confession of 1566 states in article 2, "The Means by Which We Know God," that the universe is "like a beautiful book in which all creatures, great and small, are as letters to make us ponder

the invisible things of God," https://www.crcna.org/welcome/beliefs/confessions/belgic-confession.

21. Bonaventure, *Collations on the Hexaemeron* (Darmstadt: Wissenschaftliche Buchgesellschaft, 1964), 12.14.

22. Raimundus de Sabunde, *Natural Theology, or Book of the Creatures* (*Theologia Naturalis sive Liber Creaturarum*), 146, quoted in Peter M. J. Hess, "God's Two Books: Special Revelation and Natural Science in the Christian West," in *Bridging Science and Religion*, ed. Ted Peters and Gaymon Bennett (Minneapolis: Fortress, 2003), 128–29. While some will refer to nature as God's "first book," as Sabunde does, because it appears chronologically *before* Holy Scripture, others will refer to nature as God's "second book," as I do here, because Holy Scripture remains primary, or "first," to God's self-disclosure.

23. Deborah B. Haarsma, "Galaxies, Genes, and the Glory of God," in Hiestand and Wilson, *Creation and Doxology: The Beginning and End of God's Good World*, ed. Gerald Hiestand and Todd Wilson (Downers Grove, IL: IVP Academic, 2018), 29–30. On this point, see also Todd Wilson, "Mere Creation," in *Creation and Doxology*, 53.

24. Susan Ashbrook Harvey makes this observation: "The ritual context of the liturgy established a space in which the divine and human domains mingled; the air was a permeable divide between them, a porous veil separating and bridging the seen and the unseen." *Scenting Salvation: Ancient Christianity and the Olfactory Imagination* (Los Angeles: University of California Press, 2006), 88–89.

25. Daniel W. Hardy, "Creation and Eschatology," in *The Doctrine of Creation: Essays in Dogmatics, History and Philosophy*, ed. Colin E. Gunton (London: T&T Clark, 2004), 129.

Chapter 2 The Map of the Body

1. On this point, see Ola Sigurdson, *Heavenly Bodies: Incarnation, the Gaze, and Embodiment in Christian Theology*, trans. Carl Olsen (Grand Rapids: Eerdmans, 2016), 360, cf. 16–18.

2. Cf. Tara M. Owens, *Embracing the Body: Finding God in Our Flesh and Bone* (Downers Grove, IL: IVP Books, 2015); Hillary L. McBride, *The Wisdom of Your Body: Finding Healing, Wholeness, and Connection through Embodied Living* (Grand Rapids: Brazos, 2021); Stephanie Paulsell, *Honoring the Body: Meditations on a Christian Practice* (San Francisco: Jossey-Bass, 2002).

3. "Society advises rituals, codes, and boundaries for persons' physical selves, and human bodies become the carriers of society's mores. Society interprets the body and sustains itself by means of deliberate bodily investment." Colleen M. Griffith, "Spirituality and the Body," in *Bodies in Worship: Explorations in Theory and Practice*, ed. Bruce T. Morrill (Collegeville, MN: Liturgical Press, 1999), 77.

4. Sigurdson, in *Heavenly Bodies*, 349–55, offers a summary of two terms that show up frequently in the literature: "intercorporeality" and "transcorporeality." Both are neologisms that describe the body's enmeshed meaning. Philosopher Gail Weiss coined the former term to describe the nonprivate nature of our bodies; the meaning of our bodies is always shaped by our interaction with other human bodies. Theologian Graham Ward introduced the latter term as a way to make sense of the physical body's place within larger, nonphysical bodies, such as the social body, the civic body, or the Body of Christ.

5. This is the approach used for capitalization throughout this book. For more on the body of Christ, including the ritual and mystical body, see Henri de Lubac, *Corpus Mysticum: The Eucharist and the Church in the Middle Ages*, trans. Gemma Simmonds (Notre Dame, IN: University of Notre Dame Press, 2006).

6. Cf. John Paul II, *Man and Woman He Created Them: A Theology of the Body*, trans. Michael Waldstein (Boston: Pauline Books & Media, 2006), 202–4.

7. Augustine, *Questions on the Heptateuch*, as quoted in James F. White, *Documents of Christian Worship: Descriptive and Interpretive Sources* (Louisville: Westminster John Knox, 1992), 120.

8. See Alexander Schmemann, *The World as Sacrament* (London: Darton, Longman & Todd, 1965), 16; Hans Boersma, *Heavenly Participation: The Weaving of a Sacramental Tapestry* (Grand Rapids: Eerdmans, 2011), 9.

9. It may be helpful to keep in mind that a peculiarly Catholic way of talking about physical things in the liturgy involves a tendency to prefer the vocabulary of *sacrament*. Such a tendency will show up in slogans such as "grace through nature" and "grace perfecting nature." Other church traditions may use sacramental language less and prefer instead to speak about physical things in worship in exclusively christological ways (as some Reformed communities might), while others may do so in exclusively pneumatological ways (as some Pentecostal communities may do). Each tradition, in its own way, may fail to do full justice to the expressly trinitarian work of God in the physical creation, resulting in a view that claims too much for nature and the activities of human beings and too little for the integral, co-inherent work of the Trinity.

10. Matthew A. Lapine, *The Logic of the Body: Retrieving Theological Psychology* (Bellingham, WA: Lexham Press, 2020), 350–56.

11. Highlighting the particular work of the Holy Spirit, Glenn Packiam argues in *Worship and the World to Come: Exploring Christian Hope in Contemporary Worship* (Downers Grove, IL: IVP Academic, 2020), that sacramental language "helps draw our attention to the way the Spirit works within matter" (187). One can be confident, therefore, both in the future of our resurrection bodies and in other God-given helps, such as psychology and physiotherapy, for instance, or in the God-graced activity of healing prayer that the Spirit uses for the cure of our present wounded bodies.

12. For an excellent primer on the five senses, see Lawrence D. Rosenblum, *See What I'm Saying: The Extraordinary Powers of Our Five Senses* (New York: Norton, 2010).

13. See, for instance, https://www.youtube.com/watch?v=fYvdLqPKL7M and http://breakfree2024.com.

14. This is a comment Celeste Snowber Schroeder made during a lecture that she gave on faith and dance titled "The Christian Imagination" in a course at Regent College in the spring of 1996. It is also an idea that she develops in her book, *Embodied Prayer: Harmonizing Body and Soul* (Liguori, MO: Triumph Books, 1995), esp. 58–59.

15. The Labyrinth Society offers a helpful resource for finding labyrinths around the world at https://labyrinthlocator.com.

16. Lester Ruth, Carrie Steenwyk, and John D. Witvliet, *Walking Where Jesus Walked: Worship in Fourth-Century Jerusalem* (Grand Rapids: Eerdmans, 2010), 23–24.

17. Epigenetic dynamics come into play here, and it is not too much of a stretch to say that "life-giving" physical actions within a beautiful physical environment—of gathered worship specifically—might contribute to actual physical healing in our lives. Helpful resources on this general topic include Gabor Maté, *When the Body Says NO: Exploring the Stress-Disease Connection* (Hoboken, NJ: John Wiley & Sons, 2003); Peter A. Levine, *In an Unspoken Voice: How the Body Releases Trauma and Restores Goodness* (Berkeley: North Atlantic Books, 2010); and Christopher C. H. Cook and Isabelle Hamley, eds., *The Bible and Mental Health: Towards a Biblical Theology of Mental Health* (London: SCM, 2020).

18. Scientists helpfully point out that it is actually brain memory, not muscle memory per se, that generates such experiences. See, e.g., Ainslie Johnstone, "The Amazing

Phenomenon of Muscle Memory," *Medium*, December 14, 2017, https://medium.com/oxford-university/the-amazing-phenomenon-of-muscle-memory-fb1cc4c4726.

19. Sangwoo Kim summarizes this phenomenon, often called paralinguistics, this way: "Paralanguage is 'articulation of the vocal apparatus, or significant lack of it, i.e., hesitation, between segments of vocal articulation,' which is also called 'nonverbal acoustic signs.' It includes changing tone, intonation, accent, speech, and pitch of speech, as well as making nonverbal noises, such as hissing, sighing, etc." "Embodied Prayer: The Practice of Prayer as Christian Theology" (ThD diss., Duke Divinity School, 2016), 93, https://dukespace.lib.duke.edu/dspace/handle/10161/12926. Kim incorporates the language of Mary Key, *Paralanguage and Kinesics* (Metuchen, NJ: Scarecrow, 1975), 10.

20. "If you knew the steps, it meant that you belonged to a social group," choreographer Camille Brown says in a 2016 TED talk in which she presents a visual history of social dance in twenty-five moves. To know a particular move is to belong to a specific group. The TED talk is available at https://www.ted.com/talks/camille_a_brown_a_visual_history_of_social_dance_in_25_moves.

21. Cultural contrasts exist not only across geographic, linguistic, and sociohistorical lines, they also exist within a given congregational context. I once attended a Lutheran church in Würzburg, Germany, where the Sunday liturgy followed a traditionally formal Lutheran order and tone of worship, but congregants celebrated a more charismatic service every third Friday night of the month, where hand-raising, spontaneous prayer, and praise and worship were typical. Information about this church can be found at http://www.wuerzburg-martin-luther.de.

22. See Roberta King, ed., *Music in the Life of the African Church* (Waco: Baylor University Press, 2008), 57.

23. Joseph Cardinal Ratzinger, *The Spirit of the Liturgy*, trans. John Saward (San Francisco: Ignatius, 2000), 198. But as Angela Yarber argues in *Dance in Scripture: How Biblical Dancers Can Revolutionize Worship Today* (Eugene, OR: Cascade Books, 2013), for women to dance "in the spirit of Miriam" (16), for instance, is to dance in the strength that characterizes a biblical tradition of liberation. Dancing, that is, is a sign of strength, not frailty or emotionality.

24. There is a separate category for the singular powers of the kinetic arts, which I explore in my book, W. David O. Taylor, *Glimpses of the New Creation: Worship and the Formative Power of the Arts* (Grand Rapids: Eerdmans, 2019), chap. 9, "Worship and the Kinetic Arts." Cf. Judith Rock and Norman Mealy, *Performer as Priest and Prophet: Restoring the Intuitive in Worship through Music and Dance* (San Francisco: Harper & Row, 1988); Kimberly Bracken Long, *The Worshiping Body: The Art of Leading Worship* (Louisville: Westminster John Knox, 2009), 77–88.

25. Mark Johnson, *The Meaning of the Body: Aesthetics of Human Understanding* (Chicago: University of Chicago Press, 2007), 25.

26. Annie Murphy Paul, *The Extended Mind: The Power of Thinking Outside the Brain* (New York: Houghton Mifflin Harcourt, 2021), part 1, "Thinking with Our Bodies." The tendency to think of the body in terms of a machine is a long-standing one, with pernicious effects on our ability to live integrally as humans. On this point, see Iain McGilchrist, *The Master and His Emissary: The Divided Brain and the Making of the Western World* (New Haven: Yale University Press, 2012), 438–40.

27. George Lakeoff and Mark Johnson, *Metaphors We Live By* (Chicago: University of Chicago Press, 1980), 3.

28. Lakeoff and Johnson, *Metaphors We Live By*, 20.

29. Our psychological and personal experiences of being wounded likewise draw from the language of physical wounding. We say things like "She is scarred," or "He is raw," or "This organization is a bloody mess," or "Our friendship is ruptured." On this point, see Jennie A. McLaurin and Cymbeline Tancongco Culiat, *Designed to Heal: What the Body Shows Us about Healing Wounds, Repairing Relationships, and Restoring Community* (Carol Stream, IL: Tyndale Momentum, 2021), 24–25.

30. Matthew B. Crawford, *The World Beyond Your Head: On Becoming an Individual in an Age of Distraction* (New York: Farrar, Straus & Giroux, 2015), 51.

31. "The history of Western philosophy is, for the most part, one long development of the objectivist dismissal of metaphor, punctuated rarely by bold declarations (such as Nietzsche's) of the pervasiveness of metaphor in all thought." Johnson, *Meaning of the Body*, 187.

32. Guy Claxton, *Intelligence in the Flesh: Why Your Mind Needs Your Body Much More Than It Thinks* (New Haven: Yale University Press, 2015). See also Johnson, *Meaning of the Body*, 154.

33. "Alienation from our bodies lies at the core of our alienation from our deepest self and from the world." David Benner, *Soulful Spirituality: Becoming Fully Alive and Deeply Human* (Grand Rapids: Brazos, 2011), 82.

Chapter 3 The Story of the Body

1. Decisive texts on this account include Athanasius, *On the Incarnation*, and Irenaeus, *Against Heresies*. Susan Ashbrook Harvey summarizes the theological work that sensory rich worship performed in the fourth century this way: "Liturgy provided the terms by which ancient Christian writers negotiated the body. Liturgy, like ascetic practice, was a means by which the body was reformed and remade.... Liturgy framed the Christian perception of bodily condition, discipline, and transformation." *Scenting Salvation: Ancient Christianity and the Olfactory Imagination* (Los Angeles: University of California Press, 2006), 5.

2. Cited in Gordon Lathrop, *Holy Ground: A Liturgical Cosmology* (Minneapolis: Fortress, 2003), 92.

3. Cf. "The Nairobi Statement on Worship and Culture," https://worship.calvin.edu/resources/resource-library/nairobi-statement-on-worship-and-culture-full-text/.

4. This task has already been admirably accomplished by historians, to whose work I am indebted and whose research is cited throughout this chapter.

5. Paul F. Bradshaw, *The Search for the Origins of Christian Worship: Sources and Methods for the Study of Early Liturgy*, 2nd ed. (Oxford: Oxford University Press, 2002), is an especially helpful guide on this account, raising the sorts of questions that contemporary readers may not initially recognize as necessary but that may lead to more chastened conclusions. Andrew B. McGowan makes this astute comment: "Much of what has come down to us was written to encourage, critique, and change what Christians were doing, not to describe it." *Ancient Christian Worship: Early Church Practices in Social, Historical, and Theological Perspective* (Grand Rapids: Baker Academic, 2014), 1.

6. Bradshaw, *Search for the Origins of Christian Worship*, x. Historian Peter Brown likewise warns against the temptation to extract from church history "a single Christian 'doctrine of the body,' whether to extol it or to condemn it." *The Body and Society: Men, Women, and Sexual Renunciation in Early Christianity* (New York: Columbia University Press, 2008), xl. And according to patristic scholar Andrew Louth,

> To survey the significance of the body in Western Christianity before the Reformation is not to study an established tradition, but rather to try and trace a variety of attempts to locate and value the bodily in a society that was rarely settled but

constantly subject to changing pressures. It is also to look at attitudes to the bodily that are based on very different presuppositions from our own, so much so that one is often given to doubt whether the understanding of the bodily in this society has any real continuity with any of the ways in which we relate to the bodily. ("The Body in Western Catholic Christianity," in *Religion and the Body*, ed. Sarah Coakley [Cambridge: Cambridge University Press, 1997], 111)

7. J. G. Davies, *Liturgical Dance: An Historical, Theological and Practical Handbook* (London: SCM, 1984), 36.

8. "If until the third century it is difficult to point to other material evidence that relates to actual Christian ritual, some of the activities of the early communities can be illuminated by evidence for common practices in the wider world of the ancient Mediterranean, such as for communal dining." McGowan, *Ancient Christian Worship*, 9.

9. Davies, *Liturgical Dance*, 36–37.

10. Davies, *Liturgical Dance*, 38.

11. John K. Leonard and Nathan D. Mitchell suggest extreme caution in our reading of the vocabulary of the ancient world, which "was rather fluid when it came to describing ritual postures or gestures." *The Postures of the Assembly During the Eucharistic Prayer* (Chicago: Liturgy Training Publications, 1994), 29.

12. Martin Luther, "Sermon for the Second Sunday after the Epiphany, John 2:1–11," in *The Sermons of Martin Luther*, trans. John Nicholas Lenker et al. (Grand Rapids: Baker, 1988), 2:60. It is also available online at https://sermons.martinluther.us/sermons19.html.

13. John Chrysostom, *Homilies on Genesis* 48, as quoted in Davies, *Liturgical Dance*, 20–21.

14. McGowan, *Ancient Christian Worship*, 133.

15. Davies, *Liturgical Dance*, 25.

16. Davies, *Liturgical Dance*, 56.

17. Harvey, *Scenting Salvation*, 58. Harvey continues, "Christian ritual added the visual power of pageantry, the tactile richness of procession and prostration to the sound of choirs and the taste of the Eucharist" (58).

18. "The choice of the hours of prayer and the preference for gestures like orientation toward the east, washing of hands before prayer, taking of baths, erectness and extension of hands in prayer, patterns of kneeling, kissing, etc., were part of the Greco-Roman world before being reinterpreted to embody the Christian experience." Elochukwu E. Uzukwu, *Worship as Body Language: Introduction to Christian Worship; An African Orientation* (Collegeville, MN: Liturgical Press, 1977), 18. Cf. Leonard and Mitchell, *Postures of the Assembly*, 64.

19. Joseph Cardinal Ratzinger, *The Spirit of the Liturgy*, trans. John Saward (San Francisco: Ignatius, 2000), 185.

20. Uzukwu, *Worship as Body Language*, 6–7.

21. Sangwoo Kim, "Embodied Prayer: The Practice of Prayer as Christian Theology" (ThD diss., Duke Divinity School, 2016), 95, https://dukespace.lib.duke.edu/dspace/handle/10161/12926; see also McGowan, *Ancient Christian Worship*, 197.

22. Uzukwu, *Worship as Body Language*, 18. Cf. Geoffrey Wainwright, "The Continuing Tradition of the Church," in *The Study of Liturgy*, ed. Cheslyn Jones, Geoffrey Wainwright, Edward Yarnold, and Paul Bradshaw (New York: Oxford University Press, 1992), 554–55. See also the Congregation for the Sacraments and Divine Worship, "Dance in the Liturgy," https://www.ewtn.com/catholicism/library/dance-in-the-liturgy-2167.

23. Leonard and Mitchell, *Postures of the Assembly*, 35.

24. Ratzinger, *Spirit of the Liturgy*, 205. See also Byron D. Stuhlman, *Prayer Book Rubrics* (New York: Church Publishing, 1987), 22.

25. See Leonard and Mitchell, *Postures of the Assembly*, 69. They go on to say, "By the close of the Middle Ages, kneeling to honor the sacrament at the moment of consecration had gained ascendancy over the desire to see it" (70–71).

26. Especially helpful on this question is the work of Filipino monk Anscar J. Chupungco, specifically *Liturgical Inculturation: Sacramentals, Religiosity, and Catechesis* (Collegeville, MN: Liturgical Press, 1995). See also the excellent collection of essays in Gláucia Vasconcelos Wilkey, ed., *Worship and Culture: Foreign Country or Homeland?* (Grand Rapids: Eerdmans, 2014).

27. I write about this at length in *Glimpses of the New Creation: Worship and the Formative Power of the Arts* (Grand Rapids: Eerdmans, 2019), chap. 10, "Mother Tongues and Adjectival Tongues."

28. On this matter, see Bradshaw, *Search for the Origins of Christian Worship*, chap. 10, "The Effects of the Coming of Christendom in the Fourth Century." Bradshaw shows how baptism, once a simple ceremony, after Constantine becomes a more "hair-raising," "awe-inspiring," "theatrical" event, inasmuch as church leaders of the time appropriated the pagan liturgical vocabulary of the surrounding culture. On this point, see also Geoffrey Wainwright, "The Periods of Liturgical History," in Jones, Wainwright, Yarnold, and Bradshaw, *Study of Liturgy*, 63–64.

29. McGowan, *Ancient Christian Worship*, 193.

30. McGowan, *Ancient Christian Worship*, 55.

31. It is only in hindsight that certain liturgical practices will appear, to some, as universally binding and accepted "everywhere, always, and by all," to borrow fifth-century monk Vincent of Lérins's (in)famous phrase. On this general point, see Jaroslav Pelikan, *The Christian Tradition: A History of the Development of Doctrine*, vol. 1, *The Emergence of the Catholic Tradition (100–600)* (Chicago: University of Chicago Press, 1971), 333–39.

32. Uzukwu, *Worship as Body Language*, 10. Cf. James L. Empereur, "The Cultural Bodies of Worship," in *Bodies of Worship: Explorations in Theory and Practice*, ed. Bruce T. Morrill (Collegeville, MN: Liturgical Press, 1999), 92–95. Class distinctions undoubtedly play a role in the church's historic discomfort with dance. The privileged and aristocratic classes of the Renaissance era, for instance, aimed to perfect a kind of artless, unaffected performance. Ann Wagner remarks, "Dancing could serve not only as a popular pastime but also to distinguish people of power and privilege from the common folk. The dancing engaged in by the lower ranks of society had to occur in time free from work and, when weather permitted, on the village green. Given such limited opportunities, country dancing could only have been unrefined and spontaneous, probably often bawdy and boisterous." *Adversaries of Dance: From the Puritans to the Present* (Chicago: University of Illinois Press, 1997), 12–13.

33. "Even in the liturgy, the Church has no wish to impose a rigid uniformity in matters which do not implicate the faith or the good of the whole community; rather does she respect and foster the genius and talents of the various races and peoples. Anything in these peoples' way of life which is not indissolubly bound up with superstition and error she studies with sympathy and, if possible, preserves intact. Sometimes in fact she admits such things into the liturgy itself, so long as they harmonize with its true and authentic spirit." Vatican II, *Sacrosanctum Concilium*, December 4, 1963, available at https://www.vatican.va/archive/hist_councils/ii_vatican_council/documents/vat-ii_const_19631204_sacrosanctum-concilium_en.html.

34. Uzukwu, *Worship as Body Language*, 27.

35. See "Dutch Organ Culture during the Reformation," *The American Guild of Organists*, December 4, 2017, https://www.agohq.org/north-central-dutch-organ-culture-reformation/; Frank Senn, *Embodied Liturgy: Lessons in Christian Ritual* (Minneapolis: Fortress, 2016), 59; Edward J. Yarnold, *The Awe-Inspiring Rites of Initiation* (Collegeville, MN: Liturgical Press, 1994), 76–77; Aidan Kavanagh, *Elements of Rite: A Handbook of Liturgical Style* (Collegeville, MN: Liturgical Press, 1982), 66.

36. See Leonard and Mitchell, *Postures of the Assembly*, 78–79; Uzukwu, *Worship as Body Language*, 20–21; Howard E. Galley, *The Ceremonies of the Eucharist: A Guide to Celebration* (Cambridge, MA: Cowley Publications, 1989), 51, 63; Louis Weil, *Liturgical Sense: The Logic of Rite* (New York: Seabury, 2013), 28–30. A similar issue arises with the habit of signing oneself with the cross, for this too developed largely in popular and private devotional contexts before becoming normative and ubiquitous in the official Sunday worship of the Western church.

37. Davies, *Liturgical Dance*, 19.

38. Davies, *Liturgical Dance*, 45. See also David L. Jeffrey, *The Early English Lyric and Franciscan Spirituality* (Lincoln: University of Nebraska Press, 1975), 134; Edward Muir, *Ritual in Early Modern Europe* (Cambridge: Cambridge University Press, 2005), chap. 3, "Carnival and the Lower Body."

39. Ronald Gagne, Thomas Kane, and Robert VerEecke, *Introducing Dance in Christian Worship* (Washington, DC: Pastoral Press, 1984), 59.

40. Ratzinger, *Spirit of the Liturgy*, 198–99, argues for the former position, while Uzukwu, *Worship as Body Language*, 197–207, commends the latter view.

41. St. Basil the Great, *On the Holy Spirit*, trans. Stephen Hildebrand (Yonkers, NY: St. Vladimir's Seminary Press, 2011), 104–5.

42. Basil, *On the Holy Spirit*, 104.

43. Basil, *On the Holy Spirit*, 106.

44. Carlos Eire, *War against the Idols: The Reformation of Worship from Erasmus to Calvin* (Cambridge: Cambridge University Press, 1986), 231–32.

45. Kallistos Ware, "'My Helper and My Enemy': The Body in Greek Christianity," in Coakley, *Religion and the Body*, 91.

46. Ware, "'My Helper and My Enemy,'" 99.

47. Caroline Walker Bynum, *Holy Feast and Holy Fast: The Religious Significance of Food to Medieval Women* (Los Angeles: University of California Press, 1987), 216. Equally helpful on this account is her book *Fragmentation and Redemption: Essays on Gender and the Human Body in Medieval Religion* (New York: Zone Books, 1991), esp. chap. 5. Similar issues befall non-White, marginalized, and disabled bodies. See, e.g., Willie James Jennings, *The Christian Imagination: Theology and the Origins of Race* (New Haven: Yale University Press, 2010); Esau McCaulley, "Toward a Black Anthropology and Social Ethic: Why the Humanity and Jewishness of Jesus Matters," in *Who Do You Say I Am? On the Humanity of Jesus*, ed. George Kalantzis, David B. Capes, and Ty Kieser (Eugene, OR: Cascade Books, 2020), 143–57; Khalia J. Williams, "Love Your Flesh: The Power and Protest of Embodied Worship," *Liturgy* 35, no 1 (2020): 3–9; Jana Bennett, "Women, Disabled," in *Disability in the Christian Tradition: A Reader*, ed. Brian Brock and John Swinton (Grand Rapids: Eerdmans, 2012), 427–66.

48. Bynum, *Holy Feast and Holy Fast*, 262. Bynum also shows how this tale is far more complicated, and more hopeful even, than certain historians and theologians have perhaps allowed.

49. Tertullian, *Tertullian's Treatises Concerning Prayer and Baptism*, trans. Alexander Souter (London: SPCK, 1919), 32, also available at https://www.tertullian.org/articles

/souter_orat_bapt/souter_orat_bapt_03prayer.htm. Tertullian felt rather differently about the custom of sitting after the prayers. This, he felt, ought to be prohibited, since it reflected a pagan and irreligious habit rather than a distinctly Christian one. The Council of Nicaea, a century or so later, would eventually explicitly forbid kneeling in church on Sundays as well as on the fifty days of Eastertide.

50. Augustine, *Responses to Miscellaneous Questions*, trans. Boniface Ramsey (Hyde Park, NY: New City Press, 2008), 228.

Chapter 4 The Benediction of the Body

1. I chronicle this way of viewing the body in my book, W. David O. Taylor, *The Theater of God's Glory: Calvin, Creation, and the Liturgical Arts* (Grand Rapids: Eerdmans, 2017). For more on musical instruments in the early centuries of the church, see James W. McKinnon, ed., *Music in Early Christian Literature* (Cambridge: Cambridge University Press, 1987), chap. 4.

2. Jeremy S. Begbie, *Resounding Truth: Christian Wisdom in the World of Music* (Grand Rapids: Baker Academic, 2007), 188.

3. Augustine, *Lecture or Tractates on the Gospel according to St. John*, trans. John Gibb (Edinburgh: T&T Clark, 1873–1874), 5, as quoted in David Clines, "The Image of God in Man," *Tyndale Bulletin* 19 (1968): 86.

4. P. Humbert, *Etudes sure le récit du paradis et de la chute dans la Genèse* (Neuchâtel: Secretariat de l'Université Neuchâtel, 1940), 157, quoted in Clines, "The Image of God in Man," 56. For an excellent summary of ancient Near Eastern background literature, see Werner H. Schmidt, *Die Schöpfungsgeschichte der Priesterschrift* (Neukirchen-Vluyn: Neukirchener Verlag, 1964), 127–49; see also H. Wildeberger, "Das Abbild Gottes," *Theologischer Zeitschrift* 21 (1965): 245–59.

5. Claus Westermann, *Genesis 1–11: A Commentary*, trans. John J. Scullion (Minneapolis: Augsburg, 1984), 150. So too T. C. Vriezen, *An Outline of Old Testament Theology* (Newton, MA: Charles T. Branford, 1970), 49. See also Gerhard von Rad, *Old Testament Theology*, trans. D. M. G. Stalker (New York: Harper & Row, 1962), 1:58. This reading of the Genesis narrative is strengthened, among other ways, on philological grounds. On this point, see Emil Kautzsch, ed., *Gesenius' Hebrew Grammar*, trans. A. E. Cowley (1910; repr. Oxford: Clarendon, 1976), 379; M. O'Conner and Bruce K. Waltke, *An Introduction to Biblical Hebrew Syntax* (Winona Lake, IN: Eisenbrauns, 1990), 198; Cyrus Gordon, "'In' of Predication or Equivalence," *Journal of Biblical Literature* 100 (1981): 612–13.

6. Clines, "The Image of God in Man," 80, see also 72–79. So too Schmidt, *Schöpfungeschichte*, 143n1. Contra this view, Phyllis A. Bird, "'Male and Female He Created Them': Gen 1:27b in the Context of the Priestly Account of Creation," *Harvard Theological Review* 74, no. 2 (1981): 138n22; and Westermann, *Genesis 1–11*, 145.

7. Lawson G. Stone, "The Soul: Possession, Part, or Person? The Genesis of Human Nature in Genesis 2:7," in *What about the Soul? Neuroscience and Christian Anthropology*, ed. Joel B. Green (Nashville: Abingdon, 2004), 49. See also Meredith G. Kline, "Creation in the Image of the Glory-Spirit," *Westminster Theological Journal* 39 (1977): 268.

8. John W. Kleinig, *Wonderfully Made: A Protestant Theology of the Body* (Bellingham, WA: Lexham, 2021), 29.

9. Gordon J. Wenham, "Sanctuary Symbolism in the Garden of Eden Story," in *Proceedings of the 9th World Congress of Jewish Studies* 9 (1986): 399. Jon D. Levenson adds: "Like temples, [gardens] are walled off from quotidian reality, with all its instability and irregularity and the threats these pose, and thus they readily convey an intimation

of immortality." *Resurrection and the Restoration of Israel: The Ultimate Victory of the God of Life* (New Haven: Yale University Press, 2006), 86–87.

10. Wenham, "Sanctuary Symbolism," 401.

11. See also Exod. 25:18–25; 1 Kings 6:29.

12. Peter Enns argues in *The Evolution of Adam: What the Bible Does and Doesn't Say about Human Beings* (Grand Rapids: Brazos, 2012), that Israel's temple informs its narrative of the creation story, not the other way around (73).

13. "When Genesis indicates that God rested on the seventh day, it tells us that in this account of the functional origins of the cosmos, the cosmos is being portrayed as a temple." John H. Walton, "Creation in Genesis 1:1–2:3 and the Ancient Near East: Order Out of Disorder after *Chaoskampf*," *Calvin Theological Journal* 43 (2008): 61.

14. The parallels between Gen. 1 and Exod. 25–40 are also seen by many scholars to reinforce the intimate relationship between *cosmos* and *cultus*. Work in both domains is *completed*; the Spirit of God *hovers* over both labors; the architects of both projects (God, Moses) *see* the work unfolding and then *bless* the *finished* work. Cf. P. J. Kearney, "Creation and Liturgy: The P Redaction of Ex 25–40," *Zeitschrift für die alttestamentliche Wissenschaft* 89 (1977): 375–78.

15. John Calvin, *Institutes of the Christian Religion*, ed. John T. McNeill, trans. Ford Lewis Battles (Philadelphia: Westminster, 1960), I.5.9. Cf. Taylor, *Theater of God's Glory*, chap. 5, "The Double Movement of Creation in Worship."

16. N. T. Wright, *The Resurrection of the Son of God* (Minneapolis: Fortress, 2003), 283. Cf. Marc Cortez, *Theological Anthropology: A Guide for the Perplexed* (London: T&T Clark International, 2010), 69–70.

17. See F. LeRon Shults, *Reforming Theological Anthropology: After the Philosophical Turn to Relationality* (Grand Rapids: Eerdmans, 2003), 164.

18. N. T. Wright, "Mind, Spirit, Soul and Body: All for One and One for All—Reflections on Paul's Anthropology in His Complex Contexts," paper presented at the Society of Christian Philosophers (Fordham University, March 18, 2011), 14. Wright identifies seven types of dualism that might be compatible with ancient Jewish thought: heavenly, theological, moral, eschatological, epistemological, sectarian, and psychological. A duality, however, is not to be readily equated or confused with a dualism.

19. For the disproportionately large role that "image of God" language has played in Christian theology, it is remarkable how rarely the phrase appears in the Old Testament, all of them in the early chapters of Genesis (1:26, 27 [twice]; 5:1; and 9:6). On this point, see Bird, "'Male and Female He Created Them,'" 130.

20. See W. David O. Taylor, *Open and Unafraid: The Psalms as a Guide to Life* (Nashville: Thomas Nelson, 2020), chap. 8, "Joy."

21. "In many cultures, the integral connection between the behavior involved in making music and the sound itself is clear. . . . In these settings, to make music is to dance, to move." Mary E. McGann, *Exploring Music as Worship and Theology: An Interdisciplinary Method for Studying Liturgical Practice* (Collegeville, MN: Liturgical Press, 2002), 22.

22. Tertullian, *On the Resurrection of the Flesh* 7.13–14, as quoted in Mayra Rivera, *Poetics of the Flesh* (Durham, NC: Duke University Press, 2015), 47.

23. Noteworthy here is the similarity of language that shows up in Job 2:5, where Satan challenges God to "stretch out with your hand now and touch his bone and his flesh, and he will curse you to your face."

24. Strictly speaking, which is to say metaphysically speaking, Jesus can perform his entire mission of redemption and reconciliation apart from any physical contact with others. He could simply speak a word and it would be so. This is what occurs with the healing

of the centurion's servant in Matt. 8. In response to the soldier's request, Jesus agrees to come and to cure the servant in person. But the centurion balks at Jesus's offer. "Lord, I am not worthy to have you come under my roof," he responds, "but only speak the word, and my servant will be healed" (v. 8). Amazed at the centurion's words, Jesus agrees to the centurion's terms for healing. He says, "Go; let it be done for you according to your faith" (v. 13). And as the gospel writer tells us, the servant is healed in that very moment—at a distance and on account of Jesus's direct statement. Such also is the case with the healing of the Syrophoenician woman's daughter in Matt. 15:21–28, the royal official's son in John 4:46–54, the man with the withered hand in Mark 3:5, and the Gerasene demoniac in Mark 5:1–20. Among other reasons, such touchless declarations give evidence in the Gospels to Jesus's sovereign power over all forces of chaos. But these three instances prove to be the exception to the rule. On healing as a primary Christological category, see Diane B. Stinton, *Jesus of Africa: Voices of Contemporary African Christology* (New York: Orbis Books, 2004), 54–108.

25. "When I touch," writes Rivera, "I am always, *necessarily* touched by what I touch." *Poetics of the Flesh*, 106 (emphasis in original).

26. "Letting her hair down in this setting would have been on a par with appearing topless in public, for example. She would have appeared to be fondling Jesus's feet, like a prostitute or a slave girl accustomed to providing sexual favors. It is no wonder that Simon entertains serious reservations about Jesus's status as a holy man. Even if her actions will receive a different interpretation with the narrative, within her Palestinian world they were obviously susceptible to this reading." Joel B. Green, *The Gospel of Luke* (Grand Rapids: Eerdmans, 1997), 302. See also Kenneth E. Bailey, *Jesus through Middle Eastern Eyes: Cultural Studies in the Gospels* (Downers Grove, IL: InterVarsity, 2008), 248–49.

27. Rainer Maria Rilke, *Diaries of a Young Poet* (New York: Norton, 1998), 123.

28. Paul J. Griffiths, *Christian Flesh* (Stanford, CA: Stanford University Press, 2018), 35.

29. Martin Luther, *Sermons on the Gospel of St. John*, as quoted in Kleinig, *Wonderfully Made*, 78.

30. At death we return to the dust from whence we were made (Gen. 3:19; Eccles. 3:20; Ps. 104:29), and once again our skin is enveloped by the dirt, the humus, from whence we were made.

31. Lore Ferguson Wilbert does an excellent job unpacking this aspect of Jesus's ministry in *Handle with Care: How Jesus Redeems the Power of Touch in Life and Ministry* (Nashville: B&H, 2020). See also Ola Sigurdson, *Heavenly Bodies: Incarnation, the Gaze, and Embodiment in Christian Theology*, trans. Carl Olsen (Grand Rapids: Eerdmans, 2016), 13.

32. See Griffiths, *Christian Flesh*, 146.

33. See, e.g., Wilbert, "Afterword: A Letter to Those Who Have Been Abused," in *Handle with Care*, 233–37.

Chapter 5 The Future of the Body

1. I argue the point of this chapter at greater length in W. David O. Taylor, *The Theater of God's Glory: Calvin, Creation, and the Liturgical Arts* (Grand Rapids: Eerdmans, 2017), chaps. 8 and 9. Scholars who follow this interpretive tradition include James D. G. Dunn, *The Parting of the Ways: Between Christianity and Judaism and Their Significance for the Character of Christianity* (London: SCM, 1991), 93; James Montgomery Boice, *The Gospel of John* (Grand Rapids: Zondervan, 1985), 253; Ernst Haenchen, *John 1*, trans. Robert W. Funk (Philadelphia: Fortress, 1984), 223; George Johnston, *The Spirit-Paraclete in the Gospel of John*, Society for New Testament Studies Monograph Series 12 (Cambridge: Cambridge University Press, 1970), 46.

2. John Piper, "Worship God," sermon given on November 9, 1997, available at http://www.desiringgod.org/ResourceLibrary/TopicIndex/60/1016_Worship_God/.

3. See D. Moody Smith, "John," in *The Harper Collins Bible Commentary*, ed. James L. Mays (San Francisco: HarperSanFrancisco, 1988), 956–86; E. C. Hoskyns, *The Fourth Gospel* (London: Faber & Faber, 1947); Dorothy A. Lee, *The Symbolic Narratives of the Fourth Gospel: The Interplay of Form and Meaning*, Library of New Testament Studies (Sheffield: Sheffield Academic, 1994).

4. Marianne Meye Thompson, *The God of the Gospel of John* (Grand Rapids: Eerdmans, 2001), 216–17. Similarly, Gary M. Burge, *The Anointed Community: The Holy Spirit in the Johannine Tradition* (Grand Rapids: Eerdmans, 1987), esp. 164; Rudolf Schnackenburg, *The Gospel according to St. John* (New York: Seabury, 1968), 1:437; J. Ramsey Michaels, *The Gospel of John*, New International Commentary on the New Testament (Grand Rapids: Eerdmans, 2010), 253; Herman Ridderbos, *The Gospel of John: A Theological Commentary*, trans. John Vriend (Grand Rapids: Eerdmans, 1991), 163, 164.

5. C. K. Barrett asserts that "this clause [i.e., 4:23] has perhaps as much claim as 20:30f. to be regarded as expressing the purpose of the gospel." *The Gospel according to St. John*, 2nd ed. (Philadelphia: Westminster, 1978), 238. See also Benny Thettayil, *In Spirit and Truth: An Exegetical Study of John 4:19–26 and a Theological Investigation of the Replacement Theme in the Fourth Gospel* (Leuven: Peeters, 2007).

6. So, e.g., Louis Berkhof, *Systematic Theology*, rev. ed. (Grand Rapids: Eerdmans, 1996), 42, 66.

7. Leon Morris, *The Gospel according to John*, rev. ed. (Grand Rapids: Eerdmans, 1995), 236.

8. Lesslie Newbigin, *The Light Has Come: An Exposition of the Fourth Gospel* (Grand Rapids: Eerdmans, 1982), 53. For actualist interpretations, see, among others, Hoskyns, *Fourth Gospel*, 244; Schnackenburg, *St. John*, 437; Smith, "John," 964; Michaels, *Gospel of John*, 253; Burge, *Anointed Community,* 147.

9. Thettayil, *In Spirit and Truth*, 124, identifies the various arguments surrounding the anarthrous use of *pneuma*. He reasons, rightly I believe, that the definite article is implied and that a definite Spirit, not any spirit, is in view.

10. Cf. Thettayil, *In Spirit and Truth*, 43–105.

11. Barrett, *Gospel according to St. John*, 238; Johnston, *Spirit-Paraclete in the Gospel of John*, 15. Burge argues that "personal efforts and ambitions" might be seen to replace the power of God. *Anointed Community*, 192.

12. On this point, see W. D. Davies, "Reflections on Aspects of the Jewish Background of the Gospel of John," in *Exploring the Gospel of John: In Honor of D. Moody Smith*, ed. R. Alan Culpepper and C. Clifton Black (Louisville: Westminster John Knox, 1996), 43–64.

13. See, e.g., Terry Johnson, *Reformed Worship: Worship That Is according to Scripture* (Jackson, MS: Reformed Academic Press, 2000), 21.

14. This is an argument made by B. F. Westcott, *The Gospel according to John* (Grand Rapids: Eerdmans, 1958), 73.

15. James D. G. Dunn, *Jesus and the Spirit: A Study of the Religious and Charismatic Experience of Jesus and the First Christians as Reflected in the New Testament* (London: SCM, 1975), 353.

16. Instances of the language of "Spirit" alone include John 1:32, 33; 3:5, 6, 8, 34; 4:23, 24; 6:63; 7:39; while the phrase "Holy Spirit" appears in 1:33; 14:26; 20:22.

17. See Thettayil, *In Spirit and Truth*, 128–30, 159.

18. Cf. Anthony C. Thiselton, *The Holy Spirit: In Biblical Teaching, through the Centuries, and Today* (Grand Rapids: Eerdmans, 2013), 138.

19. Frederick Dale Bruner, *The Gospel of John: A Commentary* (Grand Rapids: Eerdmans, 2012), 264 (emphasis in original). So also Stephen T. Um, *The Theme of Temple Christology in John's Gospel*, Library of New Testament Studies (London: T&T Clark, 2006), 17.

20. Gordon Fee offers a perceptive analysis of the way in which English-language Bibles, starting with the King James Version (1611) all the way through to modern versions, have translated *pneuma* in the New Testament. See his "Translational Tendenz: English Versions of *Pneuma* in Paul," in *The Holy Spirit and Christian Origins: Essays in Honor of James D. G. Dunn*, eds. Graham N. Stanton, Bruce W. Longenecker, and Stephen C. Barton (Grand Rapids: Eerdmans, 2004), 349–59.

21. C. H. Dodd, *The Interpretation of the Fourth Gospel* (Cambridge: Cambridge University Press, 1958), 223.

22. Johnston, *Spirit-Paraclete in the Gospel of John*, 45. See also Andreas J. Köstenberger, *John*, Baker Exegetical Commentary on the New Testament (Grand Rapids: Baker Academic, 2004), 157.

23. Michaels, *Gospel of John*, 255. See also Rodney Whitacre, in *John*, The IVP New Testament Commentary Series (Downers Grove, IL: IVP Academic, 1999), 106, who sums up this interpretive tradition.

24. Both Rudolf Bultmann, *The Gospel of John* (Philadelphia: Westminster, 1971), 190, and David E. Aune, *The Cultic Setting of Realized Eschatology in Early Christianity* (Leiden: Brill, 1972), 104, argue against this reading.

25. Raymond E. Brown, *The Gospel according to John*, Anchor Bible (Garden City, NY: Doubleday, 1966), 1:180. To this we might add that in the same way that, in John's Gospel, Jesus is the hypostasized *Logos* of God, so the Paraclete is the hypostasized *Pneuma* of God.

26. Explicit language of heart in John appears in few contexts, mainly related to emotional conditions, e.g., 14:27; 16:6, 22. John 12:38–41, citing Isa. 6:9–10, describes the work of God on the human heart.

27. D. A. Carson, *The Gospel According to John* (Grand Rapids: Eerdmans, 1991), 225–26, comes close to this sense but muddles a trinitarian reading with his choice of terms and irregular capitalizations, which render the Spirit in impersonal terms, while the Word is rendered in more personal ones.

28. John Marsh, *Saint John*, Pelican Gospel Commentaries (Hammondsworth, UK: Penguin Books, 1968), 218.

29. Thompson, *God of the Gospel of John*, 215, over against, say, R. C. H. Lenski, *The Interpretation of St. John's Gospel* (Minneapolis: Augsburg, 1961), 322.

30. Cf. Felix Porsch, *Pneuma und Wort: Ein exegetischer Beitrag zur Pneumatologie des Johannesevangeliums* (Frankfurt am Main: Josef Knecht, 1974), 159; Dorothy A. Lee, "In the Spirit of Truth: Worship and Prayer in the Gospel of John and the Early Fathers," *Vigiliae Christianae* 58 (2004): 280.

31. Thiselton, *Holy Spirit*, 143; cf. Thettayil, *In Spirit and Truth*, 158.

32. C. John Collins, "John 4:23–24, 'In Spirit and Truth': An Idiomatic Proposal," *Presbyterion* 21 (1995): 120–21. Collins believes that Jesus's statement to the Samaritan woman, that "real" worshipers will worship in spirit indicates in the inner self, "that is to say, in reality."

33. A. Boyd Luter Jr., "'Worship' as Service: The New Testament Usage of *Latreuo*," *Criswell Theological Review* 2 (1988): 339–40.

34. A trinitarian reading of the text is far from new. Such a reading goes back to Athanasius, Basil, Hilary, Cyril of Alexandria, and Ambrose. Cf. McHugh, *John 1–4*, 312–14. See also Anthony J. Casurella's excellent treatment of the Paraclete passages in the writings

of the church fathers in *The Johannine Paraclete in the Church Fathers: A Study in the History of Exegesis* (Tübingen: Mohr Siebeck, 1983).

35. Cf. Lee, "In the Spirit of Truth," 287–92. See also Smith, "John," 964; Burge, *Anointed Community*, 197; Schnackenburg, *St. John*, 438–40; Thompson, *God of the Gospel of John*, 214–16.

36. On this point, see Lee, "In the Spirit of Truth," 296; N. T. Wright, "Worship and the Spirit in the New Testament," in *The Spirit in Worship—Worship in the Spirit*, ed. Teresa Berger and Bryan D. Spinks (Collegeville, MN: Liturgical Press, 2009), 11; R. G. Gruenler, *The Trinity in the Gospel of John: A Thematic Commentary on the Fourth Gospel* (Grand Rapids: Baker, 1986).

37. Cf. Richard J. Bauckham, "James and the Jerusalem Church," in *The Book of Acts in Its Palestinian Setting*, ed. Richard Bauckham (Grand Rapids: Eerdmans, 1995), 425.

38. Thettayil, *In Spirit and Truth*, 122.

39. Cf. Wright, "Worship and the Spirit," 23.

40. John Calvin, *Institutes of the Christian Religion*, ed. John T. McNeill, trans. Ford Lewis Battles (Philadelphia: Westminster, 1960), 4.17.9.

41. Richard B. Hays, "The Materiality of John's Symbolic World," in *Preaching John's Gospel: The World It Imagines*, ed. David Fleer and Dave Bland (St. Louis: Chalice, 2008), 6 (emphasis in original).

42. This is a point Marianne Maye Thompson persuasively argues in "Reflections on Worship in the Gospel of John," *The Princeton Seminary Bulletin* 19 (1998): 259–78.

43. Calvin, *Institutes*, 4.17.10.

44. See Um, *Theme of Temple Christology*, 18; Lee, "In the Spirit of Truth," 284.

45. "The biblical writers do engage questions regarding the nature of humanity, but they do so implicitly." Joel B. Green, *Body, Soul, and Human Life: The Nature of Humanity in the Bible* (Grand Rapids: Baker Academic, 2008), 46. On the variety of terms that the Old Testament uses to describe the human person, see Robert A. Di Vito, "Here One Need Not Be Oneself: The Concept of 'Self' in the Hebrew Scriptures," in *The Whole and Divided Self: The Bible and Theological Anthropology*, ed. John McCarthy (New York: Crossroad, 1997), 49–88. See also Robert Jewett, *Paul's Anthropological Terms: A Study of Their Use in Conflict Settings*, Arbeiten zur Geschichte des antiken Judentums und des Urchristentums 10 (Leiden: Brill, 1971), 447.

46. Rivera argues in *Poetics of the Flesh* that the idea of a whole body is a fiction socially constructed by one group to exercise power over another. She contends that "the flourishing of diverse forms and capacities of human embodiment requires communities that recognize their inter-dependence, shared vulnerability, and the social obligation to provide the conditions to sustain carnal vitality" (7). While the body is undoubtedly subject to socially and culturally constructed ideas, Rivera takes the argument too far and falsely pits "body" and "flesh" language against each other in a way that is biblically unwarranted.

47. John Calvin, "Commentary on Romans 6:12," in *Calvin's Old Testament Commentaries*, trans. T. H. L. Parker (Edinburgh: T&T Clark, 1986). Cf. Robert H. Gundry, *Soma in Biblical Theology with Emphasis on Pauline Anthropology* (Cambridge: Cambridge University Press, 1976), 58.

48. Conversely, there is no corresponding language in Paul about a "mind of sin" or a "heart of death" or a paradoxical "carnal soul." As Jewett rightly argues in *Paul's Anthropological Terms*, however, in Romans the body is dead on account of sin, not on account of its materiality (297).

49. Cf. Udo Schnelle, *The Human Condition: Anthropology in the Teachings of Jesus, Paul, and John* (Minneapolis: Fortress, 1996), 56–57.

50. Gundry, Soma in Biblical Theology, 35.

51. Schnelle, *Human Condition*, 57. Cf. Ola Sigurdson, *Heavenly Bodies: Incarnation, the Gaze, and Embodiment in Christian Theology*, trans. Carl Olsen (Grand Rapids: Eerdmans, 2017), 371. Jewett makes the point that "unlike the word 'flesh,' *soma* can be used to depict the whole scope of salvation including the resurrection (Rom. 8:11) and redemption (Rom. 8:23) of the body and the bodily worship in the world (Rom. 12:1), which is the form of ethical activity the new aeon inaugurates and requires. The agent of this somatic salvation is the 'body of Christ' (Rom. 7:4) whose death and resurrection marked the turning of the aeons." *Paul's Anthropological Terms*, 457.

52. Jewett, *Paul's Anthropological Terms*, 261. See also Bill T. Arnold, "Soul-Searching Questions about 1 Samuel 28: Samuel's Appearance at Endor and Christian Anthropology," in *What about the Soul? Neuroscience and Christian Anthropology*, ed. Joel B. Green (Nashville: Abingdon, 2004), 78.

53. Calvin, *Institutes*, 1.11.8.

54. N. T. Wright, *The Resurrection of the Son of God* (Minneapolis: Fortress, 2003), 231.

55. Cf. Joel B. Green, "Eschatology and the Nature of Humans: A Reconsideration of Pertinent Biblical Evidence," *Science and Christian Belief* 14 (2002): 33–50.

56. Wright, *Resurrection of the Son of God*, 290.

57. "The resurrection is thus the anticipatory realization of the eschatological destiny of the whole creation." Colin Gunton, *The Triune Creator: A Historical and Systematic Study* (Grand Rapids: Eerdmans, 1998), 224. See also David Wilkinson, *Christian Eschatology and the Physical Universe* (London: T&T Clark, 2010), esp. chap. 7, "The Future of Matter."

58. Cf. Taylor, *Theater of God's Glory*, chap. 7, "A Trinitarian Theology of the Physical Body."

59. Cf. Lesslie Newbigin, *The Gospel in a Pluralist Society* (Grand Rapids: Eerdmans, 1989), 235; W. David O. Taylor, *Glimpses of the New Creation: Worship and the Formative Power of the Arts* (Grand Rapids: Eerdmans, 2019), 14.

60. John W. Kleinig, *Wonderfully Made: A Protestant Theology of the Body* (Bellingham, WA: Lexham, 2021), 137.

Chapter 6 The True Image of the Body

1. James D. G. Dunn, "1 Corinthians 15:45—Last Adam, Life-Giving Spirit," in *Christ and the Spirit in the New Testament: Studies in Honour of C. F. D. Moule*, ed. Barnabas Lindars and Stephen S. Smalley (Cambridge: Cambridge University Press, 1973), 140–41.

2. Karl Barth, *Church Dogmatics* III.1, trans. J. W. Edwards, O. Bussey, and Harold Knight (Edinburgh: T&T Clark, 1958), 346.

3. Robert Farrar Capon, *The Romance of the Word: One Man's Love Affair with Theology* (Grand Rapids: Eerdmans, 1995), 176–77.

4. Capon, *Romance of the Word*, 177.

5. Cf. W. David O. Taylor, *The Theater of God's Glory: Calvin, Creation, and the Liturgical Arts* (Grand Rapids: Eerdmans, 2017), chap. 2, "The Work of the Material Creation"; chap. 3, "The Work of the Material Symbols"; and chap. 5, "The Double Movement of Creation in Worship." See also Norman Wirzba, "Created Out of Nothing Means Created Out of Love," *The Christian Century*, November 1, 2021, https://www.christiancentury.org/article/critical-essay/created-out-nothing-means-created-out-love.

6. Cf. Makoto Fujimura, *Art and Faith: A Theology of Making* (New Haven: Yale University Press, 2020), chap. 2.

7. This is the title of a song by the musical group Passion, featuring Chris Tomlin: https://www.youtube.com/watch?v=R-WOneEXr00.

8. For a summary of this general point, see Sean M. McDonough, *Creation and New Creation: Understanding God's Creation Project* (Peabody, MA: Hendrickson, 2016), 50–57. Ian A. McFarland makes this poignant remark: "That God should not only bring creatures into being but also be present to and for them is grace upon grace." *The Word Made Flesh: A Theology of the Incarnation* (Louisville: Westminster John Knox, 2019), 75.

9. See Andy Crouch, *Culture Making: Recovering Our Creative Calling* (Downers Grove, IL: InterVarsity, 2013), 101–17.

10. Jeremy S. Begbie, *Resounding Truth: Christian Wisdom in the World of Music* (Grand Rapids: Baker Academic, 2007), 194–95.

11. No empirical investigation supports this theological conclusion. To use the language of John's Gospel, it must be revealed "from above" (3:3).

12. On this point, see Mark Johnson, *The Body in the Mind: The Bodily Basis of Meaning, Imagination, and Reason* (Chicago: University of Chicago Press, 1990); Joel B. Green, *In Search of the Soul: Perspectives on the Body-Soul Problem* (Eugene, OR: Wipf & Stock, 2010).

13. "The incarnation, no less than creation, is a work of grace. Nothing compels God to take flesh." McFarland, *Word Made Flesh*, 74.

14. It is noteworthy that *sōmata* of Rev. 18:13 carries with it the connotation of "human beings."

15. We witness such actions in John 9, where Jesus, without any apparent necessity to do so, uses mud and spit to heal the man born blind.

16. McFarland, *Word Made Flesh*, 74.

17. John W. Kleinig, *Wonderfully Made: A Protestant Theology of the Body* (Bellingham, WA: Lexham Press, 2021), 64–65.

18. As I argue in Taylor, *Theater of God's Glory*, 126–27, this is the work of the Holy Spirit. Cf. Willie James Jennings, "'He Became Truly Human': Incarnation, Emancipation, and Authentic Humanity," *Modern Theology* 12 (1996): 239–55.

19. Paul J. Griffiths, *Christian Flesh* (Stanford, CA: Stanford University Press, 2018), 27.

20. Cf. Michelle Voss Roberts, *Body Parts: A Theological Anthropology* (Minneapolis: Fortress, 2017), 122.

21. Cf. Günter Thomas, "Resurrection to New Life: Pneumatological Implications of the Eschatological Transition," in *Resurrection: Theological and Scientific Assessments*, ed. Ted Peters, Robert John Russell, and Michael Welker (Grand Rapids: Eerdmans, 2002), 270.

22. Cf. Kelly M. Kapic, *You're Only Human: How Your Limits Reflect God's Design and Why That's Good News* (Grand Rapids: Brazos, 2022).

23. On the crucial difference between the language of "limited" (which usually involves negative connotations) and "limits" (which might be regarded more positively within the realm of theology), see Deborah Beth Creamer, *Disability and Christian Theology: Embodied Limits and Constructive Possibilities* (Oxford: Oxford University Press, 2008), 93–94.

24. On this point, see Marianne Meye Thompson, *The God of the Gospel of John* (Grand Rapids: Eerdmans, 2001), 115.

25. Anthony C. Thiselton, *The First Epistle to the Corinthians: A Commentary on the Greek Text*, New International Greek Testament Commentary (Grand Rapids: Eerdmans, 2000), 1276–81. See also Alan G. Padgett, "The Body in Resurrection: Science and Scripture on the 'Spiritual Body' (1 Cor 15:35–58)," *Word & World* 22 (2002): 155–63.

26. Jeremy S. Begbie, "Looking to the Future: A Hopeful Subversion," in *For the Beauty of the Church: Casting a Vision for the Arts*, ed. W. David O. Taylor (Grand Rapids: Baker

Books, 2010), 198n6. Cf. Anthony C. Thiselton, *The Holy Spirit: In Biblical Teaching, through the Centuries, and Today* (Grand Rapids: Eerdmans, 2013), 80.

27. From Charles Wesley's hymn, "Lo! He Comes with Clouds Descending," available at https://hymnary.org/text/lo_he_comes_with_clouds_descending_once.

28. Udo Schnelle, *The Human Condition: Anthropology in the Teachings of Jesus, Paul, and John* (Minneapolis: Fortress, 1996), 59.

29. Cf. Julie Canlis, *Calvin's Ladder: A Spiritual Theology of Ascent and Ascension* (Grand Rapids: Eerdmans, 2010), 117. See also Steven R. Guthrie, *Creator Spirit: The Holy Spirit and the Art of Becoming Human* (Grand Rapids: Baker Academic, 2011), 69.

30. John Calvin, "Commentary on 1 Peter 2:5," in *Calvin's Old Testament Commentaries*, trans. T. H. L. Parker (Edinburgh: T&T Clark, 1986).

31. John Calvin, *Institutes of the Christian Religion*, ed. John T. McNeill, trans. Ford Lewis Battles (Philadelphia: Westminster, 1960), 4.17.2.

32. Quoted in McFarland, *Word Made Flesh*, 212.

33. Irenaeus, *Against Heresies* 5.2.2, quoted in David N. Power and Michael Downey, *Living the Justice of the Triune God* (Collegeville, MN: Liturgical Press, 2012), 113.

34. "This is what is new and distinctive about the Christian liturgy: God himself acts and does what is essential. He inaugurates the new creation, makes himself accessible to us, so that, through the things of the earth, through our gifts, we can communicate with him in a personal way." Joseph Cardinal Ratzinger, *The Spirit of the Liturgy*, trans. John Saward (San Francisco: Ignatius, 2000), 173.

35. Quoted in Kleinig, *Wonderfully Made*, 84.

36. Tertullian, *On the Resurrection of the Flesh* 8, as quoted in Nathan Mitchell, "The Poetics of Space," *Worship* 67, no. 4 (1993): 364.

37. Kleinig, *Wonderfully Made*, 70.

38. Ignatius of Antioch (c. 35–c. 110) writes that the Eucharist serves as "the medicine of immortality" and an antidote against the fatal effects of sin. As quoted in Alister E. McGrath, *Christian Theology: An Introduction*, 6th ed. (West Sussex, UK: Wiley Blackwell, 2017), 388.

Chapter 7 The Nature of the Body

1. See JoLyn Seitz, "The Importance of Skin-to-Skin with Baby after Delivery," *Stanford Health*, July 18, 2017, https://news.sanfordhealth.org/childrens/the-importance-of-skin-to-skin-after-delivery-you-should-know/. See also Guy Claxton, *Intelligence in the Flesh: Why Your Mind Needs Your Body Much More Than It Thinks* (New Haven: Yale University Press, 2015), 57.

2. Lise Eliot, *What's Going On in There? How the Brain and the Mind Develop in the First Five Years of Life* (New York: Bantam Books, 1999), 157.

3. Avery Gilbert, *What the Nose Knows: The Science of Scent in Everyday Life* (New York: Crown Publishers, 2008), 234.

4. Eliot, *What's Going On in There?*, 165.

5. Matthew Cobb, *Smell: A Very Short Introduction* (Oxford: Oxford University Press, 2020), 67. See also Gilbert, *What the Nose Knows*, 189–204. Scientists point out that we do not actually smell with our noses. We smell with our brains. Gilbert writes, "The sensory cells in our nose convert a chemical signal (the molecule) into an electrical signal (a nerve impulse) that travels up the olfactory nerves to the brain for interpretation." *What the Nose Knows*, 26. Cf. Eliot, *What's Going On in There?*, 158.

6. The word "scent" comes to us from the French *sentir* (to perceive or to smell), which is closely related to the term "sensory," from the Latin verb *sentire* (to feel). On sin and

smell, see Jonathan Reinarz, *Past Scents: Historical Perspectives on Smell* (Chicago: University of Illinois Press, 2014), 43–45.

7. Ambrose, *Sacraments* 1.3, in *Saint Ambrose, Theological and Dogmatic Works*, trans. R. J. Deferrari (Washington, DC: Catholic University of America Press, 1963), 270, quoted in Susan Ashbrook Harvey, *Scenting Salvation: Ancient Christianity and the Olfactory Imagination* (Los Angeles: University of California Press, 2006), 71.

8. Serapian of Thmuis, *Bishop Sarapion's Prayer-Book*, trans. John Wordsworth (Hamden, CN: Archon Books, 1964), 77; quoted in James F. White, *Documents of Christian Worship: Descriptive and Interpretive Sources* (Louisville: Westminster John Knox, 1992), 222.

9. Cf. Harvey, *Scenting Salvation*, 77.

10. In certain Japanese contexts, the goal with natural arrangements of flowers is to "let flowers express themselves," which is the literal translation of *ikebana*. On this point, see Yuriko Saito, "Letting Objects Speak: Beauty in the Japanese Artistic Tradition," in *Artistic Visions and the Promise of Beauty: Cross-Cultural Perspectives*, ed. Kathleen M. Higgins, Shakti Maira, and Sonia Sikka (Switzerland: Springer, 2017), 196.

11. Toon Overvoorde, "Liturgical Floral Arranging: Examples from a Dutch Church," *Reformed Worship* 78, December 2005, https://www.reformedworship.org/article/december-2005/liturgical-floral-arranging-examples-dutch-church.

12. Kwang-Ae Park, "A Study on Influence of Flower Work on Worship Service," *Korean Floral Art Association Magazine* 2, (2000): 95. Cf. Jung-Hee Chang, *Flower and Korean Culture* (Seoul: Kyung Sung, 2001), 19–22.

13. Howard E. Galley describes the initial reticence of early Christians to adopt the use of incense in *The Ceremonies of the Eucharist: A Guide to Celebration* (Cambridge, MA: Cowley, 1989), 56–57.

14. St. Basil the Great, *On the Holy Spirit*, trans. Stephen Hildebrand (Yonkers, New York: St. Vladimir's Seminary Press, 2011), 107.

15. Using essential oils can contribute to achieving various physiological or psychological effects. See, e.g., "Aromatherapy: Do Essential Oils Really Work?," Johns Hopkins Medicine, https://www.hopkinsmedicine.org/health/wellness-and-prevention/aromatherapy-do-essential-oils-really-work.

16. A wise and insightful resource on this topic is Warren S. Brown and Brad D. Strawn, *The Physical Nature of Christian Life: Neuroscience, Psychology, and the Church* (Cambridge: Cambridge University Press, 2012).

17. Barna Group, "Christians Struggled with Relational Health Prior to the Crisis—So What Has Changed?," Barna, September 23, 2020, https://www.barna.com/research/christians-relational-health/.

18. Jeremy S. Begbie, *Music, Modernity, and God: Essays in Listening* (Oxford: Oxford University Press, 2013), 97. See also Martin Clayton, "What Is Entrainment? Definition and Applications in Musical Research," *Empirical Musicology Review* 7 (2012): 49–56; Udo Will and Gabe Turow, "Introduction to Entrainment and Cognitive Ethnomusicology," in *Music, Science, and the Rhythmic Brain*, ed. Jonathan Berger and Gabe Turow (New York: Routledge, 2011), 3–30.

19. Nathan Myrick, "Embodying the Spirit: Toward a Theology of Entrainment," *Liturgy* 33, no. 3 (2018): 32.

20. Myrick, "Embodying the Spirit," 32.

21. Stefanie Hoehl, Merle Fairhurst, and Annett Schirmer, "Interactional Synchrony: Signals, Mechanisms and Benefits," *Social Cognitive and Affective Neuroscience* 16 (January–February 2021): 5–18.

22. William Benzon, *Beethoven's Anvil: Music in Mind and Culture* (New York: Basic Books, 2001), 28.

23. Benzon, *Beethoven's Anvil*, 43. See also Stefan Koelsch and Walter A. Siebel, "Towards a Neural Basis of Music Perception," *Trends in Cognitive Sciences* 9, no. 12 (2005): 578–84.

24. Hoehl, Fairhurst, and Schirmer, "Interactional Synchrony," 7. See also Daniel J. Levitin, *This Is Your Brain on Music: The Science of a Human Obsession* (New York: Penguin, 2006), 167.

25. On these points, see, e.g., Steven Mithen, *The Singing Neanderthals: The Origins of Music, Language, Mind, and Body* (Cambridge, MA: Harvard University Press, 2006), 208–9; Curt Thompson, *Anatomy of the Soul: Surprising Connections between Neuroscience and Spiritual Practices That Can Transform Your Life and Relationships* (Carol Stream, IL: Tyndale, 2010), 137; Eiluned Pearce, Jacques Launay, and Robin I. M. Dunbar, "The Ice-Breaker Effect: Singing Mediates Fast Social Bonding," *Royal Society Open Science* 2, no. 10 (2015), https://royalsocietypublishing.org/doi/10.1098/rsos.150221.

26. Hoehl, Fairhurst, and Schirmer, "Interactional Synchrony," 14. See also Stacy Horn, "Singing Changes Your Brain," *Time*, August 16, 2013, https://ideas.time.com/2013/08/16/singing-changes-your-brain/. C. Loersch and N. L. Arbuckle, "Unraveling the Mystery of Music: Music as an Evolved Group Process," *Journal of Personality and Social Psychology* 105, no. 5 (2013): 777–98.

27. Thompson, *Anatomy of the Soul*, 152, 180.

28. See, e.g., Daniel Weinstein et al., "Singing and Social Bonding: Changes in Connectivity and Pain Threshold as a Function of Group Size," *Evolution and Human Behavior* 37, no. 2 (March 2016): 152–58.

29. William H. McNeill, *Keeping Together in Time: Dance and Drill in Human History* (Cambridge, MA: Harvard University Press, 1995), 2.

30. Rob Moll, *What Your Body Knows about God: How We Are Designed to Connect, Serve and Thrive* (Downers Grove, IL: InterVarsity, 2014), 52.

31. On this general topic, see Levitin, *This Is Your Brain On Music*, 167; Nina Kraus, *Of Sound Mind: How Our Brain Constructs a Meaningful Sonic World* (Cambridge, MA: MIT Press, 2021).

32. Myrick, "Embodying the Spirit," 35.

33. Michelle Maiese, *Embodiment, Emotion, and Cognition* (New York: Palgrave Macmillan, 2011), 11. Jeremy Begbie notes that "music can grant an extraordinary sense of embodied togetherness (among other things, through entrainment processes), while at the same time allowing for—even encouraging—particularity and uniqueness (by virtue of its floating intentionality)." *Music, Modernity, and God*, 98.

34. Hue usually refers to the dominant "color family"—that is, one of the primary and secondary colors (red, yellow, blue, orange, violet, green). A tint is any hue to which only white is added, while a true tone is any hue to which only gray is added, and a shade is a hue to which only black is added. "Color" is the more general term that people use to describe every possible hue, tint, tone, or shade that we see.

35. American politics seems to be the exception to the rule when it comes to the colors of politics. Globally, it is usually the more liberal parties that are red, while the conservative ones are blue. In postrevolutionary Russia and Mao's China only one color mattered: red.

36. Kassia St. Clair, *The Secret Lives of Color* (New York: Penguin Books, 2017), 31.

37. David Scott Kastan, *On Color* (New Haven: Yale University Press, 2018), 2, 20–39. See also Arielle Eckstut and Joann Eckstut, *What Is Color? 50 Questions and Answers on the Science of Color* (New York: Abrams, 2020).

38. Andrew J. Elliot, "Color and Psychological Functioning: A Review of Theoretical and Empirical Work," *Frontiers in Psychology* 6.368 (April, 2015), https://www.frontiersin.org/articles/10.3389/fpsyg.2015.00368/full. Visual neuroscientist J. D. Mollon writes that "the history of color science is as much the history of misconception and insight as it is of experimental refinement." "The Origins of Modern Color Science," in *The Science of Color*, ed. Steven K. Shevell, 2nd ed. (Amsterdam: Elsevier Science, 2003), 2.

39. St. Clair, *Secret Lives of Color*, 41–42.

40. "There is evidence," writes St. Clair, "that in the Middle Ages blue was considered hot, even the hottest of colors." *Secret Lives of Color*, 26.

41. For example, historian Jo B. Paoletti tells us that in the early twentieth century boys under the age of six happily wore pink because it was regarded as a "strong" color, while a different story was told from the mid-twentieth century onward, when "pretty in pink" became the exclusive property of girls. *Pink and Blue: Telling the Boys from the Girls in America* (Bloomington: Indiana University Press, 2012), esp. chap. 5, "Pink Is for Boys."

42. This is how Josef Albers describes the relative power of color in human life in his book *Interaction of Color* (New Haven: Yale University Press, 2013), 2.

43. The church calendar, which began with a festal celebration of the Lord's Day and then over time embraced a longer period of celebration with Holy Week and then even longer periods of time like the forty days of Lent, includes two intertwining calendars: the *temporale*, which marks the great feasts and fasts surrounding Christ's life, and the *sanctorale*, which commemorates the lives of individual saints and originated around the celebration of the Eucharist at the tombs of martyrs. An excellent history of the church calendar can be found in Andrew B. McGowan, *Ancient Christian Worship: Early Church Practices in Social, Historical, and Theological Perspective* (Grand Rapids: Baker Academic, 2014), chap. 7, "Time: Feasts and Fasts."

44. Before the language of "Ordinary Time" became standard usage among churches in the late twentieth century, the time between Pentecost and Advent was marked by the number of weeks *since* Pentecost. The use of ordinal numbers, "first, second, third," and so on, may explain the original meaning of the term "Ordinary Time," which has now taken on associations with ordinary life. See Simon Chan, *Liturgical Theology: The Church as Worshiping Community* (Downers Grove, IL: IVP Academic, 2006), 164.

45. Bobby Gross, *Living the Christian Year: Time to Inhabit the Story of God* (Downers Grove, IL: IVP Books, 2009), 25.

46. Judith Couchman, *The Art of Faith: A Guide to Understanding Christian Images* (Brewster, MA: Paraclete, 2012), 173–78. Couchman also shows how the color yellow can suggest either saintly identity, as with Renaissance paintings of St. Peter, or deceit and treason, as Judas was often represented in the paintings of the era and as heretics were depicted in the artwork of the Middle Ages.

47. J. Barrington Bates, "Am I Blue? Some Historical Evidence for Liturgical Colors," *Studia Liturgica* 33, no. 1 (2003): 76. For Pope Innocent III's actual prescription, see James White, *Documents of Christian Worship: Descriptive and Interpretive Sources* (Louisville: Westminster John Knox, 1992), 32–34. See also Markus Tymister, "Liturgical Colors (Color Canon)," *PrayTellBlog*, May 19, 2018, https://www.praytellblog.com/index.php/2018/05/19/liturgical-colors-color-canon/.

48. On the use of this relatively new digital technology in worship, see Stephen Proctor, *The Guidebook for Visual Worship: Basic Training for Visual Worship Leaders* (n.p.: Illuminate.Us, 2014), https://illuminate.us/learn/. Cf. Bates, "Am I Blue?," 75–77.

49. In Alice Walker's Pulitzer Prize–winning novel *The Color Purple*, the character Shug Avery, a jazz and blues singer, remarks, "I think it pisses God off if you walk by the color purple in a field somewhere and don't notice it." She has a point, I think.

50. Around the same time Abbot Suger oversaw the construction of the Saint-Denis Abbey in Paris (c. 1130–1140) with its use of cobalt blue in the stained glass windows, "the Virgin was increasingly depicted wearing bright blue robes—previously she had usually been shown in dark colors that conveyed her mourning for the death of her son. As the status of Mary and Marian-centered devotion waxed in the Middle Ages, so too did the fortunes of her adopted color. From the Middle Ages the pigment most commonly associated with Mary was the precious pigment ultramarine [from the Latin *ultra*, "beyond," and *mare*, "sea"], which remained the most coveted, bar none, for centuries." St. Clair, *Secret Lives of Color*, 180.

51. Couchman, *Art of Faith*, 174.

52. "Around 4.5 percent of the world's population are color-blind or deficient because of faults in their cone cells." St. Clair, *Secret Lives of Color*, 14.

Chapter 8 The Art of the Body

1. This is an argument that I develop at length in W. David O. Taylor, *Glimpses of the New Creation: Worship and the Formative Power of the Arts* (Grand Rapids: Eerdmans, 2019), chap. 2, "The Meaning of Art."

2. See Simona Klimková, "A Man in Crisis: Selected Short Fiction of Joseph Conrad," *Ars Aeterna* 7 no. 2 (2015): 26.

3. Charles Spence brings to life the science and art of eating in his book *Gastrophysics: The New Science of Eating* (New York: Viking, 2017).

4. Alex Neill, "Art and Emotion," in *Oxford Handbook of Aesthetics*, ed. Jerrold Levinson (Oxford: Oxford University Press, 2005), 421; Tiger C. Roholt, *Key Terms in Philosophy of Art* (London: Bloomsbury Academic, 2013), 26.

5. On the topic of the emotions in the arts, see, e.g., Helena Wulff, ed., *The Emotions: A Cultural Reader* (Oxford: Berg, 2007); Mette Hjort and Sue Laver, eds., *Emotion and the Arts* (Oxford: Oxford University Press, 1997); and Mark Johnson, *The Meaning of the Body: Aesthetics of Human Understanding* (Chicago: University of Chicago Press, 2007), 65.

6. Jeremy S. Begbie, "Faithful Feelings: Music and Emotion in Worship," in *Resonant Witness: Conversations between Music and Theology*, ed. Jeremy S. Begbie and Steven R. Guthrie (Grand Rapids: Eerdmans, 2011), 351 (emphasis in original).

7. Begbie, "Faithful Feelings," 324. See also Jeannette Winterson, "What Is Art For?," in *The World Split Open: Great Authors on How and Why We Write* (Portland, OR: Tin House Books, 2014), 186–87.

8. Cf. Trevor Hart, *Between the Image and the Word: Theological Engagements with Imagination, Language and Literature* (Surrey, UK: Ashgate, 2013), chap. 10; Leland Ryken, ed., *The Christian Imagination: The Practice of Faith in Literature and Writing* (Colorado Springs: Shaw Books, 2002); Peter Kivy, *The Blackwell Guide to Aesthetics* (Oxford: Blackwell, 2004), chap. 1.

9. See Luke Timothy Johnson, "Imagining the World Scripture Imagines," in *Theology and Scriptural Imagination*, ed. L. Gregory Jones and James J. Buckley (Oxford: Blackwell, 1998), 9.

10. This is language that I use in my essay "The Dangers," in *For the Beauty of the Church: Casting a Vision for the Arts*, ed. W. David O. Taylor (Grand Rapids: Baker Books, 2010), 159–62.

11. This is a key argument of Jeremy Begbie in his book *Voicing Creation's Praise: Towards a Theology of the Arts* (Edinburgh: T&T Clark, 1991), 233.

12. George Lakeoff and Mark Johnson, *Metaphors We Live By* (Chicago: University of Chicago Press, 1980), 5.

13. "Metaphors: The Breakfast of Champions" is the title of the afterword in Ray Bradbury, *One More for the Road: A New Story Collection* (New York: William Morrow, 2002). American composer Leonard Bernstein argued that music, fundamentally, was "a totally metaphorical language." Quoted in Begbie, *Voicing Creation's Praise*, 243.

14. Jeremy S. Begbie, *Resounding Truth: Christian Wisdom in the World of Music* (Grand Rapids: Baker Academic, 2007), 50.

15. "Imagination is morally required because we refuse to allow the 'necessities' of the world, which are often but stale habits, to go unchanged or unchallenged when they are in fact susceptible to the power of imagination." Stanley Hauerwas, "On Keeping Theological Ethics Imaginative," in *Against the Nations: War and Survival in a Liberal Society* (San Francisco: Harper & Row, 1985), 55. Cf. W. David O. Taylor, "Discipling the Eyes through Art in Worship," *Christianity Today* (April 27, 2012), https://www.christianitytoday.com/ct/2012/april/art-in-worship.html.

16. Stephen J. Stein offers a helpful introduction to the distinctive practices of—and to the occasional innovations in—Shaker worship in *The Shaker Experience in America: A History of the United Society of Believers* (New Haven: Yale University Press, 1992), esp. 101–6, 165–200. See also Julia Neal, *The Kentucky Shakers* (Lexington: University Press of Kentucky, 1982), and *The Shakers: Two Centuries of Spiritual Reflection*, ed. Robley Edward Whitson (New York: Paulist Press, 1983), 270–82.

17. A brief synopsis for a PBS documentary gives this description: "The Shakers were celibate, they did not marry or bear children, yet theirs is the most enduring religious experiment in American history. Seventy-five years before the emancipation of the slaves and one hundred fifty years before women began voting in America, the Shakers were practicing social, sexual, economic, and spiritual equality for all members." "About the Shakers," PBS, https://www.pbs.org/kenburns/the-shakers/about-the-shakers/.

18. J. G. Davies, *Liturgical Dance: An Historical, Theological and Practical Handbook* (London: SCM, 1984), 67.

19. E. D. Andrews, *The Gift to Be Simple: Songs, Dances and Rituals of the American Shakers* (New York: Dover Publications, 1962), 17.

20. Davies, *Liturgical Dance*, 67.

21. Davies, *Liturgical Dance*, 67.

22. For examples of Shaker dancing, see "Shaker Music & Dance: Hancock Shaker Village," https://www.youtube.com/watch?v=Lhc9PK2tG5k.

23. Quoted in "'Let Us Labor': The Evolution of Shaker Dance," *The Shaker Heritage Society*, April 4, 2012, https://home.shakerheritage.org/let-us-labor-the-evolution-of-shaker-dance/.

24. Broaddus's journal entry is included in Davies, *Liturgical Dance*, 67–68.

25. Quoted in Davies, *Liturgical Dance*, 69.

26. Lillian Phelps, "Shaker Dances and Marches," Enfield Shaker Museum, https://shakermuseum.org/learn/shaker-studies/who-are-the-shakers/shaker-dancing-and-marching/. The material at this website is from Bertha Lindsay and Lillian Phelps, *Industries*

and Inventions of the Shakers: Shaker Music, a Brief History (Canterbury, NH: United Society of Believers, 1961).

27. Davies, *Liturgical Dance*, 68.

28. See Davies, *Liturgical Dance*, 68.

29. As it relates to dance more generally, the term "sacred dance" is usually used to denote the broadest category for dance in worship, while "praise dance" is a term that is frequently used by charismatic Christians to describe a spontaneous expression of affection for God or a rehearsed performance. The term "liturgical dance" usually appears in "liturgical" churches to describe movement that generally serves a specific activity in the liturgy, such as confession or thanksgiving. For a helpful summary of the nature, purposes, and practices of liturgical dance, see Kathleen Turner, *"And We Shall Learn Through the Dance": Liturgical Dance as Religious Education* (Eugene, OR: Pickwick, 2021), chap. 4.

30. See Stein, *Shaker Experience*, 4, 10.

31. Stephanie Butler, *My Body Is the Temple: Encounters and Revelations of Sacred Dance and Artistry* (Fairfax, VA: Xulon Press, 2002). A whole section could be devoted to the curative powers of laughter within the context of corporate worship, inasmuch as it enables humans to inhabit their bodies unselfconsciously and to more readily "get over themselves" in order to be more fully present to one another. A similarly beneficial study could be done with open and unembarrassed weeping in worship.

32. Phelps, "Shaker Dances and Marches."

33. For more on this topic, see Ronald Gagne, Thomas Kane, and Robert VerEecke, *Introducing Dance in Christian Worship* (Portland, OR: Pastoral Press, 1984).

34. See Angela Yarber, *Dance in Scripture: How Biblical Dancers Can Revolutionize Worship Today* (Eugene, OR: Cascade Books, 2013).

35. "Quaking Shaker" originally functioned as a derogatory term used to ridicule and to marginalize this distinctive form of liturgical dance. See Stein, *Shaker Experience*, 3–4.

36. "If one wishes to enhance the assembly's appreciation of bodily motion as a means of expressing and communicating sacred values, one might give attention to the liturgy's ceremonial choreography and to freeing the assembly from the physical restrains pews force upon it." Aiden Kavanagh, *Elements of Rite: A Handbook of Liturgical Style* (Collegeville, MN: Liturgical Press, 1982), 33.

37. On the way in which particular spaces shape our experience of sound and the arrangement of our physical bodies determines our experience of song, see Barry Blesser and Linda-Ruth Salter, *Spaces Speak, Are You Listening? Experiencing Aural Architecture* (Cambridge, MA: MIT Press, 2007), esp. 88–93. On the fundamentally tactile nature of architecture, see Juhani Pallasmaa, *The Eyes of the Skin: Architecture and the Senses* (Chichester, West Sussex: Wiley & Sons, 2012).

38. See Timothy Verdon, *Art and Prayer: The Beauty of Turning to God* (Brewster, MA: Paraclete Press, 2014), 73.

39. See, e.g., https://www.salisburycathedral.org.uk/visit-about-building/glance-floor-plan.

40. The floor plan of St. John's Abbey is available at https://saintjohnsabbey.org/commitment-to-stewardship.

41. Jean Ngoya Kidula, "Music Culture: African Life," in Roberta King, ed., *Music in the Life of the African Church* (Waco, TX: Baylor University Press, 2008), 45.

42. Working around existing seating arrangements is often difficult. Few congregations have the freedom to modify their liturgical spaces. The Anglican diocese of London offers some helpful perspective on things that could be done in "How to Replace and Reorder Church Seating," https://www.london.anglican.org/kb/replace-reorder-church-seating/.

43. An image of this painting is available at https://www.heqiart.com/store/p180/48_The-Risen-Lord_Limited_Edition.html. Roger Brown's painting, "The Entry of Christ into Chicago" (1976), might also be worth viewing. An image is available at https://whitney.org/collection/works/2522.

44. Cf. James K. A. Smith, *Imagining the Kingdom: How Worship Works* (Grand Rapids: Baker Academic, 2013), 137.

Chapter 9 The Way of the Body

1. Email correspondence, February 27, 2022.

2. What many people with disabilities face, not just in society at large but also in the church, is a stigmatization of their disability. It includes, as Amy Jacober observes, "unwelcomed looks, inappropriate comments, unsolicited touches, taunts, unnecessary questioning, ignoring, and worse . . . much worse." *Redefining Perfect: The Interplay between Theology and Disability* (Eugene, OR: Cascade Books, 2017), 50.

3. Nancy L. Eiesland, *The Disabled God: Toward a Liberatory Theology of Disability* (Nashville: Abingdon, 1994), 20, see also 67–70. Eiesland identifies three "carnal sins" that the church commits toward people with disabilities: segregationist charity (love them at a distance), virtuous suffering (mere examples of suffering for God), and sin-disability conflation (they're broken because of sin). Under this light, persons with disabilities are "either divinely blessed or damned; the defiled evildoer or the spiritual super-hero" (70). Sara Hendren helpfully distinguishes between "disabled bodies" and "disabling barriers" (a social model) that stand between bodies and the built world. "Disability in part *results* when the shape of the world—buildings and streets but also institutions, cultural organizations, centers of power—operates rigidly, with a brittle and scripted sense of what a body does or does not do, how it moves and organizes the world." When a disabled body meets a built environment that doesn't fit, it is called a "misfit" relationship to the world. *What Can a Body Do? How We Meet the Built World* (New York: Riverhead Books, 2020), 14–15.

4. For the purposes of this chapter, I will use the language of "disabled person" rather than "people with disabilities" or "differently abled" to describe this wide range of experiences. "There is no single accepted definition of disability." Jacober, *Redefining Perfect*, 5. Eiesland helpfully distinguishes between three terms: "impairment," as the loss of physiological form or function; "disability," as the consequence of one's impairment; and "handicap," as the social disadvantage that accrues from one's disability. *Disabled God*, 27.

5. In the words of John Hull, Christ's resurrected body is "a wounded perfection, a scarred perfection, and imperfect perfection." "The Broken Body in a Broken World," *Journal of Religion, Disability and Health* 7, no. 4 (2004): 18.

6. Eiesland, *Disabled God*, 100. John Swinton, in "Who Is the God We Worship? Theologies of Disability: Challenges and New Possibilities," *International Journal of Practical Theology* 14, no. 2 (2010): 273–307, rightly problematizes aspects of Eiesland's thesis and brings to light things that may remain slightly confused in Eiesland's proposal of God as disabled.

7. Hendren, *What Can a Body Do?*, 11 (emphasis in original).

8. Thomas E. Reynolds, *Vulnerable Communities: A Theology of Disability and Hospitality* (Grand Rapids: Brazos, 2008), 104.

9. It is not insignificant that Exod. 4:11–12 has Yahweh identifying himself as the author of Moses's impediment: "The Lord said to him, 'Who gave human beings their mouths? Who makes them deaf or mute? Who gives them sight or makes them blind? Is it not I, the LORD? Now go; I will help you speak and will teach you what to say'" (NIV).

10. John Swinton, "Many Bodies, Many Worlds," Baylor University Christian Reflection Project, 2012, https://www.baylor.edu/content/services/document.php/188190.pdf.

11. Eiesland, *Disabled God*, 31.

12. Hendren, *What Can a Body Do?*, 32.

13. Stanley Hauerwas, "Timeful Friends: Living with the Handicapped," in *Sanctify Them in the Truth: Holiness Exemplified* (Nashville: Abingdon, 1999), 16.

14. Amos Yong, *The Bible, Disability, and the Church: A New Vision of the People of God* (Grand Rapids: Eerdmans, 2011), 78. See also John Swinton, "Using Our Bodies Faithfully: Christian Friendship and the Life of Worship," *Journal of Disability & Religion* 19, no. 3 (2015): 228–42.

15. Rebecca Spurrier describes her experience of worshiping next to a woman named Victoria this way: "The people she touches respond to her with warmth and energy. Her hands touching their hands and shoulders creates an alternate form of connection than the unison of voices reading the creed and the prayers." *The Disabled Church: Human Difference and the Art of Communal Worship* (New York: Fordham University Press, 2019), 80. Spurrier was in attendance at Holy Comforter Episcopal Church in Atlanta, Georgia, where more than half of the church's members live with diagnoses of mental illness—including bipolar disorder, schizophrenia, and clinical depression.

16. Yong, *The Bible, Disability, and the Church*, 78–79.

17. Cf. Jacober, *Redefining Perfect*, 11; Yong, *The Bible Disability, and the Church*, 78–79. Bethany McKinney Fox offers excellent suggestions for inclusion of persons with disabilities in worship. A sampling includes offering opportunities for leadership in the worship of the church, offering opportunities for holistic response to corporate singing and to the reading of Scripture (e.g., by allowing people to draw what they think, feel, and see or by inviting someone to give a testimony to the group), and offering tangible ways to communicate a desire for physical touch. *Disability and the Way of Jesus: Holistic Healing in the Gospels and the Church* (Downers Grove, IL: IVP Academic, 2019), 159.

18. The Calvin Institute of Christian Worship includes a host of excellent resources on disability and worship, including the following articles: Allen J. Moore, "Making Worship Accessible for Persons with Disabilities," June 1, 2004, https://worship.calvin.edu/resources/resource-library/making-worship-accessible-for-persons-with-disabilities; Joan Huyser-Honig, "All God's Children Have Gifts: Disability and Worship," January 6, 2006, https://worship.calvin.edu/resources/resource-library/all-god-s-children-have-gifts-disability-and-worship; CLC Network, "Worship as One: Disability in Community," September 29, 2016, https://worship.calvin.edu/resources/resource-library/worship-as-one-disability-in-community; Thomas B. Hoeksema, "Disability and Inclusion: An Annotated Bibliography," May 16, 2016, https://worship.calvin.edu/resources/resource-library/disability-and-inclusion-an-annotated-bibliography. Also helpful are John Swinton, *Finding Jesus in the Storm: The Spiritual Lives of Christians with Mental Health Challenges* (Grand Rapids: Eerdmans, 2020); Jeff McNair, "The Power of Those Who Seem Weaker: People with Disabilities in the Church," *The Journal of the Christian Institute on Disability* 3, no. 1 (2014); Jacober, *Redefining Perfect*; Spurrier, *Disabled Church*; Lamar Hardwick, *Disability and the Church: A Vision for Diversity and Inclusion* (Downers Grove, IL: InterVarsity, 2021).

19. An image is available at https://exhibits.library.duke.edu/exhibits/show/chapel2016/stain.

20. An image of this exhibit is available at https://sites.duke.edu/dita/sadao-watanabe-exhibition-at-duke-university-chapel/. Some of Duke Chapel's other multicultural art exhibits can be viewed at https://chapel.duke.edu/art.

21. Adelle M. Banks, "Multiracial Churches Growing, but Challenging for Clergy of Color," Religion News Service, January 20, 2020, https://religionnews.com/2020/01/20/multiracial-churches-growing-but-challenging-for-clergy-of-color/.

22. See, e.g., Korie Little Edwards, "The Multiethnic Church Movement Hasn't Lived Up to Its Promise," *Christianity Today*, February 16, 2021, https://www.christianitytoday.com/ct/2021/march/race-diversity-multiethnic-church-movement-promise.html.

23. More crucial to who stands front and center, however, is the matter of who makes the final decisions about what gets sung, prayed, or preached. This is the matter of power dynamics. Sandra Maria Van Opstal writes, "Unless we have a community of diverse leaders who can speak into the situation and co-create spaces, we will repeatedly go to our favorite foods, music, decorations and event-planning processes." *The Next Worship: Glorifying God in a Diverse World* (Downers Grove, IL: InterVarsity, 2016), 80.

24. Sociologist Tia DeNora's notion of embodied security, which she explores in her book *Music in Everyday Life* (Cambridge: Cambridge University Press, 2000), 85, helpfully illumines this point.

25. Mark Charles describes the unique demand that Navajo worship places on the physical body in its experience of time this way:
Many times when people talk about contextualizing worship, they think about what instruments we are going to use or some type of style. But how do we need to change the structure of our church so that the structure itself communicates that we think this event is sacred? Many of the songs that we sing [in Navajo culture] are longer than most Christian church services. They can easily go on for an hour or two hours, all night long if they have to. The perception of time is different, so the first missionaries thought, *These Navajos don't love God; they are always late for church*. The Navajos thought, *These missionaries don't love God; look how short their service is*. Two completely different ways to understand the world." (In "Contextualizing Worship: My Journey to Worship God as a Navajo Christian," Calvin Institute of Christian Worship, January 1, 2009, https://worship.calvin.edu/resources/resource-library/contextualizing-worship-my-journey-to-worship-god-as-a-navajo-christian [emphasis in original])

26. Gerardo Marti, *Worship across the Racial Divide: Religious Music and the Multiracial Congregation* (Oxford: Oxford University Press, 2012), 195.

27. Marti, *Worship across the Racial Divide*, 155–56.

28. See W. David O. Taylor, "How to Lead Online Worship without Losing Your Soul—or Body," *Christianity Today*, March 17, 2020, https://www.christianitytoday.com/pastors/2020/march/web-exclusives/how-to-lead-online-worship-without-losing-your-soul-or-body.html.

29. For some summaries of this issue, see Michelle Boorstein, "D.C. Agrees to Pay $220,000 in Legal Fees to Baptist Church That Sued over Coronavirus Restrictions," *The Washington Post*, July 12, 2021, https://www.washingtonpost.com/religion/2021/07/09/dc-bowser-coronavirus-settlement-baptist-church-restrictions/; Kate Shellnut, "DC Settles $220K Capitol Hill Baptist Lawsuit," *Christianity Today*, July 11, 2021, https://www.christianitytoday.com/news/2020/september/mark-dever-capital-hill-baptist-church-dc-lawsuit-covid-gat.html.

30. Tom Strode, "Capitol Hill Baptist Church Sues D.C. on COVID Order," *Baptist Press*, September 23, 2020, https://www.baptistpress.com/resource-library/news/capitol-hill-baptist-church-sues-d-c-on-covid-order/.

31. Their offerings for online worship are available at https://www.life.church/online/.

32. Kate Shellnut, "When God Closes a Church Door, He Opens a Browser Window," *Christianity Today* (March 19, 2020), https://www.christianitytoday.com/news/2020/march/online-church-attendance-covid-19-streaming-video-app.html.

33. Tish Harrison Warren, "Why Churches Should Drop Their Online Services," *New York Times*, January 30, 2022, https://www.nytimes.com/2022/01/30/opinion/church-online-services-covid.html.

34. Quoted in Daniel Schultz, "Ending Zoom Church Is a Great Idea for a Column—Provided You Completely Ignore the Disability Perspective," *Religion Dispatches*, February 1, 2022, https://religiondispatches.org/turn-on-the-news-ending-zoom-church-is-a-great-idea-for-a-column-provided-you-completely-ignore-the-disability-perspective/.

35. On the powers of electricity and the videographic arts in corporate worship, see W. David O. Taylor, *Glimpses of the New Creation: Worship and the Formative Power of the Arts* (Grand Rapids: Eerdmans, 2019), "Appendix A: The Videographic Arts: Questions for Discernment."

36. Michio Kaku, *Physics of the Future: How Science Will Shape Human Destiny and Our Daily Lives by the Year 2100* (New York: Anchor Books, 2011), 17; cf. Lev Grossman, "2045: The Year Man Becomes Immortal," *Time*, February 10, 2011, http://content.time.com/time/printout/0,8816,2048299,00.html.

37. Kyle Rohane, "How Are Pastors Handling Ungathered Worship?" *Christianity Today*, March 25, 2020, https://www.christianitytoday.com/pastors/2020/march-web-exclusives/how-are-pastors-handling-un-gathered-worship.html. Collin Hansen makes a similar point in his essay, "What We Lose When We Livestream Church," *New York Times*, August 8, 2021, https://www.nytimes.com/2021/08/08/opinion/covid-church-livestream.html.

38. Curt Thompson, "A Body of Work," April 15, 2020, https://curtthompsonmd.com/a-body-of-work/.

39. Further losses include our capacity to make wise decisions in real time. The rapid pace of technological advancements often surpasses our capacity to exercise judicious choices. On this point, see Douglas Estes, *Braving the Future: Christian Faith in a World of Limitless Tech* (Harrisonburg, VA: Herald, 2018), 36; Andy Crouch, *The Tech-Wise Family: Everyday Steps for Putting Technology in Its Proper Place* (Grand Rapids: Baker Books, 2017), 189.

40. "Silence is about presence, not just absence. . . . 'Silence is felt. It is meaningful. It is not mere negation.' It is a pregnant stillness that raises heart rates and releases endorphins within the pathways of our bodies. It is about the quiet friction between individuals gathered in space. It is that eerie awkwardness, when there is an excess of silence in a church service, that makes us notice the feeling of a neighbor's presence." Chris Palmer, "A Worship Practice Zoom Can't Replicate," *The Christian Century*, January 5, 2022, https://www.christiancentury.org/article/reflection/worship-practice-zoom-can-t-replicate.

41. William H. McNeill, *Keeping Together in Time: Dance and Drill in Human History* (Cambridge, MA: Harvard University Press, 1995), 2.

42. See Katherine Willis Pershey, "We Need Our Screens Right Now. But What about Later?," *The Christian Century*, July 7, 2020, in a review of *Spiritual Restoration from Digital Distraction*, by Ed Cyzewsk (Harrisonburg, VA: Herald, 2020).

43. This represents an especially contested matter, specifically around the inclusion of virtual and augmented reality in practices of corporate worship, but more generally around the ability of digitally mediated experiences to facilitate so-called real worship. On this point, see, e.g., Kristen French, "This Pastor Is Putting His Faith in a Virtual Reality Church," *Wired*, February 2, 2018, https://www.wired.com/story/virtual-reality-church/; Andrew

Sullivan, "I Used to Be a Human Being," *New York Magazine*, September 19, 2016, https://nymag.com/intelligencer/2016/09/andrew-sullivan-my-distraction-sickness-and-yours.html; James F. Caccamo, "Let Me Put It Another Way: Digital Media and the Future of the Liturgy," *Liturgy* 28, no. 3 (2013): 7–16; Rachael Horner Starke, "Internet or Incarnation? Bridging the Digital Divide," *Christianity Today* 64 (May 2018): 83; Jay Y. Kim, *Analog Church: Why We Need Real People, Places, and Things in the Digital Age* (Downers Grove, IL: InterVarsity, 2020); Ronald L. Giese Jr., "Is 'Online Church' Really Church? The Church as God's Temple," *Themelios* 45, no. 2 (2020): 347–67; Monique M. Ingalls, "Worship on the Web: Broadcasting Devotion through Worship Music Videos on YouTube," in *Music and the Broadcast Experience: Performance, Production, and Audiences*, ed. Christina Baade and James A. Deaville (Oxford: Oxford University Press, 2016), 293–308. See also Simeon Ximian Xu, "AI Can Preach and Sing: So Why Can't It Worship God?" *Christianity Today* (August 25, 2022), https://www.christianitytoday.com/ct/2022/august-web-only/artificial-intelligence-praise-worship-body-carbon.html.

44. Teresa Berger, *@Worship: Liturgical Practices in Digital Worlds* (London: Routledge, 2018), 20.

45. As it relates to practices of baptism specifically, see John Dyer, "Digital Baptisms: What We Can Learn from Online, Virtual, and Broadcast Practices," April 18, 2020, https://j.hn/digital-baptisms-learn-from-online-virtual-and-broadcast-practices/.

46. Berger, *@Worship*, 106, 109.

47. Berger, *@Worship*, 16.

48. Douglas Estes, *SimChurch: Being the Church in the Virtual World* (Grand Rapids: Zondervan, 2009), 28.

49. David T. Bourgeois, *Ministry in the Digital Age: Strategies and Best Practices for a Post-Website World* (Downers Grove, IL: InterVarsity, 2013), 25.

50. Mirjana Spasojevic, Rachel Hinman, and Will Dzierson, "Mobile Persuasion Design Principles," in *Mobile Persuasion: 20 Perspectives on the Future Behavior of Change*, ed. B. J. Fogg and Dean Eckles (Stanford, CA: Stanford Captology Media, 2007), 119–20.

51. Estes, *SimChurch*, 25.

52. Wendell Berry, "The Body and the Earth," in *The Art of the Commonplace: The Agrarian Essays of Wendell Berry* (Berkeley: Counterpoint, 2002), 99.

53. Nathan Mitchell, *Meeting Mystery: Liturgy, Worship, Sacraments* (Maryknoll, NY: Orbis Books, 2006), 38 (emphasis in original).

Chapter 10 The Discipline of the Body

1. Lester Ruth, Carrie Steenwyk, and John D. Witvliet, *Walking Where Jesus Walked: Worship in Fourth-Century Jerusalem* (Grand Rapids: Eerdmans, 2010), 23–24. This might also describe the experience of Christians during the Feast of Fools, Children's Festival, and the Dance of Death.

2. Ruth, Steenwyk, and Witvliet, *Walking Where Jesus Walked*, 22.

3. As quoted in Ruth, Steenwyk, and Witvliet, *Walking Where Jesus Walked*, 53.

4. Ruth, Steenwyk, and Witvliet, *Walking Where Jesus Walked*, 23–24.

5. Information about this march and others is available at https://themarchforjesus.org/history/.

6. Kosuke Koyama, *Three Mile an Hour God: Biblical Reflections* (Maryknoll, NY: Orbis Books, 1979), 7.

7. Rebecca Solnit, *Wanderlust: A History of Walking* (New York: Penguin Books, 2000), 29.

8. Solnit, *Wanderlust*, 70.

9. Solnit, *Wanderlust*, 71.

10. "In walking, the means is as valuable and worthwhile as the goal itself." Arthur Paul Boers, *The Way Is Made by Walking: A Pilgrimage along the Camino de Santiago* (Downers Grove, IL: InterVarsity, 2007), 162.

11. It is always helpful, I find, to remind fellow Christians that pews were a late medieval invention and far from sacrosanct in church history, despite the protestations of plenty of contemporary Christians. See "The Oddness of Pews," *Christianity Today*, October 27, 2006, https://www.christianitytoday.com/pastors/2006/october-online-only/oddness-of-pews.html. Eastern Orthodox Christians have been less enthusiastic than Protestant or Catholic Christians about pews that keep the laity fixed in place. See "The Liturgical Effectiveness of Pews," *Orthodox Christian Information Center*, http://orthodoxinfo.com/praxis/pews.aspx.

12. "The new Rome was built as a processional city, with grand boulevards connecting the imperial palace, the government buildings, the Hippodrome, and the Great Church.... This new capital church and society were unified by liturgical processions that occurred along the boulevard from one station to another, drawing on the full forces of church and state and thousands of bystanders." Frank Senn, *Embodied Liturgy: Lessons in Christian Ritual* (Minneapolis: Fortress, 2016), 330–31.

13. Robert W. Hovda, *Strong, Loving and Wise: Presiding in Liturgy* (Collegeville, MN: Liturgical Press, 1976), 84. Aidan Kavanagh offers this word of warning against heartless and mindless ways of using our bodies in such fashion: "In most churches processions are usually perfunctory, ill-planned, poorly executed, arhythmic, and utilitarian at best, characteristics foreign to a good parade or procession." *Elements of Rite: A Handbook of Liturgical Style* (Collegeville, MN: Liturgical Press, 1982), 52.

14. I should also say here that the lines blur between prescriptive and spontaneous uses of the physical body in worship when the body is employed in a purposeful but not necessarily prescribed fashion. Hands might be raised high during a hymn of praise, for instance, not because the heart is overflowing with feeling, but rather because our will chooses to honor and to bless God, perhaps even despite the emotions of the moment. While such a practice does not involve a prescriptive use of the body, it does accomplish a similar purpose. It offers our bodies an opportunity to lead the heart and mind in the way of faithful discipleship.

15. Balthasar Fischer, *Signs, Words, and Gestures* (New York: Pueblo, 1981), 27.

16. Elochukwu E. Uzukwu, *Worship as Body Language: Introduction to Christian Worship—An African Orientation* (Collegeville, MN: Liturgical Press, 1977), 20–21.

17. Quoted in F. E. Warren, *The Liturgy and Ritual of the Ante-Nicene Church* (London: SPCK, 1897), 143.

18. Antonio Donghi, *Words and Gestures in the Liturgy* (Collegeville, MN: Liturgical Press, 2007), 10.

19. Uzukwu, *Worship as Body Language*, 22.

20. Uzukwu, *Worship as Body Language*, 22.

21. On the practice of genuflection, which one might do on entering a church in recognition that one is entering the house of the Lord, or prior to approaching the altar/table to receive the eucharistic elements, see Donghi, *Words and Gestures in the Liturgy*, 16–18. He also offers this caution: "Unfortunately, the routine nature of this gesture, which we repeat frequently in celebrations and in personal devotion, becomes such a habit that it does not always have all the internal meaning that we might desire, and it does not lead us to make of our life a profession of faith for the world to see" (17–18).

22. Donghi, *Words and Gestures in the Liturgy*, 14. Romano Guardini, *Sacred Signs*, trans. Grace Branham (St. Louis: Pio Decimo Press, 1956), 16.

23. Ezekiel 9:4 served for Christians in the early church as a key biblical reference point for signing oneself physically: "Go through the city, through Jerusalem, and put a mark on the foreheads of those who sigh and groan over all the abominations that are committed in it."

24. Tertullian, *De Corona* § 3, https://www.tertullian.org/lfc/LFC10-11_de_corona.htm, quoted in Scott Hahn, *Signs of Life: 20 Catholic Customs and Their Biblical Roots* (New York: Image, 2018), 26.

25. Donghi, *Words and Gestures in the Liturgy*, 5.

26. John R. W. Stott, *The Cross of Christ* (Downers Grove, IL: InterVarsity, 2006), 71.

27. Sangwoo Kim helpfully expounds on the historical origins of the gesture: "In the early church, the sign of the cross was made on the forehead. Later, the sign became bigger covering the upper body: from forehead to chest, from right shoulder to left shoulder, with three fingers, which is still practiced in the Eastern traditions. In the Western church, the sign was made with the whole open hand, from forehead to chest, from left shoulder to right shoulder." "Embodied Prayer: The Practice of Prayer as Christian Theology" (ThD diss., Duke Divinity School, 2016), 118n114.

28. Quoted in Bert Ghezzi, *The Sign of the Cross: Recovering the Power of the Ancient Prayer* (Chicago: Loyola, 2004), 6.

29. Martin Luther, *Luther's Little Instruction Book (The Small Catechism of Martin Luther)*, trans. Robert E. Smith, available at http://www.projectwittenberg.org/pub/resources/text/wittenberg/luther/little.book/web/book-appx.html.

30. On why some Christians make the sign of the cross by moving from right to left, or from left to right, see Ghezzi, *Sign of the Cross*, 17–25.

31. "When we cross ourselves, let it be with a real sign of the cross. Instead of a small, cramped gesture that gives no notion of its meaning, let us make a large unhurried sign, from forehead to breast, from shoulder to shoulder, consciously feeling how it includes the whole of us, our thoughts, our attitudes, our body and soul, every part of us at once, how it consecrates and sanctifies us." Guardini, *Sacred Signs*, 13.

32. Hahn, *Signs of Life*, 28.

33. Guardini, *Sacred Signs*, 14.

34. Cf. Fischer, *Signs, Words, and Gestures*, 76.

35. Cf. Guardini, *Sacred Signs*, 20–21; Donghi, *Words and Gestures in the Liturgy*, 32.

36. Donghi, *Words and Gestures in the Liturgy*, 49.

37. Howard E. Galley, *The Ceremonies of the Eucharist: A Guide to Celebration* (Cambridge, MA: Cowley Publications, 1989), 52.

38. Donghi, *Words and Gestures in the Liturgy*, 74.

39. Kavanagh, *Elements of Rite*, 66. Equally intimate is the act of kissing the altar, the act of kissing the book of Holy Scripture, and the act of kissing icons. Such practices are on par with the practice of athletes who kiss a victory cup, such as the Stanley Cup in the National Hockey League, as a way to physically signify ultimate victory and to express an intense love for something.

40. Cf. Andrew B. McGowan, *Ancient Christian Worship: Early Church Practices in Social, Historical, and Theological Perspective* (Grand Rapids: Baker Academic, 2014), 55–56.

41. "Who kissed whom, where, in what circumstances—these actions reflected, reinforced, and challenged the social order." Michael Philip Penn, *Kissing Christians: Ritual and Community in the Late Ancient Church* (Philadelphia: University of Pennsylvania Press, 2005), 15–16.

42. See Fischer, *Signs, Words, and Gestures*, 13.
43. Donghi, *Words and Gestures in the Liturgy*, 52.
44. This will not be the usual case with distinctly Eastern Orthodox worship.
45. Nathan Mitchell, "The Poetics of Space," *Worship* 67, no. 4 (1993): 363.
46. Donghi, *Words and Gestures in the Liturgy*, 66–67.
47. Kavanagh, *Elements of Rite*, 69. As I write in the chapter on history, the possibility of abuse does not negate the singular benefit that such uses of our body in worship bring to us. What is needed, as always, are pastoral wisdom, careful instruction, and liturgical sensitivity to know how the body might be employed rightly.
48. See W. David O. Taylor, "Make a Joyful Silence unto the Lord," *Christianity Today*, October 4, 2019, https://www.christianitytoday.com/pastors/2019/october-web-exclusives/church-worship-make-joyful-silence-unto-lord.html. See also Diarmaid MacCulloch, *Silence: A Christian History* (New York: Viking, 2013).
49. Donghi, *Words and Gestures in the Liturgy*, 22.
50. Donghi, *Words and Gestures in the Liturgy*, 23.
51. Kavanagh, *Elements of Rite*, 51.
52. Cardinal Robert Sarah, with Nicolas Diat, *The Power of Silence against the Dictatorship of Noise* (San Francisco: Ignatius, 2017).
53. C. S. Lewis, *The Screwtape Letters* (New York: HarperOne, 2015), 120.
54. Quoted in Ghezzi, *Sign of the Cross*, 103.
55. An excellent book that explores the connection between worship and work is Matthew Kaemingk and Cory B. Willson, *Work and Worship: Reconnecting Our Labor and Liturgy* (Grand Rapids: Baker Academic, 2020).

Chapter 11 The Freedom of the Body

1. W. David O. Taylor, *Open and Unafraid: The Psalms as a Guide to Life* (Nashville: Nelson, 2020), chap. 8, "Joy."
2. On the relationship between music, religious renewal, and embodied practices within charismatic churches such as soaking prayer, hand raising, dancing, jumping, bodily jerks, flag waving, quickened breathing, being slain in the Spirit, and resting in the Spirit, see Peter Althouse and Michael Wilkinson, "Musical Bodies in the Charismatic Renewal: The Case of Catch the Fire and Soaking Prayer," in *The Spirit of Praise: Music and Worship in Global Pentecostal-Charismatic Christianity*, ed. Monique M. Ingalls and Amos Yong (University Park: Pennsylvania State University Press, 2015), 29–44.
3. Walter Brueggemann, *From Whom No Secrets Are Hid: Introducing the Psalms*, ed. Brent A. Strawn (Louisville: Westminster John Knox, 2014), 47.
4. John Goldingay, *Psalms*, vol. 2, *Psalms 42–89* (Grand Rapids: Baker Academic, 2007), 254 (emphasis added).
5. "Communicative meaning is always, in its depths, affective; it remains rooted in the sensual dimension of experience, born of the body's native capacity to resonate with other bodies and with the landscape as a whole." David Abram, *The Spell of the Sensuous* (New York: Vintage, 1996), 75.
6. Something similar happens to Saul in 1 Sam. 19:22–24.
7. David Toshio Tsumura, *The Second Book of Samuel*, New International Commentary on the Old Testament (Grand Rapids: Eerdmans, 2019), 249.
8. "Popular use of this text to justify liturgic dance is quite beside the point, unless liturgic dance is seen as a means whereby power is reconfigured and new political legitimacy is received." Tsumura, *Second Book of Samuel*, 252.

9. Irenaeus, *Against Heresies*, 4.20.1, available at https://ccel.org/ccel/irenaeus/against_heresies_iv/anf01.ix.vi.i.html.

10. Jeremy S. Begbie, *Theology, Music and Time*, Cambridge Studies in Christian Doctrine (Cambridge: Cambridge University Press, 2000), 242, see also 223–24, 241–45.

11. Gordon Fee writes, "The word πνεῦμα occurs 145 times in the thirteen Pauline letters; the vast majority of them unambiguously refer to the Holy Spirit." *God's Empowering Presence: The Holy Spirit in the Letters of Paul* (Peabody, MA: Hendrickson, 1994), 29. See also Fee, *Paul, the Spirit, and the People of God* (Grand Rapids: Baker, 1996), 160; Fee, *Listening to the Spirit in the Text* (Grand Rapids: Eerdmans, 2000), 102; Ralph P. Martin, *Worship in the Early Church* (Grand Rapids: Eerdmans, 1964), 43.

12. Gordon D. Fee, *The First Epistle to the Corinthians*, New International Commentary on the New Testament (Grand Rapids: Eerdmans, 1987), 697.

13. Balthasar Fischer, *Signs, Words, and Gestures* (New York: Pueblo, 1981), 52.

14. Karl Barth, *Church Dogmatics*, trans. J. W. Edwards, O. Bussey, and Harold Knight (Edinburgh: T&T Clark, 1958), III/3, 49.

15. Colin Gunton, *The Triune Creator: A Historical and Systematic Study* (Grand Rapids: Eerdmans, 1998), 86.

16. Cf. W. David O. Taylor, *Glimpses of the New Creation: Worship and the Formative Power of the Arts* (Grand Rapids: Eerdmans, 2019), chap. 10, "Mother Tongues and Adjectival Tongues."

17. Barth, *Church Dogmatics*, IV/4, 22.

18. Barth, *Church Dogmatics*, III/3, 87.

19. Barth, *Church Dogmatics*, III/3, 92.

20. Barth, *Church Dogmatics*, III/3, 123, 130, 132. The Spirit, we might say, is the author of true *exstasis*, of getting "beside oneself" in order to "get over oneself," over against a life that is *curvatus in se*, absorbed and imprisoned in oneself on account of sin.

21. Jeremy S. Begbie, "Looking to the Future: A Hopeful Subversion," in *For the Beauty of the Church: Casting a Vision for the Arts*, ed. W. David O. Taylor (Grand Rapids: Baker Books, 2010), 183.

22. Begbie, "Looking to the Future," 183.

23. Wolfgang Vondey, *Beyond Pentecostalism: The Crisis of Global Christianity and the Renewal of the Theological Agenda* (Grand Rapids: Eerdmans, 2010), 132.

24. Frank J. Barrett, "Cultivating an Aesthetic of Unfolding: Jazz Improvisation as a Self-Organizing System," in *The Aesthetics of Organization*, ed. Stephen Linstead and Heather Höpfl (London: Sage, 2009), 237 (emphasis in original).

25. This is language that J. I. Packer used in his theology classes at Regent College to describe the work of the Spirit in relation to the life of the church.

26. Barry Liesch, in *People in the Presence of God: Models and Directions for Worship* (Grand Rapids: Zondervan, 1988), 213–17, matches a set of accessible movements to specific hymns as a way for a congregation to take baby steps toward the inclusion of movement in worship. On the serious business of embodied play within the context of worship, see Romano Guardini, *The Spirit of the Liturgy* (New York: Sheed & Ward, 1940), 181–82; Jürgen Moltmann, *Theology of Play* (New York: Harper & Row, 1972), 17; W. David O. Taylor, "Pursuing a Playful Liturgy," in *The Regent World* 30, no. 2 (2018), https://world.regent-college.edu/thought-action/pursuing-a-playful-liturgy; Harvey Cox, *The Feast of Fools: A Theological Essay on Festivity and Fantasy* (Cambridge, MA: Harvard University Press, 1969), chap. 10, "Christ as Harlequin."

Chapter 12 The End of the Body

1. "Your body is not a temple, it's an amusement park. Enjoy the ride." Anthony Bourdain, *Kitchen Confidential: Adventures in the Culinary Underbelly* (New York: Ecco Books, 2007), 73.

2. "Let me put the issue as bluntly and provocatively as I can: faith in Jesus requires bodily cohabitation and interaction with him. It's that or nothing!" John W. Kleinig, *Wonderfully Made: A Protestant Theology of the Body* (Bellingham, WA: Lexham, 2021), 98.

3. Joseph Cardinal Ratzinger, *The Spirit of the Liturgy*, trans. John Saward (San Francisco: Ignatius, 2000), 175.

4. John Calvin, "Commentary on Romans 12:1," available at https://ccel.org/ccel/calvin/calcom38/calcom38.xvi.i.html.

5. See Rom. 12:1; 1 Cor. 9:24–27; 2 Cor. 4:10, 13; and 1 Thess. 5:23.

6. Ratzinger, *Spirit of the Liturgy*, 176.

7. Eugene H. Peterson, *Under the Unpredictable Plant: An Exploration in Vocational Holiness* (Grand Rapids: Eerdmans, 1992), 75. In the end, we train our bodies in worship to desire the things of Christ and are trained by our bodies to continue desiring them throughout the rest of our week.

8. Steven R. Guthrie, "Temples of the Spirit: Worship as Embodied Performance," in *Faithful Performances: Enacting Christian Tradition*, ed. Trevor A. Hart and Steven R. Guthrie (Aldershot, UK: Ashgate, 2007), 104.

9. James K. A. Smith, *Imagining the Kingdom: How Worship Works* (Grand Rapids: Baker Academic, 2013), 187.

10. Sam Allberry, *What God Has to Say about Our Bodies: How the Gospel Is Good News for Our Physical Selves* (Wheaton: Crossway, 2021), 172.

11. Kleinig, *Wonderfully Made*, 95.

12. Paul J. Griffiths, *Christian Flesh* (Stanford, CA: Stanford University Press, 2018), 63–64.

13. Beth Felker Jones, *Marks of His Wounds: Gender Politics and Bodily Resurrection* (Oxford: Oxford University Press, 2007), 105–10.

14. John Stott, *The Message of Romans* (Downers Grove, IL: IVP Academic, 2020), 323.

15. Patrick R. Keifert, *Welcoming the Stranger: A Public Theology of Worship and Evangelism* (Minneapolis: Fortress, 1992), 71. On this view, I suggest that "high" liturgy is not intrinsically inhospitable, nor inimical to God's mission, in the same way that a "low" liturgy is not automatically hospitable, nor inevitably missional, to the visitor and stranger.

16. Kleinig, *Wonderfully Made*, 89.

17. For the purposes of this imaginative exercise, I have conflated geographically dispersed and liturgically distinctive practices, which nonetheless remain largely sympathetic to each other.

18. Rodney Stark, *The Rise of Christianity: How the Obscure, Marginal Jesus Movement Became the Dominant Religious Force in the Western World in a Few Centuries* (New York: HarperCollins, 1997), 73–94.

19. Jane Kenyon, "Cages," in *Collected Poems* (St. Paul, MN: Graywolf, 2005), 40.

20. Thomas Torrance, *The Trinitarian Faith: The Evangelical Theology of the Ancient Catholic Church* (Edinburgh: T&T Clark, 2016), 75.

21. Eugene F. Rogers Jr., *After the Spirit: A Constructive Pneumatology from Resources outside the Modern West* (Grand Rapids: Eerdmans, 2005), 200.

22. Dante Alighieri, "Paradiso," in *The Divine Comedy*, trans. Lawrence Grant White (New York: Pantheon Books, 1948), 183.

23. See Robin A. Parry, *The Biblical Cosmos: A Pilgrim's Guide to the Weird and Wonderful World of the Bible* (Eugene, OR: Cascade Books, 2014), chap. 11, on the song of the stars in heaven.

24. Samuel Taylor Coleridge, *Aids to Reflection*, ed. John Beer (Princeton: Princeton University Press, 1993), 236. Karl Barth describes the beginning of theology as rooted in the experience of wonder: "If anyone should not find himself astonished and filled with wonder when he becomes involved in one way or another with theology, he would be well advised to consider once more, from a certain remoteness and without prejudice, what is involved in this undertaking." *Evangelical Theology: An Introduction* (London: Weidenfeld & Nicolson, 1963), 64–65.

25. The phrase "heart-whelming wonder" is from Richard Bauckham's poetic rendering of the women's encounter with the resurrected Christ in Luke's Gospel. Cited in Jeremy S. Begbie, "Encountering the Uncontainable in the Arts," in *God and Wonder: Theology, Imagination, and the Arts*, ed. Jeffrey W. Barbeau and Emily Hunter McGowin (Eugene, OR: Wipf & Stock, 2022), 117.

26. Charles Wesley, "Maker, in Whom We Live" (1747), available at https://hymnary.org/text/father_in_whom_we_live.

27. Charles Wesley, "Love Divine, All Loves Excelling" (1747), available at https://hymnary.org/text/love_divine_all_loves_excelling_joy_of_he.

28. This language is drawn from Henry Francis Cary's translation of Canto 10 of Dante's *Paradiso*, in *The Vision; Or Hell, Purgatory, and Paradise* (London: William Smith, 1844), 444, and is available online at https://www.bartleby.com/20/310.html.

Scripture Index

Old Testament

Genesis

1:1 162
1:26 47
1:30 94
2 44, 50, 86
2:7 62
2:9 70
2:15 47, 71
2:23 5, 73
3:8 47
3:17–19 71
3:19 176n30
17 143
18 133
32:24–32 73
32:30 73

Exodus

3:12 47
4:1–17 113
4:11–12 189n9
15:20 49
15:20–21 141
23:19 83
25:6 83
28:41 47, 135
29:8 47
30:1–8 83
30:34–38 83
31:11 86
40:14 47

Leviticus

1:9 83
8:13 47
16 86
26:12 47

Numbers

12:8 73
27:18 133
28:2 47

Deuteronomy

23:15 47
34:10 73

Judges

11:34 49

1 Samuel

2 142
10 84, 142
10:1 83
10:10 142
16:12–13 135
19:22–24 196
19:24 104

2 Samuel

6 6, 142
6:5 49
6:14 49
6:16 49, 142
6:20 143
6:20–22 142
6:21 6, 143
6:21–22 139
6:22 142
7:6–7 47

1 Kings

6:1 83
6:23–28 47
18:26 49
19:16 135

2 Kings

3:14–15 142

2 Chronicles

16:14 83

Job

10:11 51

Psalms

5:7 49
8 10
19:1–2 10
22:23 128
22:29 130
23:2 94
27:4 83
29:6 49
30:11 49
33:8 5, 49
34:8 4, 70
42:5 49
45:11 49
46:10 21
47:1 5, 49
51:7 93
63:1–4 140
63:3–4 125
63:4 141
68:24–27 105
72:11 49
84:1 86
88:9 49
95:6 5, 49, 129
104 10
104:29 176n30
111:2–3 10
119:62 49
119:73 51
120–134 105
122:1 83
139:13 51
139:14–15 163
139:15 51
141:2 85
145 12
146:8 134
148 10
149:3 49
150 12
150:3–5 95
150:4 49
150:6 153

Ecclesiastes

3:4 49
3:20 176n30

Song of Songs

2:8 49
5:10 93
6:13 49

Isaiah

6:9–10 178n26
55:1 58
63:2 93

Jeremiah

31:4 49
31:13 49
31:22 49
34:5 83

Lamentations

5:15 49

Ezekiel

9:4 195n23
37 62
37:7–10 62

Daniel

3 46

Habakkuk

2:20 137

Malachi

1:11 85

New Testament

Matthew

6 137
6:22 26
8 176n24
8:3 51
8:8 176n24
8:13 176n24
8:15 51
9:25 51
9:29 51
14:35–36 51
15:21–28 176n24
17:2 93
20:34 51
25 99, 158
28:19 144

Mark

3:5 176n24
5:1–20 176n24
6:13 84, 135
7 142
7:33 51
7:37 164
9:27 51
10:13–15 51
10:15–16 43
10:16 133
11:25 148
14 135
16:1 83

Luke

1 142
1:38 137
4 144
4:40 133
5 144
5:13 51
7 52, 142
7:14 51
8:43–48 51
10 99

Scripture Index

10:39 136
13:13 73
17:11–19 51
17:16 144
22:50–51 51
24:39 73
24:39–40 52

John

1:1 73
1:14 47, 59, 61, 63, 73
1:16–18 47
1:32–33 62, 176n16
2:1–11 32
2:21 61
3:1–21 58
3:3 181n11
3:5 62, 176n16
3:6 176n16
3:8 176n16
3:34 176n16
4 57
4:7–15 58
4:22–24 55
4:23 58, 176n16
4:23–24 55, 57, 60
4:24 57, 58, 176n16
4:25–30 58
4:46–54 176n24
5:25–33 59
6:51–58 61, 77
6:63 62, 176n16
7:37–39 58
7:39 176n16
8:15 64
8:23 60
8:32 59
8:36 60
8:45–46 59
12 84, 142
12:38–41 178n26
13 52
14:6 59
14:9 73
14:16–18 60

14:26 176n16
14:27 178n26
14:31 161
15:10 161
15:26 59
16:6 178n26
16:13 59
16:22 178n26
17:17 59
17:21 61
18:37 59
19:28–30 61
19:34 61
20 62
20:19 75
20:20 75
20:22 62, 176n16
20:27 61
20:31 58

Acts

2 142, 145
8:17 133
28:8 133

Romans

1:19–20 10
3:23 47
4:1 63
6:6 63
6:13 64, 160
7 44
7:4 75, 180n51
7:14 63
7:24 63
8 44
8:3 75
8:5 63
8:9–11 63
8:11 64, 180n51
8:23 75, 180n51
8:26 78
8:26–27 145
12 158

12:1 15, 65, 158, 180n51, 198n5
12:13 158
12:20 158

1 Corinthians

1:23 130
3:16 77
6:19 26, 64, 77
6:20 5, 65, 154
9:11 63
9:24–27 198n5
11:1–2 39
12 104, 113
12:7 150
13:12 73, 107, 161
14 142, 145
14:1 149–50
14:26 145, 150
14:33 146
14:40 104
15:42–49 64
15:44 64, 75
16:13 128

2 Corinthians

1:21–22 135
2:14 83
3:18 107
4:7 50
4:10 153, 198n5
4:13 198n5
5:17 162
10:2–3 63, 64

Galatians

4:4 74
4:23 63
4:29 63
6:14 130

Ephesians

2:10 71
3:14 50

5 142
5:2 83
5:19 107
5:29–30 55
6:6 154

Philippians

2:1–11 128
3:21 75

Colossians

2:9 67, 73
3:1–4 128

1 Thessalonians

5:23 198n5

2 Thessalonians

1:10 163
2:15 29, 39, 145
3:6 39

1 Timothy

2:8 50
3:16 145

4:13 128
4:14 133

2 Timothy

1:6 50, 133

Hebrews

1:3 73, 112
1:9 135
4:16 75
12 145

James

4:10 130
5:13–14 81
5:14 135
5:14–15 84

1 Peter

2:21 125
4:8 41
5:14 50

1 John

1:1 1
4 60

Jude

1:20 145

Revelation

1 142
4:6 12
5:8 85
5:11 162
5:11–12 12
5:13 12
7 143
7:9 93
7:9–10 50, 109
19 107, 133
21:3–4 53
21:24–26 35
22 86
22:17 58, 162
22:20 162

Subject Index

Adam, 47, 50, 73
Advent, 91, 93, 185n44
aesthetics, 20, 95–98, 107–8
Albers, Josef, 90, 185n42
Ambrose, 32, 84
anointing, 52, 70, 84–85, 134, 135–36
anticipation, 12, 101, 127, 136–37, 153, 161
art, 95–100, 116–17
Augustine, 10, 32, 41, 46, 86, 129, 138

Banks, Adelle, 117
baptism, 19, 36, 53, 61, 62, 84, 91, 93, 128, 131, 134, 135, 158–60, 162
Barrett, Frank, 149
Barth, Karl, ix, 68, 147
Basil of Caesarea, 38–39, 87
Bates, J. Barrington, 92
Begbie, Jeremy, 97, 148
believers, 10, 64, 76, 77, 83, 117–18, 142, 145
Benzon, William, 88–89
Berger, Teresa, 121
Berry, Wendell, 122
Bible and tradition, 37–38
body/bodies
    abuse of, 39–40, 54, 78
    biological, 17
    cultural, 17, 71
    as despised, 7, 62
    as fallen, 12, 63, 71–72

fullness of, 12, 78–79
functions of, 20–21
as gift, 26–27, 65–66
glory of, 5–6
of grace, 40–41, 70–71
as image-bearing, 44, 45–49
language of, 18
pleasure in, 68–70
powers of, 21–25
purpose of, 5, 6–7, 8, 46–49, 162–64
as "second book," 10
as sinful, 44
social, 18
Spirit-infused, 64–65
as a temple, 26, 64, 77–78
training of, 154–58
unseen, 116–18
in worship, 8–9, 55–67
body knowledge, 22
body language, 16, 23–24
Bonaventure, 11
Book of Common Prayer, 2
Bourdain, Anthony, 154
Bourgeois, David, 122
bowing, 20, 101, 110, 133–34, 156
Bradshaw, Paul, 31
Brueggemann, Walter, 140
Bruner, Dale, 58
Bynum, Caroline Walker, 40

205

Subject Index

calendar (liturgical), 90–92
Calvin, John, 6, 11, 39, 48, 63, 76, 155
Catholic Church, 35, 86, 104, 109, 117, 121, 132
children, 18, 51, 133
chorus, 31–32
Christmas, 91
church
  art in, 99–100, 116–17
  as Body of Christ, 22, 64, 70, 75, 87, 107, 110–14, 118, 122, 146
  calendar, 90–92, 93–94
  early, 44, 128, 130, 133–34, 159, 195n23
  "free," 8, 30, 104, 128
  history, 29–31
  online, 118–21
  seating in, 105–7
  Western, 34, 136, 173n36
circumcision, 52–53
Clement of Alexandria, 32, 129
color
  importance of, 90–91, 94, 185nn41–42, 186n50
  in worship, 90, 92–93
communion
  with Christ, 24, 76–77
  with God, 27, 44, 50, 61, 73
Communion (Holy). *See* Lord's Supper
confession, 20, 66, 130, 134, 146, 188n29
Constantinian era, 31, 33
creation, 46–49, 70, 111, 130, 147, 162, 181n13
  holistic vision of, 48
  of humanity, 50–51
  new, 12, 44, 64–65, 78, 86, 162–63, 182n34
  physical/material, 10, 45, 47, 168n9
  as revelation of God, 11
  as splendor of God, 10
  story of, 46, 175n12
culture, 10, 17, 23, 30, 34, 71, 169n21
  African, 24, 35
  confusion, 35–36
  context of, 24, 166n16
  Japanese, 23
  Latin American, 23
  Middle Eastern, 23
Cyprian, 160

dance, dancing, 24, 49, 139–41, 148, 172n32, 188n29, 196n8
  in African churches, 24
  in the Bible, 49, 142–43
  contexts for, 32–33
  of David, 6, 49, 135, 142–43
  liturgical, 31–32
  prohibitions against, 32–33
  in the Shaker church, 101–5
  in worship, 36–37
Dante Alighieri, 162–63
David (king), 6, 34, 49, 135, 142–43
Davies, J. G., 31–33, 36, 101, 103
death, 44, 52, 74, 82, 90, 94, 100, 133, 160, 161, 176n30
  of the body, 2, 51, 55
  and resurrection, 64–65, 131, 160
deficiency, 7
digital worship, 118–23
Dionysius of Alexandria, 160
disabilities, 109–15, 121, 173n47, 189n3, 189n6
  Christ and the broken body, 111–12
  "cult of normalcy," 112–13
  and hospitality, 113–14
  and the *imago Dei*, 114
  of Moses, 113
diversity, 191n23, 117–18
  lack of, 116–17
Dodd, C. H., 59
Donghi, Antonio, 129, 130, 133, 136, 137
dualisms, 40, 175n18
Duke Chapel, 116–17

Eastertide, 92
Eden, 47–48, 86, 174n9
Egeria, 126
Eiesland, Nancy, 110
Eliot, Lise, 82
embodied presence, 24–25
emotion(s), 18, 89, 97, 100–101, 102, 104, 140, 152, 186n5, 194n14
entrainment, 88
Epiphany, 91
eschatology, 12, 103

Subject Index

Estes, Douglas, 122
Eucharist, 76, 112, 171n17, 182n38, 185n43.
  See also Lord's Supper

faith, 20, 33, 62, 67–68, 75, 84, 87, 104, 120, 126–27, 156
  confession of, 38, 66, 128
  family of, 99, 158
  gestures of, 162
  journey of, 86
  trinitarian, 61, 131, 162
fasting, 136
Fischer, Balthasar, 146
flesh, 16, 18, 50–51, 68, 72
  of Christ, 5, 26, 30, 39, 44, 52, 76–77, 79, 154, 157, 161
  intelligence in the, 26
  and physicality, 57, 62–64
  and sin, 43–44, 75
  Word made, 39, 73–77, 181n13
  See also body/bodies
flowers, 86–87, 183n10
food, 43, 74, 76, 82, 191n23
footwashing, 52, 61, 176n26
functions of the body, 20–21

Galen, 34
Gaudí, Antoni, 97
gesture, 34, 54, 129–30, 133, 134, 136, 147, 194n21, 195n27, 195n31
Gnosticism, 7, 30
God
  body as belonging to, 5–6
  communion with, 50–51
  grace of, 4, 19, 26, 30, 70–74, 137, 148, 156
  redemptive work of, 48, 144, 147–48, 162
  as Spirit, 57–58
  triune, 4, 39, 56–57, 61, 66, 115, 132, 157
  work of, 4, 48, 69, 76, 133
Goldingay, John, 140
grace, 17, 38, 61, 113, 115, 145, 147, 151, 160, 168n9, 181n8, 181n13
  body of, 40–41
  of God, 4, 19, 26, 30, 70–74, 137, 148, 156
Greco-Roman practices, 33–35, 171n18

Gregory of Nazianzus, 32
Griffiths, Paul, 52–53, 157
Guardini, Romano, 132
Gunkel, Herman, 46

Haarsma, Deborah, 11
hands, 132–33
  empty, 128–29
  folded, 34, 129
  open, 129
  raised, 128–29, 141, 156, 194n14
Hardy, Daniel, 12
Hauerwas, Stanley, 114
Hays, Richard, 61
healing, 26, 53, 65, 71–72, 79, 84–85, 135–36, 156, 168n17, 175n24
  prayer, 4, 25, 146, 168n11
  touch of God, 44, 160
Hendren, Sara, 112, 114

icons, 18, 98, 112, 195n39
imago Dei, 45–49, 50, 114
incense, 85–86
inertia, 25
Innocent III (pope), 92
Irenaeus, 5, 61, 76, 144
isolation, 1–3
Israel, 37, 44, 47, 74, 83–85, 91, 105, 115, 129, 142, 175n12

Jennings, Laura, 99–100
Jesus
  anointing of, 52
  body/flesh of, 67–68, 72–73, 112
  bond with humanity, 154–55, 157–58
  healing touch of, 51–52
  humanity of, 30, 51
  ministry of, 50, 85, 133, 144, 162
  physicality of, 52–53, 73–74
  as redeemer and reconciler, 50, 75–76, 154
  resurrected, 30, 52, 64–65, 75, 155
  woundedness of, 75, 111–12
John Chrysostom, 11, 32–33, 131
Johnson, Mark, 25

Johnston, George, 59
Justin Martyr, 134

Kavanagh, Aidan, 134, 137
Kidula, Jean N., 106
kissing, 22, 24, 35, 38, 52, 134–35, 159, 195n41
   of icons, 195n39
Kleinig, John, 47, 73, 157, 158
kneeling, 6, 20, 34, 36, 41, 110, 129–30,
   171n18, 172n25, 173n49
Knego, Samir, 119
Koyama, Kosuke, 126

labyrinth, 21, 127, 168n15
language, 35, 64, 175n19
   about the body, 18
   of the body, 4, 63, 120
   of dance, 32
   flesh and body, 57, 62, 179n47
   heart, 147, 178n26
   Johannine, 56–58, 181n11
   metaphorical, 187n13
   of Psalms, 49–51
   of Revelation, 68
   of sacrament, 19, 168n9, 168n11
   of smell, 83
   of the Spirit, 148, 177n16
   trinitarian, 55
   of worship, 8
laying on of hands, 23
Lent, 86, 91, 93, 185n43
Lewis, C. S., 138
liturgy, 6, 8, 21, 34, 38, 44, 57, 92, 97, 110,
   141, 146, 156, 168n9, 170n1, 188n29
   "high," 198n15
   historic, 128
   "of the neighbor," 123
   public, 142
   Roman Catholic, 35, 92, 172n23
Lord's Supper, 4, 19, 21, 25, 36, 56, 76–77,
   136, 146, 171n17, 182n38, 185n43
love, 6, 53, 59, 63, 68–69, 76, 94, 96, 99, 103,
   118, 120, 147, 153, 155–56, 158, 164
   disordered, 44, 72
   divine, 4

   of God, 50–51, 57, 66, 92, 115, 127, 133, 137
   law of, 54, 156
   movements of, 162–63
   of neighbor, 97
   reconciling, 65
   sacrificial, 23
   vulnerable, 161
Luther, Martin, 32–33, 53, 76, 131

March for Jesus, 21
Marti, Gerardo, 118
McNeill, William, 89, 121
metaphor, 26, 98, 99, 147
Miriam, 34, 44, 49, 142, 169n23
mission, 63, 92, 122, 158, 175n24, 198n15
Mitchell, Nathan, 4, 123
Moll, Rob, 89
Morris, Leon, 57
muscle memory, 22
music, 88–89, 97–98, 103–4, 117–18, 149–50,
   175n21, 184n33, 187n13, 191n23, 196n2
Myrick, Nathan, 88

Newbigin, Lesslie, 57
new creation, 12, 44, 64–65, 78, 86, 162–63,
   182n34
Nicene Creed, 20, 67, 134
nonverbal communication, 23–24

odor, 81–87
online worship, 118–22
orans, 35
Origen, 40, 129, 134
originalism, 36–37

Paraclete, 60, 178n25, 178n34
passing of the peace, 22, 23, 120, 134–35
Paul (apostle), 10, 63, 73, 76, 130, 145–56
   anthropology of, 48, 77
   language of, 64, 75
Pentecost, 92, 162, 185n44
Peterson, Eugene, 5, 10, 155
pilgrimage, 21, 125–26
Piper, John, 56

Subject Index

posture(s) in worship, 34, 39, 40–41, 96, 128–30
  bowing, 20, 101, 110, 133–34, 156
  of humility, 6, 133–34
  kneeling, 20, 34, 36, 41, 110, 129–30, 171n18, 172n25, 173n49
  penitential, 93
  sitting, 40, 127, 130, 135–36, 173n49
  standing, 20, 34–36, 38, 40, 127–29, 140, 159
practices of the church, 30, 36–37
praesul, 31
prayer, 7, 21, 65, 68, 79, 84–86, 94, 103, 114, 120, 129, 196n2
  healing, 25, 146, 168n11
  kneeling, 34, 41
  liturgical, 4
  Lord's, 54
  ministry, 23
  posture for, 34, 35, 38, 40–41, 133, 169n2, 171n18
  silent, 146
  standing, 34, 35, 38, 41
  unanswered, 78
  walks, 127
Psalter, the, 5, 44, 49–50, 141

Quakers. *See* Shakers

racial disparity, 7
Ratzinger, Joseph (cardinal), 24, 34, 154
Raymond of Sabunde, 11
redemption, 75, 175n24, 180n51
revelation, 10–11, 59, 145
Reynolds, Thomas, 113
Rilke, Rainer Maria, 52
Rivera, Mayra, 8, 176n25, 179n46
Rogers, Eugene, 162

sacrament(al), 5, 18, 19, 30, 53, 56, 71, 85, 115, 154, 159, 168n9, 172n24. *See also* baptism; Lord's Supper
sacrifice, 134, 140, 152, 155–56, 158
Sarah, Robert (cardinal), 138

sarx, 18, 63, 73
scent(s), 13, 83–84, 87, 94, 134, 182n6
  of a human, 81–82
  of worship, 7
  See also odor
Schnelle, Udo, 75
Schroeder, Celeste, 20
Scripture, 37–39, 45, 48–49, 84, 87, 96, 105, 117, 135, 143, 145, 150
"second book" of God, 10
self-discipline, 155–56
senses, 70–71, 96–97
Shakers, 101–5, 187n17
sight, 12–13, 83, 94, 100, 159, 163
sign of the cross, 20, 38, 130–32, 159, 195n27
signs, 18–19, 136, 169n19
Sigurdson, Ola, 16
silence, 137–38
sin, 43–44, 63, 66, 71–72, 78, 83, 130, 133, 146, 154, 156, 161, 179n48, 182n38, 189n3
singing, 25, 87–89
sitting, 40, 127, 130, 136, 173n49
Smith, James K. A., 156
Solnit, Rebecca, 127
sōma/sōmatikōs, 18, 48, 63, 73, 180n51
soul, 62
soul only worship, 3–4
sound, 2, 6, 83, 88–89, 94, 98, 159, 188n37
Spirit of God, 55–62
  activity of God as, 57–58
  and truth, 58–62
spontaneity in worship, 139–52
  appropriateness of, 143–44
  as freeing, 146–48
  misuse of, 151
  as ordered improvisation, 148–50
  Spirit-of-the-Moment, 145–46
  as surrender, 149
  as unifying, 150–52
standing, 128–29
Starks, Rodney, 160
Stations of the Cross, 127
Stott, John, 131, 158
suffering, 63, 65, 72, 78, 100, 189n3

symbols, 19, 21, 70
synchrony, 88

taste, 6, 20, 70, 82, 153, 159, 165n6
temple
  the body as a, 26, 64, 77–78
  Christ as a, 154
  the church as a, 98
  of God, 76
  Jerusalem, 143, 175n12
  language, 64, 154
  practices, 85
  of the Spirit, 86, 107, 157
Tertullian, 41, 50, 77, 130, 134, 159, 173n49
Thompson, Curt, 120
Thompson, Marianne Meye, 56, 59
touch, 4, 16–18, 20, 70, 82, 99, 115, 122, 126, 147, 153, 175n23, 176n25
  as act of devotion, 52
  as healing, 53
  physical, 25, 50–54, 190n15, 190n17
  as restorative, 52, 114
touch deficiency syndrome, 3
tradition, 37–38, 39
training in Christlikeness, 154–64
  as preparation for the age to come, 162–64
  for service to neighbors, 158, 160
  stripping off the old self, 159
  as vulnerability, 161
  as witnesses for Christ, 154–58
trust, 23, 115, 164
Tsumura, David Toshio, 142

unity, 103–4, 151
unseen bodies, 116–17
Uzukwu, Elochukwu, 34, 35

van der Kolk, Bessel, 3
Vondey, Wolfgang, 149
vulnerability, 17, 114, 161

walking, 125–28
Ware, Kallistos, 40
water(s), 53, 69, 159
  baptismal, 38, 131
  blood and, 74
  changed into wine, 18–19
  holy, 70, 135
  living, 58, 61
weakness, 44, 65, 75, 113, 130
Wesley, Charles, 163
Westermann, Claus, 46–47
woman/women, 40, 49, 51–52, 74, 85, 134, 142, 159
  story of the Samaritan, 55–56, 178n32
  who anoints Jesus's feet, 52
wonder, 12, 163–64, 199n24
worship, 23, 47, 55–56, 63–64
  ambulatory, 125–28
  bodily, 49–50
  colors in, 90–94
  corporate, 8, 18–19, 20–21, 110–11
  dance in, 101–5
  disabled bodies in, 109–15
  goal of, 12–13, 163
  kneeling in, 129–30
  multiethnic, 117–18
  online vs. in-person, 118–23
  seating in, 105–7
  silence during, 137–38
  singing in, 87–89
  in spirit and in truth, 55–56
  spontaneous, 141–52
  standing, 128–29
Wright, N. T., 48, 64, 175n18

Yong, Amos, 114

Zoom, 119–21

www.ingramcontent.com/pod-product-compliance
Lightning Source LLC
Chambersburg PA
CBHW031426150426
43191CB00006B/414